Christianity and the Igbo Rites of Passage
The Prospects of Inculturation

European University Studies

Europäische Hochschulschriften
Publications Universitaires Européennes

Series XXIII

Theology

Reihe XXIII   Série XXIII
Theologie
Théologie

Vol./Bd. 462

PETER LANG

Frankfurt am Main · Berlin · Bern · New York · Paris · Wien

Charles Ok. Onuh

Christianity and the Igbo Rites of Passage

The Prospects of Inculturation

PETER LANG
Frankfurt am Main · Berlin · Bern · New York · Paris · Wien

Die Deutsche Bibliothek - CIP-Einheitsaufnahme

Onuh, Charles Ok.:

Christianity and the Igbo rites of passage : the prospects of
inculturation / Charles Ok. Onuh. - Frankfurt am Main ; Berlin ;
Bern ; New York ; Paris ; Wien : Lang, 1992
    (European university studies : Ser. 23, Theology ;
    Vol. 462)
    Zugl.: Rom, Univ. Teresiana, Diss., 1991
    ISBN 3-631-44974-7

NE: Europäische Hochschulschriften / 23

ISSN 0721-3409
ISBN 3-631-44974-7

© Verlag Peter Lang GmbH, Frankfurt am Main 1992
All rights reserved.

Printed in Germany 1   3 4 5 6 7

DEDICATION

in evergreen memory of my dear father

Late Mr. Joseph O. Onuh,

To

my lovely and dear mother

Mrs. Josephine Ade Onuh

my brothers and sisters,

who, in solidarity with me, have shared

the gift of life, and especially

the gift of Christ, meant for all peoples and cultures;

and

the new Diocese of Nsukka.

ACKNOWLEDGEMENTS

Not to us, Lord, not to us,
but to your name give the glory
for the sake of your love and your truth! (Psalm 113B)

I thank immensely the Almighty God, who made this work possible through His inspirations and at the intercession of the Blessed Virgin Mary, the patroness of my studies!

I express my gratitude to his Lordship Rt. Rev. Dr. M. U. Eneja, my former Bishop, who offered me the opportunity for further studies and had also financed the first phase of it. The same thanks go to his successor and my new Bishop, Rt. Rev. Dr. F. E. O. Okobo, who, in spite of the personnel problems, allowed the completion of this work.

My thanks go to all my Professors in Teresianum and Gregorian Universities, whose lucid lectures laid the foundations for this doctoral work. I am also grateful to Prof. Dr. G. Fittkau for his private academic advice. To the Rector, Students and the Domestic Staff of Collegio Olandese in Rome, where I had my first accommodation, and the Archdiocese of Köln, who gave me a domicile to complete this work, I give my appreciation.

In a special way, I thank my chief moderator, Prof. Bruno Moriconi for the kind, fatherly and patient direction of this work. His interestedness, suggestive criticisms and humane approach have been a great incentive for the completion of this work. My thanks go also to the other Readers of the work, Profs. Virgilio Pasquetto and Edwin Diniz, who, in spite of their academic loads and administrative functions, had time to read and criticise

VIII

the work.

The assistance from the libraries of the White Fathers, Holy Ghost Fathers, Sedos, Teresianum, Gregorian and Urban Universities in Rome, Universities of Regensburg and Dusseldorf in Germany, the University of San Francisco and the Catholic University of Washington D.C., helped to solve the literature problems for the work. To them as well as to all the research informants, who frankly supplied me with the concrete cultural facts, I remain indebted. In this regard I thank Chief P. Omeje, Rev. Dr. O. Anigbo and his Students, Fr. D. Agbo and his former parishioners, Fr. M. Nkachukwu, Messrs A. Eze, M. Ude, E. C. Anichebe, D. Ozokolo, and G. Onah.

This work could not have been possible without the support - moral and financial, encouragements, prayers, advice, criticisms of my colleagues, friends, and well-wishers. Hence I thank Fathers J. Okoye, D. Anih, G. Onah, A. Ezugwu, Sr. A. Magri, Miss E. Wolter, Mrs K. Schmoll, Mrs Jeanne Borg and relations, Family W. M. Müller and relations, Family J. Geissler, Mrs Ifeoma Abangwu, Don Poli Noberto and his parishioners, and many other friends in Brühl, Köln-Poll and Troisdorf.

May the Lord bless and reward all abundantly.

Charles Ok. Onuh

Rome, 3rd February, 1992

TABLE OF CONTENTS

XIV

ABBREVIATIONS

AAS	Acta Apostolicae Sedis
AA.VV	Various Authors
Acts	Acts of the Apostles
AFER	African Ecclesiastical Review
AMECEA	Association of Members of Episcopal Conference of East Africa
art. cit	Article cited
CHIEA	Catholic High Institute of Eastern Africa
CIWA	Catholic Institute of West Africa
Col.	Colossians
Cor.	Corinthians
Dr.	Doctor
e.g	example
et. al	And Others
Fr.	Father
G.S	Gaudium et Spes
Heb.	Hebrew
Ibid.	Ibidem (the same reference)
Id.	Idem (same)
i.e	id est (that is)
Jn	John

LG	Lumen Gentium
Lk	Luke
op. cit.	Opus citatis (in the work cited)
Phil.	Philippians
Prof.	Professor
Ps	Psalm
Rev.	Reverend
Rt.	Right
SC	Sacrosanctum Concilium
SECAM	Symposium of episcopal Conferences of Africa and Madagascar
Sr.	Sister
UNN	University of Nigeria Nsukka
viz	videlicet (namely)

MAPS

A MAP OF THE IGBOLAND

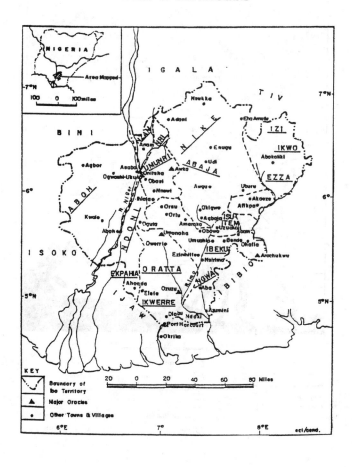

MAP 2

THE ECOLOGY OF THE IGBO CULTURE AREA

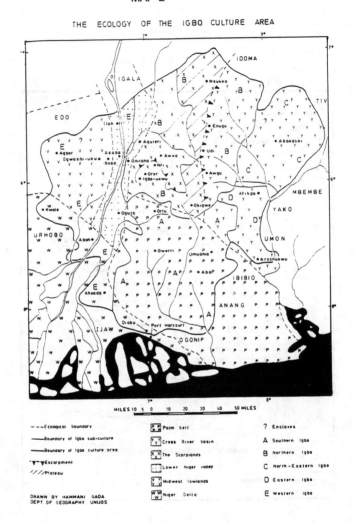

INTRODUCTION

At various times in the past and in various different ways, God spoke to our ancestors through the prophets; but in our own time, the last days, he has spoken to us through his Son, the Son that he has appointed to inherit everything, and through whom he made everything there is (Heb. 1:1).

This passage of the Scripture seems to contain a vivid truth that forms the central point of our theme. The Incarnation of Christ - an eventual and definitive divine intervention in human history, and the apex of God's self-communication to man in space and time - is the base-rock of Christianity. It is the greatest boon ever given to man. The Son of God was incarnate within the context of the Jewish people, assuming their mentality, customs, and traditional ways of life. "The Word was made flesh, and dwelt among us"(Jn 1:14). Even though the Incarnation was realised within this geographical and historical context, it is a gift to the whole of humanity. As such, it transcends cultural and geographical boundaries, since Christ, thereby, becomes a part of humanity.

The purpose of the Incarnation demands that Christ penetrates every time, place and people, in order to transform them into sons of God, since "to all who accept him, he gave power to become sons of God"-(Jn 1:12). Hence, ". . . the Church has been sent to all ages and nations and, therefore, is not tied exclusively and indissolubly to any race or nation, to any one particular way of life, or to any customary practices, ancient or modern".[1] The Incarnation principle dictates also that Christianity is expected to incarnate in the various cultures that constitute the whole of humanity. The Holy Father Pope Paul VI clarifies this point when he teaches in Evangelii Nuntiandi:

> The gospel, and therefore evangelization, are certainly not identical with culture, and they are independent with regard to all cultures. Nevertheless, the kingdom which the gospel proclaims is lived by men who are profoundly linked to a culture, and the building up of the kingdom cannot avoid borrowing the elements of human culture or cultures. Though independent of cultures, the gospel and evangelization are not necessarily incompatible with them; rather they are capable of permeating them all without becoming subject to any of them.[2]

This message of Christ came to Igboland through the indomitable and self-sacrificing apostolate of the Missionaries only a century ago. The Missionaries, despite all odds, planted the seeds of Christianity in Igboland. After a hundred years, the planted seeds have begun to yield fruits. The

---

[1]VATICAN II, Gaudium et Spes, n.58, AAS 58 (1966), 1080.

[2]Pope Paul VI, Evangelii Nuntiandi, Papal Encyclical, n. 20.

After a hundred years, the planted seeds have begun to yield fruits. The products of this apostolate reveal a flamboyant external and a peripheral development set up on very weak and fragile roots. It is undeniable that in any part of Igboland there stand out in eloquent testimony, obvious monumental contributions of the Missionaries in the field of Education, Hospitals, Maternity homes, Church Buildings, Orphanages, and other social services. But it is equally disturbing to discover, as Godfrey Onah clearly and rightly puts it, that

> Nearly all our church buildings have become too small for the teeming population of Christians surging to them for worship and devotion day in, day out. Yet these same Christians are in the offices embezzling; in the markets cheating and swindling; on the highways robbing and killing; in the homes and brothels fornicating and desecrating the matrimonial beds; in the clinics aborting; in the Law courts lying; at the boarders smuggling; at the 'juju' shrines apostatising; in the secret societies syncretizing.[3]

In Igboland one finds the 'baptised but not converted' Christians. This is even confirmed by the Bishops of Igboland, who remarked:

> Some desirable changes have been made in the personalities of many people due to Christianity, but the extent of such changes must not be exaggerated. There is abundant evidence to show the prevalence of superstitious native customs and beliefs as well as materialism under a thin veneer of Christianity among many of our Christians.

They continue:

> A settled spiritual allegiance is not yet a realised fact in the Christian life of our many converts. Most of our Catholics do not find any incompatibility in plural belonging . . . . Easily, airily, they slide out of one skin into another or rather by some miracle peculiar to themselves they comfortably wear both skins at once.[4]

A majority of Igbo Christians are, so to speak, double-faced. One face is that of Christianity, which hangs on them as a coat which one puts on as long as the vicissitudes of life find one in joy and peace; and the other, the traditional face, which naturally belongs to them to the core - being part and parcel of their traditional and cultural communities. This face is manifested and projected in life's crises. Confronted with illnesses, misfortunes, deaths,

---

[3]Fr. Godfrey Onah, "Baptised but not Converted", An Address delivered at the Centenary Lectures in Enugu Diocese, (1985), pp. 10-11.

[4]Catholic Bishops of Onitsha Ecclesiastical Province, Put out Into deep Water, Pastoral Letter, 1985, pp. 11-12.

and barrenness, the double-faced Christian adheres to the traditional methods for solution to these life's problems. This tallies exactly with the observation of Augustine Nebechukwu, who writes:

> It is a fact, that a good percentage of traditional religious men and women would not embrace Christian faith, but also that, a sizeable percentage of Christians sneak to the villages to perform traditional practices in search of answers to their problems of life.[5]

Michael Mozia confirms this observation, identifying the same situation from a social point of view. He writes:

> . . . many Christians find themselves living in two completely different communities: the Christian community and the traditional one. Thus they feel themselves bound together by two seemingly opposed solidary forces. Thus they try to play their parts independently in these two camps, for they seem to see nothing in common between them.[6]

This leaves a lot of questions regarding the conversion in Igboland. According to Luzbetak,

> . . . "Conversion" means a "turning" away from old ways toward new ways, a basic reorientation in premises and goals, a wholehearted acceptance of a new set of values affecting the "convert" as well as his social group, day in and day out, twenty-four hours of the day and in practically every sphere of activity - economic, social, and religious.[7]

However, this view of the Igbo christian is at variant with the life of an authentic Igbo traditionalist, who is so sincere and consistent in his religion, that he is described as eating, walking, dancing, and acting religiously. The Traditionalist radiates and transmits his religious convictions into the various sectors of his life. Therefore, it is necessary to ask questions about this double-faced existence exhibited by the Igbo Christians. The answer is simply that the Christian faith remains on top of the Igbo christians as a sort of blanket. Christianity was presented to them in such a way that its acceptance meant for the Igbos a total abandonment of their traditional way of life, culture and religion. As a result, Christians find themselves at cross-roads when they are confronted with real cultural problems and situations

---

[5]AUGUSTINE NEBECHUKWU, "Beginning Inculturation Theology of Life (in Igbo Culture)", in Lucerna, vol. 6, no. 1, p. 22.

[6]MICHAEL I. MOZIA, Solidarity in the Church and Solidarity among the Igbos of Nigeria, Claverianum Press, Bodija-Ibadan, 1987, p.27

[7]LOUIS J. LUZBETAK, The Church and Cultures, William Carey Library, California, 1984, p. 6.

that demand their reaction as the people of a particular race and culture, as definitely these situations are bound to come up. This was a fundamental mistake. Professor Chinua Achebe, in the borrowed lines of W. B. Yeats, laments the situation which he sees as

> Turning and Turning in the widening gyre
> The falcon cannot bear the falconer;
> Things fall apart; the centre cannot hold;
> Mere anarchy is loosed upon the world.
> (W. B. Yeats :'The Second Coming')[8]

Christians simply find themselves suspended between two systems - one being a Western-oriented way of life, whose social and cultural values clothed the Christianity brought to the Igbos; the other being an Igbo Traditional world of values. In between these two worlds are the Igbo Christians, groping this time, in one camp, and, at another time, in the other. The Igbo Christian cannot pinpoint at his veritable and proper cultural base.

The citation from the letter to the Hebrews above, furnishes a positive attitude in going into some of the cultural values of one's ancestors to discover some link that could form a sound and authentic base on which an engrafting work can be achieved. While recognising the uniqueness and prime of place of the eventual speech of God in Christ, one is convinced that for Christianity to have a meaning and relevance and be able to command a complete control of a person, it cannot come so superficially and in a totally alien way, unconnected with the word of God spoken to a people's ancestors though creation, and which has found a certain response in some beliefs and life-styles of these ancestors, even though this is manifested in an ambiguous approach. This is the truth recognised and proclaimed by the Church in Ad Gentes as "seeds of the Word which lie hidden among them".[9]

In search for the fundamental lacuna in the life of the Igbo Christians, Father Luke Mbefo gives expression to the problem thus:

> Our aim thereby seems to be the discovery and the rehabilitation of the cultural heritage of our ancestors, . . . There is a widespread conviction that our ancestors had a certain self-understanding, a view of their world, and of their place within it, a life style that was their own making and in which they felt at home, a religious attitude that responded to their experience of transcendence and that satisfied their expectations of the transcendent in the immanent. . . . if we could reclaim such a cultural originality, we would be able to develop within its structural parameters a theology that is

---

[8]CHINUA ACHEBE, Things Fall Apart, Heinemann Educational Books Ltd., London, (1958), p. v

[9]Vatican II, Ad Gentes, n.9 & 11

authentically Christian . . ."[10]

It is this idea that comes to mind in undertaking this work. It is meant to be a research into the cultural roots, life and the religion of the Igbos to discover those good values and potentials which should serve as solid foundations in the consequent Inculturation of the Christian Faith among the Igbos. This would surely provoke a deeper commitment in the Igbo christians. The intention of this work is to search out for ways through which christianity may enter the very blood and veins of the Igbos, make it answer their aspirations and anxieties, make Igbo christians recover their unique identity rather than live a dualistic life with one foot in the faith, the other in the traditional world.

This research is greatly encouraged by the Holy Father Pope Paul VI in his address to the African Bishops in Kampala:

> . . . you may, and you must, have an African Christianity. Indeed, you must possess human values and characteristic forms of culture which can rise up to perfection such as to find in Christianity, and for Christianity, a true superior fullness, and prove to be capable of a richness of expression all its own, and genuinely African.[11]

The same encouragement finds a perfect resonance in Evangelii Nuntiandi, where the same Pope spells out the implications of the work of evangelisation:

> Evangelisation loses much of its force and effectiveness if it does not take into consideration the actual people to whom it is addressed, if it does not use their language, their signs, their symbols, if it does not answer the questions they ask, and if it does not have an impact on their concrete life.[12]

Cecil Mc Garry reminds us that

> . . . 'Christianity as such' does not exist. It exists when people believe; and it becomes deeply rooted when it touches people and their lives where and as they are. The faith is not a culture, but it can only find expression and live within cultures. Faith must remain faith but it only becomes living in terms of culture, understanding by culture the integral life of men and

---

[10]LUKE MBEFO, "Theology and Inculturation - Problems and Prospects, - The Nigerian Experience", The Nigerian Journal of Theology, vol. 1, no. 1, Published by CATHAN, p. 55.

[11]PAUL VI, Address to the closing session of the Symposium of African Bishops in Kampala, 31st July 1969.

[12]Pope Paul VI, Evangelii Nuntiandi, Papal Encyclical, n. 63.

women and their values.[13]

If the faith finds its expression in certain good cultural elements among the Igbos, it could be considered as a fertile ground for the germination and flamboyant bearing of fruits in abundance of Christianity among the Igbos.

In the progress of this work, one keeps constantly in mind the serious warnings of the Holy Father Pope Paul VI who, against the negative tendencies arising from the politically motivated calls for the restoration of culture, gives guidelines and principles to be followed:

> If you are able to avoid the possible dangers of religious pluralism, the danger of making your Christian profession into a kind of local folk-lore, or into exclusivist racialism, or into egoistic tribalism, or into your own interpretation of the Christian life, you will be able to formulate Catholicism in terms congenial to your own culture. You will be capable of bringing to the Catholic Church the precious and original contribution of **nègritude** which she needs particularly in this historic hour.[14]

The motive force for this research comes from the personal provocations of the New Era of Evangelisation proclaimed by the Holy Father Pope John Paul II during his first-ever visit to Nigeria, and indeed to Igboland in 12th - 17th February 1982, which new era is to be characterised by the Inculturation of the Gospel into the lives of the people. One searches for ways of making Christian values find a comfortable home in the Igbo cultural structure, so as to rightly play the role, which the Holy Father, admonishing the Bishops, advocated:

> The Catholic people under your pastoral leadership, have the opportunity, the privilege and the duty . . . to bring the Gospel into the very heart of their culture; into the fabric of their everyday lives. . . . help them to bring forth from their own living tradition original expressions of Christian life, celebration and thought.[15]

By the use of the term 'Incarnating' in the title of this work, one sees evangelisation work as being preoccupied with making Christ feel at home in all places and cultures. The term 'incarnation' is used to mean 'the taking shape of Christianity in a culture'. It is interchangeably used with the term 'inculturation'. For John Waliggo, it

means the reformulation of Christian life and doctrine into the

---

[13]CECIL MCGARRY, in AA.VV., Inculturation : Its Meaning and Urgency, St. Pauls Publications, Africa, (1986), p. 8.

[14]Pope Paul VI, Address to African Bishops.

[15]JOHN PAUL II, Address to the Nigerian Bishops in Lagos, 15th Feb. 1982, AAS 1982, p. 615-616.

very thought patterns of each people. . . . It is the continuous endeavour to make Christianity truly "feel at home" in the cultures of each people.[16]

Specifically, one chooses the Igbo traditional birth rites and the rite of traditional Headship as concrete areas to research into. The value of the beginning and end of life for the Igbos is so great that one can regard these two sectors as pressure points of the Igbo Culture. On account of the cultural value of these two aspects and their importance, they are highly ritualised. Most of the problems that confront Christians in Igboland, for which reason they resort to the parallel attitude rotate around the gift of life, especially at its beginning and its conclusion. In all cultures, these two phases of life are always strategic. Incidentally, this is an area where Christianity has to do a lot of research among the Igbos.[17]

At this juncture the question arises, why this research is limited to Igbo Culture instead of a wider cultural ambient. The choice of an ethnic group may suggest a myopic and a sectionalistic character, and even raise doubts as to the universal value of such a work. Far from being the case, the choice is rather for a more practical and concrete treatment of the topic in question. It is chosen for objectivity purposes. An abstract and colossal treatment of a subject such as Inculturation is bound to arrive at an abstract conclusion, which serves little or no use in solving inculturation problems. The specific limitation of this work to an ethnic group - the Igbos - is meant, therefore, to serve as a model for any similar study among other ethnic groups in any other cultural area of the world. One is convinced that the more specific and concrete a subject is, the more detailed and less abstract such a subject is approached. André Droogers recommends that,

> In any attempt to Africanise Christianity and the church in Africa, primary attention should be given to local situations . . . The actual cultural situation should be studied and analyzed in detail, particularly in connection with the question regarding the extent to which spontaneous adaptations of Christianity to the local culture have occurred.[18]

It must be borne in mind that every area has its own peculiar problems,

---

[16]J. M. Waliggo, "Making a Church that is Truly African", in AA.VV., Inculturation : Its Meaning and Urgency, p. 12

[17]"Beginning from the sacraments of christian initiation through marriage to the anointing of the sick, the church in Nigeria has yet to begin a serious investigation on their resemblance and manner of association with the cultural rites of passage corresponding to the stages in life." - B. K. NWAZOJIE, "The Nigerian Hierarchy and Liturgical Inculturation in the Nigerian Church", in CATHOLIC SECRETARIAT OF NIGERIA, Inculturation in Nigeria, Proceedings of Catholic Bishops' Study Session, Nov. 1988, p. 74.

[18]ANDRÉ DROOGERS, "The Africanisation of Christianity", in Missiology, vol.V, no. 4, October 1977, p. 454.

attitudes, and cultural background. Hence, one researches on the prospects of Inculturation within the Igbo Culture and particularly in the specified parameters of the Culture.

CHAPTER I

1 **GENERAL IGBO BACKGROUND**

1.1 **Geographical and Ethnological Background**

'Igbo'[1] is both the language and the name of an ethnic group in Nigeria. This ethnic group is knit together by geographical, linguistic, social, political and cultural factors. Igboland is found in the southeast of Nigeria within the southern coast of West Africa. The Igbos occupy the eastern, part of the midwestern, and parts of the delta area of Nigeria. They can be geographically traced within the parallels 6° and 8° east longitudes and 5° and 7° north latitudes. In the present political structure in Nigeria, the Igbos make up the Enugu, Anambra, Imo, Abia, and parts of the Delta, Cross River, Akwa Ibom and Rivers States of Nigeria. They share common boundaries with other ethnic groups: northwards - with the Igalas, the Idomas and the Tivs; eastwards - with the Ekoi; southwards - with the Ibibios, Efiks, Ijaws and the Ogonis; westwards - with the Binis and the Isokos. The 1963 Nigerian census had the Igbo population to be at ten million. So, today, with Nigeria having an estimated population of about one hundred and twenty million, it is to be expected that the Igbos may have an estimated population of approximately thirteen million people.[2]

A large portion of Igboland falls within the tropical rain forest region stretching towards the north with a wood and savanna type of vegetation. Igboland is very thickly populated especially in the heartland of Okigwe areas where the population density is about one thousand persons per square mile.[3] Located in the dense tropical region, Igboland is heavily and specially blessed with forest resources, and, as such, can boast of abundant varieties of economic trees, especially the oil palm trees, which are mostly cultivated and greatly valued. Being naturally more favoured than the other parts of Nigeria, Igboland has an entirely different landscape, different climatic and vegetative conditions, and therefore, has different types of occupation from the rest of the country. There are two seasons in the year - the wet and the dry seasons; the wet lasting from April till the end of November, while the dry season fall within the months of December and March. The hottest

---

[1] 'Igbo' as a term, has an alternative - 'Ibo', being the equivalent used by foreigners because of the difficulty in pronouncing the Igbo double consonant 'gb'.

[2] Cf., Special Report on Nigeria in Time, 2nd March 1987, p.33.

[3] D. FORDE & G. JONES, The Ibo and Ibibio Speaking Peoples of Eastern Nigeria, London, 1950, p.11 & 13.

period in the year is in the months of February and March, when the temperature rises up to 87°F. Because of the favourable weather, Igboland has a very rich potential for agriculture, and this accounts for their general occupation which is farming, although this is on peasant level.

The Igbos form one of the three largest linguistic groups in Nigeria, second only to the Hausa speaking group.[4] Basden describes the Igbos as having "bridgeless noses and wide open nostrils . . . and thick protruding lips and the powerful jaws."[3] It is difficult to trace the origin of the Igbos. The difficulty rests largely on the fact that there had been no written records from the ancient times of the history of the Igbos. The only available facts have either come from the local and oral traditions/history transmitted from one generation to another. Such oral traditions have their handicaps, for, as Leith-Ross observed,

> Local ancestries go far back but vary with each telling. The old men sit in the meeting house, telling old tales, squabbling and contradicting. The youngmen are content to have no past, so long as they can have a future.[4]

Another author refers to the problem of the origins of the Igbos as "a very maze within a maze".[5]

These difficulties are based on the fact that the Igbos, made up of about two hundred or more dialectical cultural groups and villages, being independent and relatively small polities, have always posed a lot of difficulties for any scientific treatment of their traditions. However, some information can be gathered from the oral traditions, as against the impression being created by some authors, who say that the Igbos have no history.[6] On the contrary, because the Igbos have a culture, therefore, they have a history, even if this is yet on the level of oral tradition. Ethnological research based on these oral tradition reveals the Igbos as having a history that stretches as far back as five thousand years ago. Archaeological discoveries confirm the similarity of pottery fabricated about five thousand years ago with that made today at Nsukka in the northern part of Igboland.[7] There is a strong conjecture that first human inhabitants must have originated from the northern part of Igboland.

---

[4]Each of the three language groups in Nigeria has not less than three hundred dialects, distinct customs and traditions.

[3]G. T. BASDEN, Among the Ibos of Nigeria, Frank Cass & Co Ltd., (1966), p. 31

[4]S. LEITH-ROSS, African Women, London, (1939), p. 56.

[5]A. LEONARD, The Lower Niger and Its Tribes, London, (1906) p. 31.

[6]cf., V. C. UCHENDU, The Igbo of Southeast Nigeria, Holt, Rinehart and Winston, London, 1965, p. 2.

[7]DONALD D. HARTLE, "Archaeology in Eastern Nigeria", in Nigeria Magazine 93 (June 1967), 136-7.

The Igbos have very striking similarities with the Hebrews. Basden testifies to this fact in his writings:

> There are certain customs which rather point to Levitic influence at a more or less remote period. This is suggested in the underlying ideas concerning sacrifice and the practice of circumcision. The language also bears several interesting parallels with the Hebrew idiom.[8]

The Igbos are a strongly built race, with a very resourceful character; they are hard-working, ambitious, progressive, proud, intelligent, optimistic, and would hardly accept a defeat in any human enterprise. They have a strong sense of character. These qualities corroborate the views expressed above, which trace a link between the Igbos and the Jewish race. Some authors trace the origin of the Igbos to an immigration from Egypt in 1870 B.C on account of the Nubian wars. This view has it that some Egyptians came to settle in Yoruba and certain Igbo sub-tribal areas.[9] It seems, then, that Basden is right in thinking that,

> The Ibo people like their Yoruba neighbours, at some remote time, either actually lived near or had very close association with the Semitic races. The successive waves of invasion from the North-East Asia down through Egypt pressed these people to the South-West. As wave after wave came, they were borne onwards until finally, the Igbos came to rest where we find them today, and throughout ages, they have retained ideas and customs handed from generation to generation.[10]

In the absence of contrary evidence, one may hold on to this as the most probable.

As already mentioned above, due to the small units of the ethnic Igbo grouping, the consciousness of being one, whole ethnic entity has not always been there in Igboland. This sense of cohesion of all the Igbos is something of a recent past. The Nigeria and Biafra war re-awakened them to this consciousness. During this war, all the Igbos for the first time in history, stood together and made their experience as a people.

The major occupation of the Igbos is farming. Since there exists many important trade centres, some become traders and merchants. Others occupy themselves with such jobs as wood works, crafts, and arts. As the social structure of the Igbos is to be treated later, suffice it here to say that on the social level, Igbo solidarity and sense of community is superb. The Igbos are a forward-looking race, and it is this aspect that has led them into all nooks and corners of Nigeria. In fact, Geoffrey Parrinder is correct when

---

[8]G.T.BASDEN, op. cit., p. 31

[9]cf., P. AMAURY TALBOT, The Peoples of Southern Nigeria, vol. I, Oxford University Press, London, 1962, p. 19.

[10]G. T. BASDEN, Niger Ibos, Franc Cass & Co Ltd., London, p. 411.

he remarked that the "Ibo people of Eastern Nigeria . . . have remained an active and progressive people with a high population which led them into the delta . . . and into contacts with the outer world."[11]

1.2 **Igbo Vision of Life and World View**

Emefie Metu defined the world view of any people as the "complex of their belief and attitudes concerning the origin, nature, structure of the universe and the interaction of its beings, with particular reference to man."[12] Therefore Igbo vision of life and world view would reveal the attitudes and beliefs of the Igbos about the world around them, and their conception of the interaction of beings in the world. From the vision of life, one gains an access into the mentality of the people and their philosophy of life.

Underlying the Igbo mentality and philosophy is the principle that every effect must have a cause. One finds this principle operating in every system of life of the people. Accidents have no place in Igbo mentality, since every effect is traceable to a cause. The world is seen as an effect of an artifice. The universe for the Igbo is a complex, single whole with two phases - the visible and the invisible sectors of the one single reality. As Metu describes, the Igbos see the world as "one fluid, coherent unit, in which spirits, men, plants, and animals, and the elements, are engaged in continuous interaction."[13] Uchendu testifies to this interaction:

> . . . the Igbo world is a 'real' one in every respect. There is the world of man, peopled by all created beings and things, both animate and inanimate. The spirit world is the abode of the creator, the deities, the disembodied and malignant spirits, and the ancestral spirits. It is the future abode of the living after their death. There is a constant interaction between the world of man and the world of the dead; the visible and the invisible forces.[14]

The invisible sector is inhabited by God, the spirits, and the ancestors, while the visible part is occupied by man and other lower beings. Man occupies the centre in this world as a pivot where he "seeks through rituals to maintain an equilibrium and a harmonious relationship with all the beings

---

[11]E. G. PARRINDER, West African Religion, Epworth Press, London, 1978, p. 5.

[12]EMEFIE I. METU, God and Man in African Religion, Geoffrey Chapman, London, 1981, p. 48.

[13]Id., African Religions in Western Conceptual Schemes, Claverian Press, Ibadan, 1985, p. 4.

[14]V. C. UCHENDU, op. cit., pp. 11-12

and forces that impinge on his life and being".[15]

The Igbos believe that God created the world. For them the concept of creation and providence is fundamental in their concept of God, the Supreme Being. This God is considered as transcendent and immanent in his effects through the intermediary action of the deities and other spirit world, who are looked upon as divine messengers and representatives in the visible world. This God who created all is specially bound to each one through a personal spirit - 'chi', his personal emanation as well as one's destiny, dictating the natural package for every one - one's 'akala aka': which means literally one's natural palm-prints. The Igbos have a proverb which says that 'akala aka onye n'edu ya' - (one is always led by his palm-prints). Isichei explains, "the 'chi' a personalised providence, comes from Chukwu and reverts to him at a man's death. Each man has his own 'chi' who may be well or ill-disposed".[16] Also Francis Arinze on this 'chi' writes: "Most Ibos believe that each individual has a spirit, a genus, or a spiritual double, his 'chi', which is given him at conception by Chukwu and which accompanies this individual from the cradle to the grave".[17]

The Igbos believe that God has not only created the world, but also continues to sustain it, hence, they also call God 'Elili ji obele', meaning, the rope suspending the calabash, where the world is seen as a calabash, and God as the all-important rope holding the calabash in being.

Besides God, the invisible world is replete with other spirits and deities.[18] The actual relationship between Chukwu and these deities remain ambiguous. But generally the Igbos regard these deities as messengers and manifestations of Chukwu. The spirits are generally personified forces found in nature. They can be very useful as they can also be very dangerous depending of whether they are properly controlled or mishandled. As Arinze explains,

> These 'alusi' are like electric wire; they do not consider bona fide transgression. Not even the most rapacious thief would dare to take anything kept under their protection. These spirits have the reputation of wasting no time in tackling such unholy

---

[15]E.I.METU, African Religions in Western Schemes, p.4.

[16]E. ISICHEI, A History of the Igbo People, The Macmillan Press Ltd., (1976), p. 24.

[17]F. A. ARINZE, Sacrifice in Ibo Religion, Ibadan University Press, 1970, p. 15.

[18]"The invisible world is the spirit world (Ani mmuo). Spirits are called Mmuo. There are two types of Mmuo - Ndi Mmuo - human spirit (the dead) and Mmuo (spirits who were never humans). Spirits can be grouped into four broad categories: Chukwu (the Creator), Mmuo (deities), Alusi (spirit-forces), and Ndi Mmuo (the living dead)." E. I. METUH, African Religions in West, Concept., p. 38.

14

offenders.[19]

The interaction with the ancestral spirits are not left out in their world view. The ancestral spirits are the spirit of good people who have ultimately reached the land of the spirits. It is the firm belief of the Igbos that the 'alusi' and the bad spirits looming large in the physical world of experience causing confusion and havoc are no other than "the unhappy spirits who die bad deaths and lack correct burial rites", therefore, "cannot return to the world of the living or enter that of the dead. They wonder homeless and dispossessed, expressing their grief by causing harm among the living."[20] Man steers clear of these by sacrifices. The interaction and cooperation between the ancestors and God is responsible in bringing new lives into existence.

Diviners, being key figures in ascertaining the mind of the spirit world, play the intermediary roles in the interaction between man and the spirits. Since for the Igbos human situations and conditions depend not on physical, nor social nor mechanical factors, but rather on the relationship with the spirits, therefore, anything that happens, be it good or bad, is traced to the intervention of the spirits, who may have returned with a blessing or a punishment respectively. The diviners are the arbiters of whichever case it is.[21] Thus an equilibrium is maintained, based on the principle of reciprocity in the pragmatic sense, for the Igbos have a proverb that states: 'aka nni kwo aka ekpe, aka ekpe akwo aka nni' (meaning : both hands reciprocate in washing one another). To ward off the negative intervention of the spirits, the traditional norms called 'Omenani', are meticulously observed. These norms are supposed to have been handed down by the ancestors through successive generations up to the present.

On the interaction among the humans in the world, it is interesting to note that the Igbos are strongly attached to each other. The bond of attachment is indeed very strong. In Igboland, each person is considered as a being in relation. Thomas Merton's title of his book "No man is an island" is indeed an appropriate description of the Igbo sense of belonging. This point is so important that a person is always defined in terms of the group to which one belongs. It is in fact abnormal for one not to inhere in any group, in terms of either a family, kindred, age-group or grade. For the Igbos, as Arinze puts it,

. . . to exist is to live in the group, to see things with the

---

[19]F. A. ARINZE, op. cit., p. 12.

[20]E. ISICHEI, op. cit., pp. 25 - 26.

[21]"Whatever menaces the life or property of an individual or society, is an indication to the traditional Igbo that something is wrong somewhere, and that it must be set right before it is too late. A necessary consequence to this is the frequent consultation of diviners (dibia, affa) to find out the hidden causes of the danger signal." S. OBIUKWU, "'Ala' in Igbo Culture and Traditional Religious Beliefs",(Ph.D Thesis) Urban University, Rome, 1978, p. 25

group, to do things with the group. Life is not an individual venture, each one for himself. This powerful social instinct has been harnessed to produce wonderful results in community development projects. The Ibos help one another to build a house or to cut a new road, to celebrate a marriage or to solemnise a funeral.[22]

This bond of relationship is not only on a socio-biological level, but takes even religious and ontological dimensions. Each one is inserted within an extended family structure. The principle that underlies this mentality is the fact that might is great. It is taken for granted that no man is independent of the others. Obiukwu rightly expatiated this point when he said that

> . . . man in this world needs another in order to realise his life's objectives. This truth is so vivid in the average mind of the Igbo that he thinks communally, feels communally, and tries to live communally . . . . This sense of collective responsibility is very beautifully summarised in Igbo proverbial saying, namely, 'ofu aka luta mmanu, otezue ndi ozo'.[23]

(This literally means that when a finger is smeared with oil, it eventually involves the other fingers.)

With regard to life in general, the Igbos conceive life as the greatest possession of man, to which nothing can be given in exchange. Certain Igbo nomenclature such as 'Ifeyinwa' (nothing is like the gift of a child); 'Ndukaku' (life is greater than wealth); 'Ndubuisi' (life is prior to everything), confirms this. This accounts for the great love for children in Igbo families, where traditionally the birth of nine or ten children is taken as quite normal The Igbos believe that life comes only from God with the cooperation of the ancestors. Death is not considered as the termination of man's life, but is only an end of a phase in the continuous rounds of human existence. Hence there is a belief in Reincarnation. Igbos believe that life involves a cyclic process of birth, death, and rebirth. They want to live and continue to live with a strengthened life-force in each cycle of life. They consider a very long and healthy life the greatest blessings; while the misfortune of having to die without an offspring or childless is regarded as the greatest curse in life. In line with this is the mysterious and superstitious belief in 'Ogbanje', a feature which attributes the death of very young children to mysterious reincarnated spirits called 'ogbanje'.

This vision of life of the Igbos is enmeshed with an integrated religious sense that permeates all aspects of life of the Igbos. This mentality, in no small way, influences and characterises the entire Culture of the Igbos as would be seen below.

---

[22]F. A. ARINZE, op.cit., pp. 4 - 5.

[23]S.OBIUKWU, op.cit., p. 26.

1.3   **Igbo Cultural Background**

Before scaning through Igbo Culture, it is essential to draw attention to the observation made by a certain author, who said that, "no one individual is ever familiar with the total culture of his society, still less required to express all its manifold patterns in his overt behaviour."[24] It would be deceptive, then, to think of an exhaustive and comprehensive outline of Igbo Culture on account of its complexity. One can only attempt a description of some cultural elements of the Igbos.

One glaring difficulty in treating Igbo Culture, which it shares with other African cultures, is the already mentioned fact of absence of literary records of the past. So much remain unarticulated scientifically. But this should not be interpreted as 'not there', as some outsiders arbitrarily conclude. An observation of the Igbos even from a distance would immediately reveal them as having a very rich and complex culture. Igbo cultural elements emerge from their vision of life. This vision of life, as in many other African cultures, has its deep roots in religion, as Ukpong rightly points out:

> . . . in traditional African world view there is a unity in the realm
> of values with religion as the integrating force. This gives rise
> to a thought system in which there is no separation of the
> sacred from the profane, both being seen as a unity with the
> profane subordinated to the sacred.[25]

Elements of Igbo Culture branch off from this religious base, each highly charged with a deep religious character. Hence, one considers first and foremost in Igbo Culture, man's relationship with the supernatural beings and superhuman forces, namely the Supreme Being, minor deities and ancestral spirits, as well as the lower spirit forces - all these come under the umbrella of religion.

1.3.1 Igbo Traditional Religion

The most fundamental characteristic of Igbo Culture, as pointed above, is that it is so intertwined and rooted in religion that one can say that the Igbos have a religious Culture or a cultural Religion. From this religious source, every aspect of the culture bears a religious imprint. Hence it is difficult to observe a dichotomy between the sacred and the profane in Igbo Culture. An interesting comparison can be made between the Igbo world outlook and the biblical Old Testament outlook. In the Old Testament outlook the divine and the mundane are so intricately intertwined and

---

[24]RALPH LINTON, The Cultural Background of Personality, Routledge & Kegan Paul Ltd., London, 1968, p. 36.

[25]JUSTIN S. UKPONG, "Contextualizing Theological Education in Western Africa" in Chiea : African Christian Studies, vol. 3, no. 3, Sept. 1987, p. 64

penetrate one another, in such a way that each turning point of history is interpreted as a divine intervention, and the handwork of the Most High is seen everywhere.[26] It is just the same in Igbo Culture. It is difficult to think of an ambient that is completely mundane without a religious implication. Of course, one would expect such, because "in societies which have not been secularised to any considerable degree, worldly activities such as work, government, learning, etc. are surrounded by religious observances . . ."[27]

There is no sector of Igbo Culture that has posed serious problems to ethnologists, anthropologists and Christian Missionaries as the Igbo Traditional Religion. Igbo Traditional Religion defies any easy classification and definition. Some people have tended to see it as primitive religion. But as Parrinder would clarify, this is not true. He writes,

> The famous French writer Lévy-Bruhl, although he held that many races were 'prelogical', yet recognised that the Ashanti possessed a real religion above the primitive level. The same could be said of the intricacies of Ewe, Yoruba, or Ibo belief.

He explains why this is so:

> Instead of being confounded with a universal substratum of 'primitive religion' it may be claimed that these central and important groups of West Africans have had traditional religious beliefs which deserve consideration in comparison with some of the races of Europe and Asia. Though there are no scriptures and little known history, the subtlety of many religious beliefs shows them to be developed well beyond the primitive.[28]

There has also been a tendency to consider this religion as 'fetishism'. If fetishism stands for "the doctrine of spirits, embodied in, or attached to, or conveying influence through certain material objects . . . including the worship of 'stocks and stones' and . . passes by an imperceptible gradation into idolatry"[29], then, it would be incorrect to qualify Igbo traditional religion with this term, since it gives a distorted and unfair representation of the religion. One must note that

> The Africans are more capable of abstract thought than is generally recognised, and they believe in a latent energy in

---

[26]Cf., GERHARD von RAD, Old Testament Theology, vol. 2, SCM Press Ltd., (1965), pp. 336-356

[27]THOMAS F. O'DEA, The Sociology of Religion, Prentice-Hall, Inc., Englewood Cliffs, New Jersey, 1966, p. 115.

[28]E. GEOFFREY PARRINDER, West African Religion, Epworth Press, London, (1949), 1969 edition, p. 7.

[29]E. B. TYLOR. Primitive Culture, vol.II, New York, Harper Torchbooks, (1871) 1958, p. 143ff.

things which is not visible in outward appearance but can be seen in the effects produced by use.[30]

It is a fact that in Igbo traditional religion there are sacred animals, trees, stones, rivers, and places, but one has to strongly note that sacred objects are only symbols. A study of symbolic systems is essential for a right interpretation of Igbo Religion. Just like some other African religions, Igbo Religion as Parrinder still testifies,

> . . . is not just the worship or the use of the work of men's hands. It is known today that no 'heathen in his blindness bows down to wood and stone'. The 'heathen' worships a spiritual being, who may be approached through a material object. But all Africans believe that there are other spiritual forces than those associated with 'idols'. The great Creator has very few temples or images, but is almost everywhere believed in. Many other gods and ancestors are prayed to without any material representations of them being used.[31]

Another author, who has exclusively written about Southern Nigeria, of which the Igbos make up a major part, reinforces this objection. He observes:

> True Fetishism, in which the object of worship is not symbolic but is worshipped for itself and not as connected with, or representing a deity or spirit, is absent from this country.[32]

Some Missionaries have referred to Igbo Religion as pagan. This would also be totally wrong, since paganism originally used to refer to a village dweller or a countryman, a person who lives away from the civilised community; a term used to denote a rustic, unpolished and unsophisticated person, which only later by extension, came to have a religious connotation. It was applied in a derogatory sense to religions thought to be inferior to other religions considered as superior. It is taken as synonymous with magic. It should not, however be limited only to the African religions as many have hitherto done.

Is the traditional religion of the Igbos to be taken for animism? Animism is the system of belief and practices based on the idea that objects and natural phenomena are inhabited by spirits or souls.[33] Many authors oppose vehemently any attempt to ascribe the term to only African religions.

---

[30]E. G. PARRINDER, African Traditional Religion, Sheldon Press, London, 1974, p. 23

[31]E. G. PARRINDER, African Traditional Religion, pp. 15-16.

[32]P. A. TALBOT, The Peoples of Southern Nigeria, Oxford University Press, London, 1926, vol. II, pp. 20ff.

[33]Cf., J. S. MBITI, Introduction to African Religion, Heinemann, London, 1975, p. 17.

A religious scholar warns,

> . . . 'animism' properly defined cannot be predicated as a
> monopoly of African or any other race, . . . Animism can . . .
> be predicated as part definition of every religion. But it is
> inappropriate as the name for African traditional religion: the
> derogatory and abusive nomenclature of Africans as 'animists'
> should cease."[34]

Igbo traditional religion has really traces of animism. But it is much more
than a belief in the spirit of objects and natural phenomena. Even if these
are approached with spiritual sentiments, who is however worshipped
through these natural objects, is, of course, the Supreme God, whom the
Igbos see as the overall head of all spirits.

One is left with the alternative of regarding Igbo traditional religion as
polytheism. Even at that, there remains a big problem, for, among the
Igbos, although they have several minor deities, yet the supremacy of God
does not come into question. God as the Supreme Being is upheld
everywhere and is accorded the ultimacy demanded by monotheism.
Confronted by this problem, Talbot refuses to call Igbo traditional religion a
polytheism, and had to conclude thus:

> On the whole, the religion strongly resembles that of the
> ancient Egyptians, who combines a belief in the existence of
> an omnipotent and omniscient Supreme God . . . with that in
> multitude of subordinate deities . . . [35]

So, the true term that could describe adequately the religion of the Igbos
is yet to be found, but should, however, vacillate between mono- and
polytheism or what Idowu would like to refer to as 'diffused monotheism'.[36]

Briefly, one can distinguish Igbo traditional Religion in four dimensions.
A panoramic view of these dimensions may be necessary.

1.3.1.1   **The Supreme God**

The Igbos strongly believe in the existence of the Supreme God.
This Supreme God is variously referred to as: 'Chukwu' (Chi-ukwu) - the
Greatest Spirit, 'Chineke' - the creating Spirit, and 'Osebuluwa' - the
Upholder of the Universe. G. T. Basden referring to this God says,

> Among the Ibo people there is a distinct recognition of a
> Supreme Being - beneficent in character - who is above every

---

[34]E. BOLAJI IDOWU, African Traditional Religion, SCM Press Ltd.
London, 1973, p. 134.

[35]P. A. TALBOT, op. cit., p. 15

[36]Cf., E. B. IDOWU, op. cit., p. 135

other spirit, good or evil. He is believed to control all things in heaven and earth, and dispenses rewards and punishments according to merit. . . . But Chukwu is supreme, and at His service are many ministering spirits whose sole business it is to fulfil His commands . . . [37]

Throughout Igboland one finds so many names given to God the Supreme Being. The firm and unshakeable belief in the Supreme God finds a very rich and eloquent expression in Igbo nomenclature, which is always a compendium of divine attributes. Such names given by parents to their children is always a guide for understanding the Igbo concept of God. Such Igbo names reveal God as very real and near to the Igbos and convey the purest expression of their religious thinking and experience. An experience of the daily life of the Igbos would immediately reveal the impact and essence of these divine names, and reflect the Igbo sense of divine presence, divine care, and protection, - all these are reflected in their attitude to this Supreme Being. For instance, the following names reveal so much of the divine that is expressed in the Igbo nomenclature :

'Nwokike' - son of the Creator;
'Chinenye' - God gives;
'Chima' (Chukwuma) - God knows;
'ArizeChukwu' - were it not for God's sake;
'OkeChukwu' - creature of God;
'NgoziChukwu' - God's Blessings;
'Chukwuka' - god is the greatest;
'IfeanyiChukwu' - nothing is impossibe to God;
'KeneChukwu' - Thank God;
'Chizoba' (Chukwuzoba) - May God save etc.

These names show as Idowu would agree that "to them, Deity is the Living One who is the ever present, ever active, and ever acting Reality in the world".[38] Westermann is also of the same conviction as he observes:

People acknowledge him . . . He is God of the thoughtful . . . ., in the sayings of this people . . . the figure of God assumes features of a truly personal and purely divine Supreme Being . . . it cannot be overlooked that he is a reality to the African, who will admit that what he knows about God is the purest expression of his religious experience . . . [39]

With special reference to the supremacy of God in Igbo religion, Parrinder writes,

---

[37]G. T. BASDEN, Among the Ibos of Nigeria, p. 215

[38]E. B. IDOWU, op.cit., p. 28

[39]DIEDRICH WESTERMANN, Africa and Christianity, Oxford University Press, 1937, p. 65ff

That God is almighty is one of the most obvious assertions, since supremacy implies it. All-powerful is a common name for him and he receives many similar titles: creator, allotter, giver of rain and sunshine. These attributes imply the transcendence of God and to some extent his immanence.[40]

From the above it is doubtless that God is real to the Igbos. He is unique and the absolute controller of the universe. He created everything, knows everything, and has no equal. Although there are no cult symbols, nor statues, nor shrines for the Supreme God among the Igbos, He is the final recipient of sacrifices offered through the minor deities, who, as will be seen below, are regarded as the messengers, manifestations and mediators of the Supreme Being. Igbo morning prayers and prayers at other circumstances of life, which are a compendium of expressions and attitudes of complete dependence and utter submission, are directly addressed to the Supreme God. Hence Cronin is correct in saying that

> Every African people recognize the Supreme God as one: there may be other spirits or nature gods but there is always one supreme or high God. When Africans of different ethnic groups meet, they recognize that the different names they have for God refer to the one supreme God. God is not a tribal God but a supreme Lord.[41]

For the Igbos, then, the Supreme Being is personal, not human like the minor deities, who are looked upon as the promoted ancestors. The Igbo Supreme God is the ultimate arbiter of all matters and the final Judge of man. From such a concept, an authentic christian theology can have a solid base among the Igbos.[42]

1.3.1.2   Belief in the Minor Deities

Besides the belief in the Supreme Being, the Igbos have minor deities. It is on account of these minor deities that confusion arises as to the nature of God of the Igbo traditional religion. It is wondered and asked what roles these minor deities play, and their relationship with the Supreme God. From the explanations given above, these deities are considered as messengers, and mediators whose role exists in the execution of the will of the Supreme Being. It is on account of these deities that Igbo religion has

---

[40]E. G. PARRINDER, Africa's Three Religions, Sheldon Press, London, 1969, p. 39

[41]BRIAN CRONIN, "Religious and Christian Conversion in an African Context", in African Christian Studies, vol. 3, no. 2, June 1987, p. 25

[42]Cf., E. G. PARRINDER, Africa's Three Religions, p. 39

been seriously accused of polytheism. So, a clarification is necessary. Arinze clearly explains this point:

> The Ibos have . . . a strong belief in the non-human spirits. These are often personification of natural phenomena: there are spirits of rivers, hills, farms, and lightening. The four days of the Ibo week are also personified. Then there are spirits of destiny, of the household and of fertility. . . . they have super human power to help or to hinder.[43]

On the relationship of these deities with the Supreme Being as well as their nature, Arinze continues:

> The spirits are invisible . . . are above man but below God. They, or at least the good spirits, are God's messengers although God seems to give them much liberty of action. The spirits are all created by God.[44]

Metuh also views the apparent paradox of accepting the Supreme Being and at the same time recognising many deities as not problematic for the Igbos, because according to him,

> . . . it would seem that in line with their ideas about kingship and nobility, the number and power of subordinate deities enhance the importance and supremacy of Chukwu, just as the prestige of a king is sometimes measured by the number and power of his subordinate chiefs. So it would be normal and logical to the Igbo to affirm in one breath the unity and Supremacy of God, and the greatness and multiplicity of the deities.[45]

But that is not all. Some of the spirits are taken to be the ancestors who have been deified. Some are thought, therefore, to have been human and have been eventually made divine.[46]

To clear the impression of polytheism, it may be necessary to view the remark made by Paul Tillich, who holds that,

> Polytheism is a qualitative and not a quantitative concept. It is not a belief in a plurality of gods but rather the lack of a unifying and transcending ultimate which determines its

---

[43]F. A. ARINZE, op. cit., p. 12

[44]Ibid.

[45]EMEFIE I. METUH, God & Man in African Religion, p. 61

[46]Cf., E. G. PARRINDER, West African Religion, p. 26

character.[47]

If one takes note of this remark, then the doubts are clarified. From the structural conception of the spirits in Igbo traditional religion, one can say that they have no absolute existence, since they are in being only as a result of and for the purposes of mediation. This point is strongly emphasised by Arinze, who insists that

> when the Ibos pray to the spirits or offer sacrifices to them, they sometimes tell the spirits expressly to intercede for them before Chukwu . . . . The Iboman . . . simply will not accept that they exist of themselves. That is why he takes God as the final court of appeal when these intermediaries prove themselves unequal to the task . . . . What is crystal clear is that no Iboman will put God on a level with any alusi (spirits), be that spirit ever so powerful.[48]

Shelton, on the same point, further clarifies,

> Worshipping of the lesser deities is an act of worshipping the high god, who is considered to be immanent in subordinate beings or is symbolised by the images of lesser deities. In any case, whatever powers the inferior deities possess, these powers are ultimately derived from God, the source. . . . but it is also understood that the deities are descendant powers, especially considered of Chukwu, (chi, okike, Chineke).[49]

Hence the power of these spirits and deities are meaningless if severed from the supreme Being. The spirits can be considered as functionaries in the theocratic control of the universe. Therefore, they are not ends in themselves but only means to an end - to the Supreme Being. On the status of these deities, Parrinder throws more light, when, speaking of African religion in general, he remarks

> although African gods are said to be personal, having names, temples, images, priests, and cults, the personification need not be taken too literally, but rather as poetical expression through the use of abundant metaphor.[50]

Having made these fundamental clarifications, one takes a particular look at some of the Igbo deities and spirits.

---

[47]PAUL TILLICH, Systematic Theology, vol. I, 1953, p. 246

[48]F. A. ARINZE, op. cit., p. 13

[49]A. J. SHELTON, "Recent Interpretation of Deus Otiosus: Withdrawn God in West African Psychology", in Man, Jan. 1964, p. 53

[50]E. G. PARRINDER, Africa's Three Religions, p. 48

1.3.1.2.1   The Sun Deity - "Anyanwu"

The Igbos have a varied cult of the sun. 'Anyanwu' is worshipped as a deity of fortune, and the provident of wealth. The deity is prayed to for profit in the market and for good harvest. Metuh observes,

> generally Anyanwu is called the son of Chineke and sometimes his emanation. The special and close association of the Sun with the Supreme Being is . . . seen in the fact that some sacrifices made to the supreme Being are made through Anyanwu.[51]

1.3.1.2.2   The Sky or Thunder Deity - 'Igwe' or 'Amadioha'

The god of Thunder which is worshipped under various names viz: 'Igwe', 'Amadioha', 'Kamalu', and 'Ofufe', is regarded as a powerful deity. Igwe expresses this power and anger in thunderbolts and lightnings.[52] It is believed that in disputes involving serious and malicious accusations, the divine verdict is always transmitted and expressed by the agency of Amadioha, which usually strikes down culprits. Such deaths are denied befitting burial, since they are considered as punished from God. Speaking of this Igbo deity, Parrinder reveals that

> He is one of the most important gods . . . . Amadioha is seen in the lightning and heard in thunder, and punishes sorcerers, witches, and those who break his laws. But since he sends rain he is also a giver of fertility and prayers are made to him both for increase of crops and for children in the home.[53]

1.3.1.2.3   The Earth goddess - 'Ala'

The most prominent and most important of the Igbo deities is the Earth goddess - 'Ala'. She is regarded as the president of the earth below, and the one who takes care of all dead and alive. This should not be a wonder to anyone, since the earth is the leveller of all, and all mortals make their final embrace to her when they die and are laid to rest. She is taken to be the giver of fertility to men, animals, and crops. Men are born to live on earth, they feed on the products of the earth and they die, and are

---

[51]E. I. METUH, African Religion in Western Conceptual Schemes, p. 41

[52]Cf., V. C. UCHENDU, op. cit., p. 97

[53]E. G. PARRINDER, West African Religion, p. 33

buried in the earth.[54]   Ala is regarded as the custodian of the laws and customs - 'Omenani' - of the land, whose infringement by such crimes as adultery, incest, homicide, theft, poisoning, must be specially purged by sacrificial rites.   As Metuh observes,

> The cult of Ala is one of the most powerful integrating forces in Igbo societies which are characterised by the absence of centralised political authority.   Her cult is organised at the family, village, and clan level so that there are family shrines, village shrines, and clan shrines to Ala.[55]

In Meek's view,

> 'Ala' is in fact the unseen president of the community, and no group is complete without a shrine of Ala.   The common possession of a shrine of Ala is, indeed, one of the strongest integrating forces in Ibo society.[56]

From these testimonies, the importance the Igbos attach to land becomes very understandable.

Besides these deities, there are still others like the deity of yam - 'Ifejioku' (yam is the most staple food for the Igbos).   Sacrifices are offered to Ifejioku before and after the planting seasons for successful growth of yam.   There are also water deities that are regarded as the guardians of rivers, and lakes, and to whom sacrifices are offered when traditional laws guiding such places are violated.

As already said above, no matter the power attributed to these deities and spirits, none can be equated to or seen in the same platform as the Supreme being.   All these spirits take orders from Him.

1.3.1.3   **Ancestral Veneration**

Generally speaking, all people manifest a devotional attitude towards the dead.   This gives an impression that there is always a kind of communication and relationship between the living and the dead, even if this relationship is on the symbolic level.   One sees the almost daily visits to the cemeteries and burial places, as well as the special adornment of the graves with flowers, which practice is observable among all people, as a kind of expression of this relationship.

Among the Igbos, as already stated in the world view, there exists a strong bond of relationship between both the living and the dead.   This is as a result of the extended family system, where membership is not limited only

---

[54]Cf., W. R. C. HORTON, "God, Man, and Land in Northern Ibo Village-Group", in Africa, 26 (1956), p. 18

[55]E. I. METUH, God and Man in African Religion, p. 67

[56]C. K. MEEK, Law and Authority in a Nigerian Tribe, p. 25

to the visible living family members, but includes also the dead members of the family, and even those yet to be born. In such a context, the contact and relationship with the dead surpasses the symbolic level and acquires a sort of concrete reality. Parrinder had to remark:

> Not only are the ancestors revered as past heroes but they are felt to be still present watching over the household, directly concerned in all the affairs of the family and property, giving abundant harvests and fertility.[57]

That the relationship with the ancestors is strong and seen as something very real is testified to by Idowu, who writes:

> The ancestors are regarded still as heads and parts of the families or communities to which they belonged while they were living human beings: for what happened in consequence of the phenomenon called death was only that the family life of this earth has been extended into the after-life or supersensible world. The ancestors remain, therefore, spiritual superintendents of family affairs and continue to bear their titles of relationship like 'father' or 'mother'.[58]

That is why the Igbos do not break their heads debating whether they are worshipping or giving reverence to their ancestors. They have high regard and respect for their seniors, especially their parents, for it is believed that one's parents, by virtue of their fatherhood or motherhood are endowed with power to bless or curse an offspring. Hence it is no wonder that this belief in such powers of one's parents, who may have passed into ancestral region, is thought to have an enhanced and continuous effect on their offspring. Cullen is, therefore, absolutely correct in his remarks, which can be relevantly applied to the Igbos. He says:

> The African community is a single, continuing unit, conscious of no distinction, in quality, between its members still here on earth, and its members now there, wherever it may be that the ancestors are living.[59]

It is the same point that Marc Ela clarifies when he expatiates that

> Drink and food offered to the ancestors are symbols, . . . of the continuity of the family and of this permanent contact. In the African mind, these offerings express an attitude that is unchanged by death, which is the passage into the invisible.

---

[57]E. G. PARRINDER, West African Religions, p. 115

[58]E. B. IDOWU, op. cit., p. 184

[59]CULLEN YOUNG, African Ideas of God, quoted in E. G. PARRINDER, African Traditional Religion, p. 65

Accordingly, the African always behaves as if the ancestors were still living. Offering one's dead father a meal is a simple act of filial piety.[60]

Hence, ancestral reverence occupies a very prominent position in Igbo religion and culture.

The ancestors are called 'Ndichie' or 'Ndi Nna anyifa'. But it is interesting to note that not all the dead qualify to be ancestors. To qualify, one must have been good; must have been survived by at least a male child - for, women generally speaking, and all who die childless are not regarded as ancestors. Living well means living in accordance with the norms, customs, and traditions of the land - the 'Omenani'. Other requirements are the attainment of a ripe old age, dying a good death, and being accorded a befitting funeral rite.[61] One may be tempted to say that the ancestors are the traditionally canonised saints of the Igbos, and names of such ancestors are immortalised by newly born infants being named after them.

On the role which the ancestors are supposed to play, the Igbos regard them as intermediaries with God in transmitting life and looking after their living ones. They are 'symbols of peace, unity and prosperity in the family. At the same time, as protectors of traditional laws and customs, and welfare of their families, they may punish offenders'.[62] Since they are the elder members of their families, they have enhanced powers to protect the interests of their own. The Ancestors are responsible in maintaining discipline in their families. In the words of Ela,

> Thanks to the kinship system, the ancestors remain linked to
> their families and continue to protect the living, caring for them
> and acting as their intermediaries, while receiving their respect,
> reverence, and solicitude.[63]

On the attitude given to the ancestors, the categorical statement of J. H. Driberg is particularly appropriate to the Igbos. He writes:

> No African prays to his dead grand father any more than he
> 'prays' to his living father. In both cases the words employed
> are the same: he asks as of right, or he beseeches, or he
> expostulates with, or he reprimands . . . but he never uses in
> his context the words for 'prayer' and 'worship' which are strictly
> reserved for his religious dealings with the Absolute Powers and

---

[60]JEAN-MARC ÉLA, My Faith as an African, Orbis Books, Maryknoll, New York, 1988, p. 19

[61]I. P. ANOZIA, "The Religious Import of Igbo Names", Doctoral dissertation, Urban University, Rome, 1968, p. 9

[62]E. I. METUH, God & Man in African Religion, p. 96

[63]J. ELA, op. cit., p. 17

the divinities. The Latin word 'pietas' probably best describes the attitude of Africans to their dead ancestors, as to their living elder.[64]

In any case, daily remembrance of ancestors are made at meals and during morning prayers. In the year there is an annual feast in honour of the ancestors. This is called the 'Ilo-mmuo ' feast. During this feast the entire family is reunited and family ties are strengthened. The ancestors are invoked at the family gatherings and in such family ceremonies as festivals, births, marriages, in sicknesses, and funerals of the family.

On whether to refer to this as worship or not, it may suffice to consider the point made by De Napoli, when he remarked,

> There is little doubt that there is a cult of the dead in many cultures. But to conclude that this is worship can scarcely be proved and indeed is disproved by more recent studies. The cult of the dead is a good example of a practice found in non-Christian cultures which could easily be purified and inculturated by sound Christian doctrine.[65]

Important in the ancestral reverence is the aspect of the symbol of authority. There is what is known as the 'Ofo', which is the visible material symbol of authority. This symbol represents the person and the authority of the ancestors. The lineage 'Ofo' symbol is the external sign of the presence of the ancestors, and must therefore, be displayed when important family discussions are held and serious decisions are taken. The 'Ofo' derives its value from the fact that it has been successively handed on to the first-born son called 'okpala' through several generations ending up with the present oldest son in the lineage. This oldest in the lineage is the custodian of this symbol of authority, and on account of this lineage 'Ofo', the oldest man is accorded a very great prestige, homage and respect, as the visible representative of, and the nearest living contact to the ancestors. In Igboland, especially when a Christian grows to be the oldest living in the lineage, a lot of problems are confronted especially as regards the performance of the traditional roles. This is why the Igbo Old age system and its ceremonies is singled out to be specially treated in the model chapter of this work.

1.3.1.4   **Evil Spirits and Forces - 'Arusi'**

On the negative side, there are evil spirits referred to as 'Arusi'. These are non-human and, therefore, unknown spirits that harass people.

---

[64]J. H. DRIBERG, The Secular Aspects of Ancestor Worship in Africa, quoted in E. G. PARRINDER, African Traditional Religion, p. 64

[65]GEORGE A. DE NAPOLI, "Inculturation as Communication", in MARIA DE LA CRUZ AZYMES et al., Effective Inculturation and Ethnic Identity, Pontifical Gregorian University, Rome, 1987, p. 92.

As malevolent spirits, they "delight in inflicting suffering almost capriciously and at the least provocation. They are offered sacrifices only to appease them and to invite them to do harm to one's enemies".[66]

The attitude of the Igbos towards these malignant evil spirits and forces is to endeavour as much as possible to ward off and dodge these spirits, and steer clear of them and treat them as if they were electric conduits.

Aligned to these spirits, are other mystical forces which feature greatly among the Igbos. These forces are identified with the use of charms, witchcraftcy, sorcery and poisonous potions, referred to in Igbo as 'nsi'. Witchcraftcy is more practised in riverine areas. The Igbos have much faith in traditional medicine. Although there is the positive aspect of the traditional medicine, in the sense of medicinal herbs and concoctions for the cure of certain ailments such as snake bites, malaria, convulsions, or the like; but there are the negative dimension of traditional medicine, which is employed for harmful and offensive motives. This takes the form of poisoning - 'iko nsi'. This has much to do with the use of magical powers. It must be noted that here one deals not with spirits but natural forces controlled by man, but negatively made use of for sinister motives.

We have seen above the various aspects that make up the traditional religious dimensions of the Igbos. Let us now focus the attention on the other aspects of the culture.

1.3.2 The Social and Political Elements

These consist of the social, recreational and political structures and institutions which treat of man's relationship with the human family and means of social control. These concretely are such spheres as the family, social and political organisations - the age grades, title institution, associations and groups, societies, the Masquerades etc. The recreational sector treats of celebrations, festivals, music, folklore, dancing, etc. these are intended to provide the Igbo with relaxation especially during the relaxed moments in his life.

1.3.2.1 Igbo Social Elements

A deep sense of solidarity, as already highlighted, is an underlying factor in all Igbo group cohesion and social stratification.

1.3.2.1.1 Igbo Social Structure

The Igbos have a social structure which is modelled on the extended family system. Generally speaking, the family is the nucleus of any society. But the Igbo family is extended, in the sense that it is made up of not only the nuclear family - 'ezi-na uno'-, but of all the various nuclear families

---

[66]F. A. ARINZE, op. cit., p. 14

bound together by blood relationship. No nuclear family in the classic sense of the term, is therefore autonomous. Each is necessarily connected to other nuclear families, so that a complete family is generally very large. This image of the family widens further to include the kindred - the extended patrilineal family called the 'Umunna', the lineage - the 'ebo', which is a collection of kindred. This eventually widens to form what is the village - the 'ogbe' - a collection of lineages. This is not the limit of the Igbo social unit. There is still the town - 'obodo' - which is the conglomeration of all the villages.

It is interesting to note that at the head of each successive level of grouping, is the eldest, who, by virtue of being the first surviving son in the group, assumes the spiritual as well as the administrative head of the group. Such a one inherits the traditional ancestral staff of authority. It is not difficult to discover from this extended family structure the Igbo concept and philosophy of universal fraternity, for the universe is seen as a spider's web in which all beings are interwoven by a network of relationships which influence each other. It is exactly to this interaction that Jean-Marc Ela refers, when, speaking of the mountain Cameroonian community, who share this characteristics of the Igbos - being the nearest neighbours of the Igbos - he observed that all - young and old alike "are joined in one feeling of communion that reinforces the unity and cohesion of the entire ethnic group".[67] This sense of feeling and interaction in the extended family is transmitted into the wider ambient of the society. Hence a bond of union exists between families, kindred, lineages, and this extends even up to the town level. The strong sense of solidarity is manifested in all situations of life - be it joyous as in the case of births of new members of the community, as well as in sorrowful situations as in tragedies or death of community members, or in sickness. It is, therefore, unheard of for anyone to die of hunger or to go naked, or have no shelter as long as the one adheres to his group in the community. In such situations, a great communitarian spirit is manifested. This social attitude is transmitted in community activities and projects such as road constructions, farm work, erection of houses, etc. Green describes this community attitude thus:

> The system of living in house groups and the fact that most activities - pounding palm nuts, cracking kernels, making palm oil - are carried on out of doors, means that even when an individual is engaged alone on a job, he or she is not solitary. Often work such as hoeing is done by teams. And team work may be accompanied by singing, with a consequent heightening of a sense of solidarity which also finds expression in the dancing of the men on market days, and of the women in the market place on other days. Solitude is held to be a mark of wickedness, . . .[68]

The family and the village structures of the Igbos, by their very

---

[67] JEAN-MARC ELA, op. cit., p. 17

[68] M. M. GREEN, Igbo Village Affairs, Frank Cass & Co. Ltd., London, 1964, p. 253.

nature, enhance social interaction. In the villages, adjoining various homes at strategic points are the village squares or traditional parks referred to as 'ilo' or 'mbala ezi', a veritable traditional rendez-vous for group meetings, or children's play ground. Village meetings are held in these squares. Commenting on these village open spaces, Basden writes,

> The public meeting ground 'Ilo', is a charming spot; a large open space shaded by one or more Awbu trees . . .
>   Meetings for many purposes are held in these open spaces: for the adjustment of differences between individuals or households; for the celebration of fixed feasts; . . . Frequently the 'ilo' serves also as the market place, in which case it is the rendez-vous of great crowds.[69]

Perhaps Basden's vivid description of the activities that take place in the square may furnish one with a concrete picture and give an idea of the social interaction that can emerge from such a structural context. He observes:

> In the Ilos . . . the children are playing in the sand: a company of boys are imitating the ju-ju ceremonies, and probably a bevy of merry girls are dancing with wholehearted enjoyment. The men lounge round in a leisurely manner; a few of the younger perhaps, engage in archery contests. In one corner, a group of older men sit together deeply interested in a game of 'okwe'.[70]

The group interaction and cohesion is greatly favoured and influenced by the traditional context of the squares.

1.3.2.1.2   Igbo Hospitality

One of the aspects of Igbo sociology is their unparalleled hospitality. As Basden points out, "all persons, irrespective of age, sex, or rank, salute each other as they meet. None . . . would fail to return the customary greetings unless, indeed, he were mourning for the dead. . . ".[71]

This sense of belonging of every one in the community is not limited only to the members of the traditional community, it is even specially manifested to strangers, who are always accorded very hearty and warm reception. A visitor's arrival is normally signalled from afar by ushers of welcome. One is

> indiscriminately embraced, hugged, and showered with a barrage of words of welcome . . . ; people visiting the

---

[69]G. T. BASDEN, op. cit., p. 49

[70]Ibid., p. 46

[71]Ibid., p. 269

community will be flabbergasted by the amount of words of
welcome poured out to guests . . . the greater the repetition,
the greater assurance of welcome and intimacy.[72]

Visitors are presented with 'kola-nuts' - a symbol of love, cordiality, intimacy
and solidarity among the Igbos. "The kola-nut is the first thing to be shared
with a visitor. It is the traditional welcome".[73] No visitor may depart from
any house without partaking of kola-nut or some equivalent.[74] Once kola-
nut is presented and shared, one automatically becomes a friend.[75] Of
course, food and drinks are offered to visitors without being demanded, and
for no return. In the case of unfamiliar visitors, such offers are tasted by
the host to give the assurance and guarantee that it is harmless and free
of poison.[76] Travellers and strangers have no cause for alarm. They have
only to formally identify themselves, after which adequate accommodation to
pass the night will be provided to them without charge, and at times, to the
discomfort of the host, who may even surrender his own accommodation to
the visitor. Green testifies to this ready and warm hospitality of the Igbos
to strangers. He writes,

> With Ibo sociability goes that pleasant hospitality which prompts
> every woman to ask the passing caller 'Shall I cook for you?'
> and which means that the host will bring out oji - kola or a
> substitute - and palm wine to pass the time of day.[77]

Basden reinforces this view, remarking that the Ibo is very hospitable, and
refers to many of the chiefs as 'nature's gentlemen'. He affirms,

> Travelling in this simple manner, I was never once molested,
> and have never had cause to grumble at the treatment meted
> out to me at any of the places visited . . . [78]

1.3.2.1.3 Group Associations among the Igbos

The principle of aggregation, being a fundamental human factor, is
not unique only to the Igbos. In the Igbo context, however, characterised

---

[72]O. A. C. ANIGBO, Commensality and Human Relationship among the
Igbos, University of Nigeria Press, Nsukka, 1987, p. 158

[73]F. A. ARINZE, op. cit., p. 4

[74]G. T. BASDEN, Among the Ibos of Nigeria, p. 269

[75]Ibid., p. 43

[76]O. A. C. ANIGBO, op. cit., p. 159

[77]M. M. GREEN, op. cit., p. 253ff

[78]G. T. BASDEN, op. cit., pp. 43-44

by a strong sense of solidarity, this human aggregation finds a very rich expression in the existence of various associations and interest groups.

Resulting from the social structure based on the sense of solidarity, which is first and foremost cultivated and nurtured in the family level, as soon as one grows to a certain maturity, one becomes aware of group aggregation. It becomes clear to one that no individual lives isolated from the others. Rather one understands that in order to achieve one's existential identity, a belonging to a social group for various motives: social, recreational, political and even spiritual, is imperative. So, early in life, one begins to associate with others and develops this sense of aggregation.

On a fundamental level stands the extended family interaction and interrelationship. One associates first and foremost with his extended family members. To this primary grouping belongs everyone - both male and female, born or married into the extended family. The president of this primary grouping is the traditional first-born son, who, as it were, should be the oldest in the family. Belonging to this grouping is not optional but compulsory, even though it has so many social, religious, and political implications. This is exactly where and why the Igbo Christians find it extremely difficult, since they are compelled and drawn by entirely two different forces, that demand their allegiance. While on the one hand, they naturally belong to the family grouping, on the other, they are Christians. It is necessary to note here that any dissident member in the extended family association normally attracts the penalty of being ostracised. For one to be ostracised by one's extended family is tantamount to "an Igbo without citizenship both in this world of men, and in the world of the ancestors".[79]

Apart from the extended family associations, there are many other free associations or groupings, which exist for various purposes such as entertainment, musical, purely social, and even as insurance scheme, since well organised official life insurance scheme are glaringly lacking in the traditional system. Therefore there are such groups as age-grades, titled institutions, craft and trade associations, dancing groups, credit fraternities, at times secret group associations of which the Masquerades and occult fraternities are outstanding.

Since some of these associations are political arms of the traditional administration, they will be mainly treated in the subsequent section that deals with the political structure of the Igbos. For the purpose of sampling, it may be interesting to expose here one of such social associations - the 'Umuada' - a traditional association of the women.

The village women association - the 'Umuada' or 'Umuokpu' as they are called, is a very powerful grouping in all parts of Igboland. Membership to it is naturally restricted only to the womenfolk. It is made up of all women born into the village, whether they stay in their village or are married out elsewhere. It is an association organised to create a communicating link between the women in the village. The reason for their aggregation is fundamentally for creating social order among the women, although they wield a strong political influence in the villages, and have also recreational and religious functions. The women are so knit together that they form a well-defined group "more homogenous and closely woven than any grouping

---

[79]V. C. UCHENDU, op. cit., p. 12

one finds among the men".[80]   Basden speaks of this group thus:

> In every town, there is a sort of committee of women which
> controls all women's affairs and exercises great influence in
> various directions. . .

Of their responsibilities in the community, he continues,

> The Committee further controls everything in the town relating
> to women. In judging cases where both men and women are
> involved the chief must call upon the members . . . for their
> opinions and assistance. The committee makes its own laws
> for the women of the town irrespective of the men.[81]

Concerning this women association, Isichei further reveals,

> . . . they brought much pressure to bear on any bad things
> that were going on in the town or village . . . but they went
> far to make sure that women married into the town from other
> towns were conforming to the norms of the town. They
> disciplined the offending women through very serious sanctions
> that ranged from seizure of property, to the isolation of the
> culprit from their affairs.[82]

Therefore this grouping also performs arbitrating and peace-making
functions. They take it upon themselves to see that justice is done. At
times, they act as enforcement agents among the women of the decisions
of the elders. In a special way, they are the mouthpiece, the organ of
expression of the womenfolk, and they have a special right to be listened
to. This association has an overriding influence in the community, and their
arbitrations are never disputed.

Their roles in funerals are noteworthy. During funerals, each of them
provide food for the celebration as an expression of their solidarity to their
member.   They organise wake-vigils and thereby keep their bereaved
members company that can last for days. Generally assessing this women
grouping, Leith-Ross writes:

> When one has listened to their meetings, seen the order, the
> good sense, the knowledge of human nature displayed, . . .
> listened to those quiet voices, one cannot help feeling what a
> pity it is that not more use can be made of these women and

---

[80]M. M. GREEN, op. cit., p. 187

[81]G. T. BASDEN, Among the Ibos of Nigeria, pp. 94-95

[82]E. ISICHEI, Igbo Worlds, Macmillan Education Ltd., London, 1977, p.
74

their surprising organisations.[83]

From this exposition, one can have an idea of what it amounts to, if one, in the name of religion goes contrary to the rulings of such a traditional grouping in the village. And many a time this women group adheres strictly to the demands of traditional religion, which, at times, are opposed to christian way of life. Here one sees immediately the reasons for double allegiance of the Igbo Christian. This reinforces the need for Inculturation.

1.3.2.1.4 **The Igbos and Recreation**

The Igbos are a strongly built and serious looking race. Generally, as farmers, they are most of the time occupied in the demanding exigencies of the farm. However, they are equally a humorous and hilarious race. Therefore, after the discharge of their seasonal, agricultural commitments, they spend their time celebrating cultural festivals, which serve as a sort of relaxation and recreation, as well as for religious motives. Such celebrations punctuate their calendrical cycles annually. Igbos celebrate various feasts ranging from ancestral, deity, harvest thanksgiving, to births, family feasts, masquerade seasonal feasts such as 'Odo', 'Omabe' especially in the northern areas. Such festivals have overriding influence that they attract home from abroad all members of each community. These feasts are very important features in Igboland, and draw together the entire community, amidst entertainments of all sorts ranging from dancing, singing, wrestling contests to amusements and folktales in the village squares. The celebrations are intermittently punctuated by very booming cannon gunshots and fireworks. Really, on such festivals, there is always veritable interaction of the entire community. Commensalism is also one of the distinguishing marks of such festivals. People stay together, make fun together, eat together, and try to manifest their fundamental existential unity and solidarity. It is striking to note that christians are advised to keep off from these festivals and village traditional celebrations, and thus are prevented from interacting with, and, therefore, alienated from their kith and kin, simply in order not to be defiled.

Besides these festivals, in the normal life of the Igbos, music and dancing play a fundamental role. As Arinze reveals, "Ibos love music. Whether they are dancing or walking, paddling a canoe or hoeing the field, one will hardly find a group of Ibos silent".[84] Echezona reinforces this view as he attests,

> . . . music not only accompanied Nigerian life, it was part of life. Every stage of life, from cradle to death, was connected with one type of music or the other. . . . Music constituted part of such traditional ceremonies as weddings, initiation of boys

---

[83]LEITH-ROSS, African Women, Routledge and Kegan Paul, London, 1939, p. 109

[84]F. A. ARINZE, op.cit., p. 6

into adulthood, feast of gods or ancestral heads and festivities like new yams in Igbo. In these celebrations music and dance assume prominence.[85]

Hence, in this aspect of music, the Igbos share the same attitude with other Africans as was pinpointed by Bishop Milingo, who noted that in Africa, composers of music are found in every field. "They make it naturally. We have music for pounding maize. We have music for evening recreation in the moonlight. We have funeral music, initiation music, and marriage music".[86]

An expression is given to this musical inclination in dancing, which is generally done by everybody. Besides the social and recreational motives for dancing, the Igbos have a religious motive for it as well. As Basden observes, "such dancing is always the physical expression of joy and thanksgiving". Dancing has always a profound psychological effect on the Igboman's spiritual disposition.

> The more one listens to the native music, the more one is conscious of its vital power. It touches the core of man's inmost being, and stirs his primal instincts. It demands the performer's whole attention and so sways the individual as almost to divide asunder . . . mind and body . . . . Under its influence, and that of accompanying dance . . . men and women pass into a completely dazed condition, oblivious and apparently unconscious of the world around them.[87]

1.3.2.1.5 Igbo Linguistics

Language is an important element in any culture, and the key for decodifying any culture. It is also the primary vehicle for sharing and transmitting culture. Communication among people is made possible by language and the people's system of signs and symbols.

It is interesting to note that the term 'Igbo' is used to denote both the language and the ethnic group. The word 'Igbo', as Anigbo reveals, can, in fact, have three different meanings: it refers to the Igbo territory; to the domestic speakers of the language, and to the language spoken by them.[88] Igbo Language, although unique, has some affinities to Latin language in its characters. It has its own consonants and their combinations

---

[85]W. W. C. ECHEZONA, "Nigerian Music - Then and Now", in OGBU U. KALU, ed., Readings in African Humanities: African Cultural Development, Fourth Dimension Publishers, Enugu, 1978, pp. 224-225

[86]E. MILINGO, Demarcations, pp. 135-136, quoted in The World in Between, C. Hurst & Company, London, 1984, p. 74

[87]G. T. BASDEN, Among the Ibos of Nigeria, pp. 185-193

[88]O. A. C. ANIGBO, op. cit., p. 24

which foreigners find very difficult to pronounce. It is very interesting to note that accents play very important role in the language. A single word can have several meanings, depending on how one employs the accents. For instance, a word like 'akwa' can variously mean : clothes, egg, bed, to sew, to cry, moaning, and 'to push', depending on how one accents the term. This role of accents makes it difficult in learning the language, especially for foreigners.

Furthermore, Igbo language has so many significant variations that it poses a real problem even for the Igbos themselves. It is no wonder that "a villager from a Southern Igbo village group may require the aid of an interpreter to make himself understood by his counterpart in the north".[89] Hence, there exists several dialects of the Igbo, but generally, these are reducible to two major dialectical differences popularly referred to as 'Onitsha' and 'Owerri' tongues.

Making matters still worse in learning the language, it is noteworthy that in Igbo language, "proverbs, fables, and stories enter very intimately into the ordinary conversation of the people, and some acquaintance with them is absolutely necessary in order to take an intelligent interest in any subject of discussion".[90] Proverbs are to the Igbo language, what sauce is to any solid food. For the Igbos, 'to speak always in very plain and simple language is to talk like inexperienced little children'.[91] Proverbs play the role of crystallising "the accumulated wisdom handed down by the ancients. They reveal profound thoughts, the soul of the people. This field is often closed to outsiders".[92]

Folklore also plays an important part in Igbo language, being "inventions of fertile imaginations using the natural phenomena as excuses for weaving delightful and quite often instructive tales".[93] So, folklore have emotional, etiological and hence, ethical values, since these stories serve "the communities as means of entertainment, as avenues for the acculturation of the young ones, and as shorthand methods for adults to express ideas proverbially".[94] Through these avenues, fundamental moral values and behaviourial patterns are inculcated into the younger generation. At times, some corrective and satirical lessons are conveyed by songs and verses, impersonifying the people concerned.

From this exposition of the linguistic elements of the Igbos, one can, then, appreciate more the challenges through which the early Missionaries in Igboland passed. So much of these still stare even the present evangelisers in the face, since attention has to be given to the linguistic

---

[89]Ibid., p. 25

[90]G. T. BASDEN, Among the Ibos of Nigeria, p. 273

[91]F. A. ARINZE, op. cit., p. 3

[92]Ibid.

[93]D. I. NWOGA, "African Traditional Literature" in OGBU U. KALU, ed., op. cit., p. 64

[94]Ibid.

elements in the transmission of the Christian Message, so as to tap deeply the roots of the Igbo people. It is to be expected that adequate use should be made of the proverbs, folklore, and verses, which are the authentic traditional transmission channels, in conveying meaningfully the christian dogmas and conclusions to the Igbo people.

1.3.2.2 **Political Aspects of the Igbos**

From what has been seen in the Igbo social structure, the Igbos organise themselves by a system, whereby the heads of the family, kindred, clan, and village units, as well as the elders, the titled institution, age-grades, masquerade society, the daughters' union, and in some places - the Chiefs[95] - all these arms cooperate and play important roles in the traditional government of the Igbos.

1.3.2.2.1 **Traditional Administration**

M. M. Green once remarked,

> There is . . . no Ibo State, no central authority which welds the people into a political whole. Thus, having no paramount Chief or other organ of government common to them all, they lack what to other peoples may be powerful symbols of unity.[96]

This remark may leave the impression that anarchy reigns supreme in Igboland. Granted that there is no unifying system of authority in the modern formal sense, that binds all as a unit, and that each town stands by itself, yet it is an indubitable fact that the Igbos have a strong system of government, which satisfies all expected governmental needs and exigencies of the Igbos. The highest political unit in Igboland is the town unit. Occupying positions of authority, the extended family heads are responsible for the internal family affairs. On the higher level, the Umunna head is responsible for the Umunna, with the help of the nuclear family heads. The same obtains on a higher level with reference to the clan. The climax is the village and town levels, where the oldest clan supplies their head, who, therefore, should be the oldest in the whole village or town. As should be expected, on account of old age, such a head has always a deputy, who should be a middle-aged son, who runs his errands. The traditional political administration is a system whereby the lower unit participates in the higher by representation so that there results ultimately a central governing council made up of the village heads and the representatives of the smaller units. These, with the titled class, as well as the representatives of the other arms such as the masquerade society, the age-grades, and at times, the village

---

[95]Generally speaking, the Igbos have no kings. This is expressed commonly as an adage among the Igbos thus: 'Igbo enwe Eze'.

[96]M. M. GREEN, op.cit., pp. 5-6

daughters' union - these being regarded as the executive arm of the system - all form the planners and policy makers of the community. They enact laws for the town, enforce them, control the community, and see to it that peace and order exist in the community. So, there is no gainsaying that the Igbos have political structure. Hence Olisa had to write,

> . . . authority and leadership are exercised at the village - group level by a loosely structured council of elders who direct discussions and sum up decisions in the assembly of the whole village-group. At the sub-village level down to the extended family - the Okpara (elder) of the relevant unit is the leader and his leadership is based on being the oldest man as well as the keeper of ofo of the unit he leads.[97]

However, it should be known that the Igbos exercise a sense of democracy. Therefore, even though the oldest man has the last say, he is by no means a dictator. On whatever level any matter is discussed, opportunity is given to all to freely air their views and contribute ideas and deliberations, even though it is the Council of the Elders that exercise the legislative, judicial and executive powers. Hence, Uchendu is quite correct as he remarks,

> The village group government is neither a federation nor a confederation. . . . What laws or decisions it makes are not binding on any village which is not represented or which disagrees with the others. The power of the village-group is based . . . rather on the consensus of the village.[98]

Isichei evaluates this traditional administration as a very democratic system. According to her,

> . . . traditional Igbo government gave its citizens more real participation in decision-making processes than is possible in a western-styled democracy.[99]

As parts of this political system, it is essential to see the structure of the Age-grades, titled and masquerade societies.

1.3.2.2.2   The Age-Grades

An Age-grade is simply a category of persons who happen to fall

---

[97]M. S. O. OLISA, "Political Culture and Stability in Igbo Society", in The Conch, III, Nsukka, Nigeria, 1971, p. 19

[98]V. C. UCHENDU, op. cit., p. 44

[99]E. ISICHEI, Igbo Worlds, p. 95

within a particular culturally distinguished age range.[100]   Among the Igbos, Age-grades

> are formed by men (sometimes by women) of about the same age. They help to maintain law and order, bring suspected criminals before the elders, collect fines and give general help in public works.[101]

Members are initiated into their respective Age-grades between the ages of fifteen and eighteen. In some places this is done simultaneously with initiation into the masquerade society. As part of the initiation rite there is the taking of a new additional name and motto of the Age-grade. As soon as one is initiated into the group, he is launched into a responsible belonging to the Age-group in contributing one's proper role to the community. To each Age-grade is assigned a specific function and service for the community. Each group is anxious to make impression and project a good image of itself before the public and maintain its good name in the community, hence each Age-grade establishes means of control and discipline for its members. The Age-grades constitute such an important wing in the organisation of the village that they ought to be recognised and adequately utilised. The Church in Igboland has hitherto rarely taken any cognizance of the age-grades, and therefore, has not benefitted from their potentiality. As already remarked, the age-grades participate in the policy making function of the community. Even from their functions in the community, they are of service, as Uchendu reveals:

> Besides serving as a social indicator which separates the seniors from juniors, the age-grade association is a means of allocating public duties, guarding public morality through the censorship of the members' behaviour and providing companionship and mutual insurance for the members.[102]

1.3.2.2.3   Titled Institution

Another very important social and political association among the Igbos is the titled institution. People become influential and assume positions of honour in the community by entry into this institution, of which the most famous is generally the 'Ozo' title. By entry into these institutions, a great rise in social status is acquired and guaranteed, since the various titles are considered by the Igbos as marks of excellence. An untitled person has no voice in the community. Merely taking a wife and having children, no matter how highly these two values are regarded among the

---

[100]CAROL R. EMBER-MELVIN EMBER, Cultural Anthropology, Prentice-Hall, Inc., Englewood Cliffs, New Jersey, 4th ed., 1985, p. 205

[101]F. A. ARINZE, op. cit., p. 5

[102]V. C. UCHENDU, op. cit., p. 42

Igbos, does not necessarily make one fulfilled. Title-taking is regarded as the crowning factor in one's personal fulfilment in life.[103] This is the only traditional way by which one is publicly proclaimed famous, and through which one is declared affluent and well-to-do.[104]

One enters this institution by spending a considerable sum of money. Green sees it as a sort of insurance. He writes,

> Title-taking . . . is . . . a form of mutual insurance. When an individual is admitted to the taking of a title he has to expend a considerable sum of money and produce food and drink, all of which is divided among those who have already taken title.[105]

Admission into the title is done through a sort of initiation, which is punctuated by rituals. It is important to note that not everyone is admitted to the titles. Only freeborn of the town are free to take titles. Among the prerequisites besides the financial factor, is that one must be of irreproachable character, and must have distinguished himself in good conduct. He must be trustworthy and truthful. He should be above suspicion. On the expected quality for taking a title, Isichei writes,

> An Ozo title holder is supposed to be an honest man. He must not enter into anything that is dirty, and the cord is a witness between him and the gods, that he is now different from other human beings. He is regarded as pure all through, and he wears a bell, so that wherever he goes the bell jingles . . . . He is no more a hidden person. He will never enter any secret thing.[106]

Hence , as a titled man, one accedes to an enviable position in the community, and thereby participates in the governance of the community, functioning as an important consultant, and having an active voice in any decisions of the community. As Basden points out,

> . . . the members exercise a widespread influence and they administered all the affairs of the town. They were treated with the utmost respect . . . and feared . . . . They had the power of life and death, and were the fully accredited rulers of the town.[107]

---

[103]Cf,. TONY UBESIE, Odinala Igbo, Oxford University Press, Ibadan, 1978, p. 121

[104]M. M. GREEN, op. cit., p. 58

[105]Ibid., p. 48

[106]E. ISICHEI, Igbo Worlds, p. 66

[107]G. T. BASDEN, Among the Ibos of Nigeria, p. 264

On the influence which the titled people wield among the Igbos, Arinze has this to say:

> The Ozo men had great power in Ibo society in the past and often decided major issues together with the other elders and the chief.[108]

In fact, they are even considered as the highest traditional judges of the land.

> After the decisions of the Ozo, no more appeal. At times, they condemned somebody to death, and it was final.[109]

Therefore, titled holders constitute major policy makers of the traditional community. That is why it is very disturbing that Christians were forbidden in Igboland from taking titles right from the early days of Christianity in Igboland, simply on grounds of the superstitious rituals involved in the traditional conferment of titles. This has much consequences for the present day situation of the Church, since Christians find themselves elbowed out of the decision making body in the community. It is no wonder, then, that Christians are being treated as second class citizens, and castigated upon, since they have no say in the traditional community. In order to be able to take traditional titles, so many christians had to bow exit to Christianity, and were thus lost permanently.

1.3.2.2.4   **The Masquerade Society**

The Masquerade society is a social but secret association, with an essentially political function among the Igbos. By its qualification as a secret society, it is meant that absolute secrecy is enjoined on its members. Any divulging of their secrecy attracts one the penalty of death, or a threat of an equivalent punishment. It is a closed association surrounded by mysterious beliefs and activities, with a restricted membership only to males initiated into it. Women are not only prohibited from membership, but are even debarred from appearing in the presence of a masquerade under the pain of severe punishment.

Masquerades are variously called 'Muo', or 'Mmanwu', or 'Egwugwu', according to the various zones. There are the mysterious masquerades found in the northern parts of Igboland. These are called 'Odo' and 'Omabe' in the Odo-ozo and Nsukka areas respectively. As Arinze describes,

> The Mmanwu are men robed in unusual clothing from head to foot, with raffia strapping and sometimes artistically carved heads. The person speaks in a weird guttural voice . . . .

---

[108]F. A. ARINZE, op. cit., p. 5

[109]E. ISICHEI, Igbo Worlds, p. 67

The idea is to have a spiritual appearance.[110]

This is because it is the general belief that 'Mmuo' is the dead who has come to life in the sense of a visitor from the ancestral lands to participate in special celebrations. Meek is therefore correct in saying that

> Mmuo are in fact ancestral spirits personated by maskers who appear in public at seasonal periods, at festivals and at celebrations of funeral rites.[111]

Entry into this secret society is by participation in special initiation rites supposed to unveil the mask secrecy to the novices. This initiation rite takes the form of passing through terrifying and excruciating ordeals of various types, meant to toughen and harden the young man, and to instil in him, a sense of manliness, courage and endurance. At times, this is achieved by masquerades flogging the candidates mercilessly; giving them dry bones to chew - purported to be bones of the ancestral spirits; and the ultimate unveiling of the secret of the mask to the aspirants, which secrecy one is now bound by oath under the pain of death to keep.[112]

Initiation rite gives one the right to join the masquerade world, right to accompany and participate in their activities. As already remarked, the initiation is a prerequisite for taking titles. One who is not initiated is considered a woman equivalent and called 'ogbodu', and has no rights to any title in the land. It has also been remarked that the masquerade society is one of the political arms of the village administration. Masquerades function as means of social control, compelling individuals in the society to comply to traditional standards and way of life, as well as guarding community property against intruders. So, they are the enforcement agents within the traditional set-up. Isichei observes:

> . . . much of the function of these masquerades is to effect obedience to the sanctions of the town on a culprit. These could invade a culprit's home, and seize all his belongings until the owner paid the stipulated fine for his crime . . .[113]

Therefore, working in cooperation with the policy makers the masquerade society is a pressure point in the traditional system. The youths are greatly influenced by this society and give it a wide following. All efforts from the Church circles to restrain youths from participating in the masquerade society have always proved of no avail. The Church has always seen the

---

[110]F. A. ARINZE, op. cit., p. 18

[111]C. K. MEEK, Law and Authority in Nigerian Tribe, Oxford University Press, London, 1937, pp. 66-75

[112]E. G. PARRINDER, West African Religion, pp. 133-134. Cf. G. T. BASDEN, Among the Ibos of Nigeria, pp. 235-243

[113]E. ISICHEI, Igbo Worlds, pp. 74-75

masquerade society only negatively because of the mysterious superstitious rituals and charms surrounding the masquerade society. But it ought to be observed that, while certain masquerades exist purely for amusement and entertainment purposes, some, however, have unfortunately degenerated into agents of harassment of innocent members of the society. In any case, being a part of the political pressure points of the traditional set-up, it should not be brushed aside simply on account of its negative excesses. There remains a possibility of purifying this society, limiting its functions to social controls and for amusement purposes, especially if the superstitious elements are done away with.

1.3.3 Igbo Morality

Igbo Morality treats of man's comportment resulting from the link with the Supreme Being. As can be seen from the ethical values attached to fables and folklore, which are meant to inculcate the rudiments of morality, the Igbos have a strong moral standard. In line with every other moral system, the Igbo moral standard has its reference point in the voice of conscience. One should not lose sight of the Igbo world view, which is ultimately rooted in the supernatural order. This vision of life, and the Igbo belief in the principle of causality determines Igbo Morality. According to this mentality, if, for instance, the lightening strikes down a person, or his house, the Igbo would immediately judge such a one as having done something evil. He must have offended the gods to have attracted their immediate vengeance.[114] The Code of conduct which serves as an objective point of reference is the inherited set of customs and traditions - the 'Omenani' - handed down by the unbroken lineage of ancestors from the earliest times.

Igbo morality has both spiritual and social dimensions. As Arinze explains,

> Ibo religion and morality are closely related . . . it is helpful to bear in mind that among the Ibos, law and custom, tradition, etiquette and religion, all go by the same name, and are included under the word 'omenani'.[115]

On the other hand, on account of the Igbo solidarity, it is believed that any infringement of the moral standard, sets in motion series of chain reaction. Hence Igbo morality has very much social implications. This accounts so much for the public punishments attached to any infringement of the Omenani. Basden testifies:

> In the majority of Ibo towns a very clearly defined code of morals exist . . . infringements of these laws may lead to

---

[114]E. G. PARRINDER, West African Religions, p. 199

[115]F. A. ARINZE, op. cit., p. 30

severe penalties being inflicted . . . [116]

In Igbo morality, absolute observance of the moral prescription is demanded. There is no parvity of matter. Such values as honesty, respect, justice, marital fidelity, truth etc. are highly esteemed. It is no wonder that these values are brought to bear when one takes the title.

As has already been highlighted, the earth deity and the ancestors are the custodians of Igbo morality. In order, therefore, not to attract their vengeance, one has to behave in accordance with the traditional 'dos' and 'don'ts' - the taboos - the infringement of which are considered as crimes - 'nso-ani'.[117] Crimes are looked upon as abomination, for which purification on both personal and communal levels are necessary. Crimes include such acts as murder, theft, incest, and adultery. In the past, giving birth to twins was also seen as a crime because it was considered abnormal for human beings - it was thought as belonging only to the animal world to give birth to more than one at a time. In the same light were seen such diseases as small-pox and leprosy, which were considered as expressions of divine vengeance. Hence, if one were to die of any of these diseases, one would not be accorded a burial, but would be thrown away into the jungles and thick forests.

In Igbo morality no crime goes unpunished. Even certain personal hidden crimes are always redressed by open confessions at death-bed by the offenders at the prick of conscience. Since crimes are always seen as disruptions of the harmonious unity and interaction of the beings in relationship, and are directly offence against the deities and the ancestors, there exists the mediation of the diviners and traditional native priests, whose role in interpreting the mind of the gods is considered as important.[118] The diviners are consulted as intermediaries for ascertaining from the spirit world what must be done to redress any such crimes. Besides this function the diviners mediate in such practices as fortune-telling, sorcery, charms, and magic, interpretations of dreams and palms, and in the tracing of re-incarnational persons.

In as much as there are positive aspects in Igbo morality, such as the strong moral standard, and the readiness and disposition to accept mysteries, yet, so much ought to be done to ward off the superstitious elements, and redress or purify the traces of inhuman acts and dehumanising practices. In treating of the Igbo taboos, however, care has to be taken in order not to give a licence to commit crimes. One sees in the taboos a strong sense of moral control.

However, one major problem that confronts the Igbo Christian, is the dilemma in choosing between a Christian and a tribal norm of morality.

---

[116]G. T. BASDEN, Among the Ibos of Nigeria, p. 34

[117]E. I. METUH, African Religions in Western Conceptual Themes, p. 74

[118]"Since the spirits have very great influence over human life, the dibia has very close dealings with the spirits. In fact, the dibia are believed to get their powers of healing from Agwu, deity of medicine." - E. I. METUH, ibid., pp. 33-35.

Robert Moore highlights the dilemma thus:

> Where the issue is pressing, tribal morality will usually prevail.
> But if the Christian defies tribal morality in an important matter,
> and insists on following a Christian conscience, he may undergo
> an kind of ostracism. He may become a 'desocialised person'.
> This condition is no more conducive to normal Christian living
> than is polygyny or the practice of infanticide.[119]

The Christian is simply forced into the stereotyped role expectancies
imposed by the traditional structure. It is for solving such dilemmas that
one speaks for inculturation.

1.3.4 Igbo Rites of Passage in general

In Igbo Culture there is yet an important dimension that treats of the
various rituals and ceremonies that punctuate the phases of life of man on
earth, such phases as birth, childhood, passage from puberty into adulthood,
marriage, old age, death and passage into the next world. These are
generally called the rites of passage. It is this particular dimension that
attracts our major attention in this work. It is as a result of their conviction
that life is the most precious gift, and therefore, most sacred. The Igbo
"does not think of life as possible without due attention being paid to the
invisible higher powers". He insures himself to the spiritual powers to have
this life. For "the Ibo wants life above all else, . . . convinced that as long
as one is still breathing he can still hope".[120]

Right from birth one is surrounded by rituals. Then, come the
circumcision and naming ceremonies. At the ripening age of maturity, formal
initiation rites are celebrated, which opens the way to the different traditional
groups: the age-grade, masquerade society, and if a girl, presents her as
mature and ready for marriage. The most elaborate in the rites of passage
is the traditional rite of marriage. Lastly come the funeral rites, which are
based on the highlighted Igbo view of death. The Igbos strongly believe in
the life after death. Hence funeral rites are intended to assure an entrance
into the spirit land.

To sum up, the Igbos love life, and accompany that life with assuring
rituals right from the cradle to the grave, and even beyond to the after-life.

This general background of the Igbos has furnished us with a working
knowledge of the mentality of the Igbos, as well as supplied a framework on
which to operate in making use of the exposed salient aspects of the culture
in inculturation.

---

[119]ROBERT O. MOORE, "Towards an African Catholic Culture", in AFER,
Vol. 19, no. 4, 1977, p. 239

[120]F. A. ARINZE, op. cit., p. 111

CHAPTER 2

2   **CULTURAL AND PSYCHOLOGICAL PRESUPPOSITIONS**

2.1   **CULTURAL PRESUPPOSITIONS**

Since this work is missiologically inclined and anthropological, it involves an entrance into the field of culture. Entrance into culture involves a knowledge of the fundamentals and dynamics of culture. Inculturation presupposes a lot of these fundamentals. As such, it becomes necessary to take a look at the concept and the characteristic elements of any given culture, as well as the presuppositions. This would ultimately lead one to the right understanding of the essentials in Igbo culture, which should be considered in any attempts at constructing a faith-orientated inculturation.

2.1.1 The Concept of Culture

If there is a term that has constituted an obstacle to anthropologists and sociologists as regards a generally accepted definition, it is the term 'culture'. It has been an object of heated debates and arguments to give it a definition and to outline its essential characteristics. Geertz remarks:

> . . . the term culture has by now acquired a certain aura of ill repute in special anthropological circles because of the multiplicity of its referents and the studied vagueness with which it has all too often been invoked.[1]

The lack of agreement is understandable since each anthropologist emphasises his special field and interest in giving a definition. The problem escalates with the everyday usage of the term 'culture' to mean the "desirable quality we can acquire by attending a sufficient number of plays and concerts and trudging through several miles of art galleries".[2] This work demands an anthropological understanding of culture, which differs greatly from the above layman's view. Ralph Linton clearly distinguishes between the two:

> It (culture) refers to the total way of life of any society, ...
> Thus, culture, when applied to our own way of life, has nothing

---

[1]C. GEERTZ, The Interpretation of Cultures, Basic Books, Inc., New York, 1973, p. 89.

[2]CAROL R. EMBER - MELVIN EMBER, Cultural Anthropology, Prentice-Hall, Inc., New Jersey (1973), pp. 17-18.

to do with playing the piano or reading Browning. For the social scientist, such activities are simple elements within the totality of our culture. This totality also includes such mundane activities as washing dishes or driving an automobile, and for the purposes of cultural studies this stands quite on a par with "the finer things of life". It follows that for the social scientist there are no uncultural societies or even individuals. Every society has a culture, no matter how simple this culture may be, and every human being is cultured, in the sense of participating in some culture or other.[3]

As a concept, culture originally indicated one who is informed, well prepared, cultivated. It seemed to be derived from the latin verb 'colere', which has nearly the same meaning with 'educere' - (to draw out, make to flow, develop some innate capacity). In this light the term does not differ much with the term civilisation, which is the quality of getting refined, arising from some development of one's way of life. Considered anthropologically it is a substantive meaning something that does not only belong to an individual as a quality, but also to a society, and thereby expresses a collective knowledge and behaviour. It is J. G. Herder who distinguished the form taken by culture in the individual as education, and that which is a social patrimony which he referred to as Culture. Influenced by the voyages which put him in contact with diverse peoples, Alexander Humboldt specified the concept of culture, using the term not only as a generic singular but as plural - 'cultures'- to underline their variety and diversity.

It was, however, the German Gustav Klem who attempted the first scientific definition of culture as "customs, information, and techniques, domestic and public life in time of peace and in war, religion, knowledge and art."[4] In a bid yet to arrive at a summarised formulation that would be acceptable to most social scientists, C. Kluckhohn and A. L. Kroeber carried out a research on as many as three hundred possible definitions of culture. As a fruit of this research, culture was considered as consisting

. . . of patterns explicit and implicit, of and for behaviour acquired and transmitted by symbols, constituting the distinctive achievement of human groups, including their embodiments in artifacts; the essential core of culture consists of traditional (i.e. historically derived and selected) ideas and especially their attached values; culture systems may, on the one hand, be considered as products of action, on the other, as conditioning elements of further action.[5]

---

[3]RALPH LINTON, The Cultural Background of Personality, New York, Appleton - Century Crofts, 1945, p. 30.

[4]Cf., C.TULLIO-ALTAN, Antopologia, Feltrinelli, (1985), Milano, p. 148.

[5]ALFRED L. KROEBER & CLYDE KLUCKHOHN, "Culture: A Critical Review of Concepts and Definitions", Harvard University Peabody Museum of American Archaeological Papers, Vol. 47 (1952) p. 181.

Following this research so many anthropologists have come up with so many definitions of culture. For instance, Lowie defined culture as the

> sum total of what an individual acquires from his society - those beliefs, customs, artistic norms, food-habits, and crafts which come to him not by his own creative activity but as a legacy from the past, conveyed by formal or informal education.[6]

Kluckhohn again proposed culture as "the total way of life of a people, the social legacy the individual acquires from his group".[7] Gillin is of the mind that culture "consists of patterned and functionally interrelated customs common to specifiable individual human beings composing specifiable social groups or categories".[8] Keesing sums up and thinks of culture as "the totality of man's learned, accumulated experience which is socially transmitted, or, more briefly, the behaviour acquired through social learning".[9] Clifford Geertz denotes culture as

> . . . an historically transmitted pattern of meanings embodied in symbols, a system of inherited conceptions expressed in symbolic forms by means of which men communicate, perpetuate and develop their knowledge about and attitudes towards life.[10]

But the most chartered and well-known definition is that of E. B. Tylor who stated that

> Culture or civilisation taken in its wide ethnographic sense, is that complex whole which includes knowledge, belief, art, morals, law, custom, and any other capabilities and habits acquired by man as a member of society.[11]

There are, therefore as many definitions of culture as there are anthropologists. But Tylor's definition is considered as the basis of most modern theories of culture with modifications here and there. Whichever

---

[6]ROBERT H. LOWIE, The History of Ethnological Theory, Rinehart, New York, 1937, p.3.

[7]C. KLUCKHOHN, Mirror for Man : The Relation of Anthropology to Modern Life, New York & Toronto, McGraw hill, 1944, p. 17.

[8]JOHN GILLIN, The Ways of Men: An Introduction to Anthropology, New York, Appleton- Century- Crofts, Inc., 1948, p. 181.

[9]FELIX M. KEESING, Cultural Anthropology: The Science of Customs, New York, Rinehart, 1958, p. 18.

[10]C. GEERTZ, op. cit., p. 89.

[11]E. B. TYLOR, Primitive Culture, New York, Harper Torchbooks, 1958 (originally published 1871), p. 1.

definition one prefers, some basic essential facts are revealed. Let us see those essential factors of culture.

2.1.2 Culture as an Organised Way of Life

In history, man has always been confronted with the basic problems of life. He has always reacted to these problems in one way or another. Man has consistently sought for the solutions of these problems in order to satisfy his human needs in several ways. What is referred to as culture evolved as the systematised answers to these human problems. Hence, culture is viewed as a designed system of responses, a way of life, by which man in society in the spatio-temporal conditions, has been able to adjust to his environment. Culture is something which man interposes between himself and his environment in order to ensure his security and survival. This coping with the environment is manifested in food-getting, housing, clothing, eating-habits, mating practices, marriage, family organisations, kinship systems, status, social class, ownership, inheritance, trade, government, war, law, religion, magic, and language. These solutions of life's problems have been so systematised and institutionalised that they become as it were unconscious aspects of life. Culture, therefore, embraces everything which helps man to survive and solve his human, spiritual, physical, biological, social and psychological needs. That is why so many social scientists have had a functional view of culture, since all aspects of a people's culture has some functional value in the society. Hence, one can say that culture is a way of life, a design for living of a people.

2.1.3 The Peculiarity of Culture

Culture reveals a sort of paradox. Although it is universal in the sense that every group of people has a culture and shares a way of life, yet each culture is unique. In each region of the world different sets of experiences are uniquely and variously manifested, in relation to the peculiar way of life of the society that lives it. Because of this fact, any evaluation of culture has to be made with a sense of detachment or ideally from the perspectives of its participants. This is technically referred to as cultural relativism, which advocates a transcending or elimination for the moment one's own cultural conditioning and values, and assumption of a subjective ethnocentric attitude and mentality of an adherent or a participant in the culture, in the evaluation and interpretation of any given culture.[12] This demands some empathy in the observer, so as to be able to see others in their culture as they see themselves or wish to be seen. In this regard, one guards against ethnocentrism which, as the opposite extreme, is an uncritical prejudice in favour of one's own culture and the distorted biased criticism of an alien culture.

2.1.4 Culture is not Innate

---

[12]Cf., International Encyclopedia of the Social Sciences, vol.3 & 4, (1972), s.v. "Cultural Relativism".

Culture is a set of learned beliefs, values, and behaviours of a group or society. Hence it is not something innate, but what one acquires as one consciously gets acquainted with the society to which one belongs. What is innate in man are the general response capacities, which culture regulates as man comes into contact with cultural patterns. Geertz tries to expatiate why this is so. According to him,

> At some particular stage in his phylogenetic history, a marginal genetic change of some sort rendered him capable of producing and carrying culture, and thenceforth his form of adaptive response to environmental pressures was almost exclusively cultural rather than genetic. As he spread over the globe, he wore furs in cold climates and loincloths (or nothing at all) in warm ones; He didn't alter his innate mode of response to environmental temperature. He made weapons to extend his inherited predatory powers and cooked foods to render a wider range of them digestible. Man became man, . . . when . . . he became able to transmit knowledge, belief, law, morals, custom to his descendants and his neighbours through teaching and to acquire them from his ancestors and his neighbours through learning.[13]

2.1.5 **Culture as communitarian**

For anything to be cultural, it has to be commonly shared by a certain population or group of individuals. Cultural characteristics are shared by segments of a population who share the same ethnological conditions of life. But this does not mean that everything shared by a people is cultural. For instance, a people may share the same colour of the skin or a type of hair. This is not cultural. Culture should also be distinguished from personal habits.

2.1.6 **Transmission of Culture**

It is always a wonder to notice how various cultural traits and way of life are uninterruptedly practised by every member of any given culture. The transmission of culture accounts for this. Every culture provides its members with the knowledge of the various ways of solving the ordinary problems of life through the agency of cultural transmission. Learning is an important aspect of culture, required in order that culture be transmitted. It does not suffice that something be shared for it to be cultural. If culture is a way of life of a certain population, and is not something innate, then, it has to be transmitted somehow. Parents play an important role in this regard. As some authors point out,

> Because parents have a common culture and, thus, shared ideas about how to treat their offspring, all the members of a

---

[13]C. GEERTZ, op.cit., pp. 46-47.

fairly stable group (i.e. not changing too quickly) will have had similar experiences in childhood. Parents with a common culture teach their children much the same things. This is how culture is transmitted, and this transmission is part of every individual's childhood.[14]

This is achieved through the process of learning the culture, which is technically referred to as 'enculturation'. Since learning may be formal or / and informal, the formal learning of one's culture is through express and direct instruction - education - of the individual, while the informal learning of culture may be either by deliberate observation and imitation, or through unconscious imitation and a kind of absorption - the unconscious copying of behaviour.[15]

Learning is important in culture because most cultural patterns are transmitted in significant symbols. Access to such systems of symbols as language, art, myth, ritual, technology, religion etc. is only possible through learning. Geertz explains that ". . . men build dams or shelters, locate food, organise their social groups or find sexual partners under the guidance of instructions encoded in flow charts and blueprints, hunting lore, moral systems and aesthetic judgements : conceptual structures moulding formless talents".[16] Man needs to decode the symbolic system in order to get to the cultural roots. In an eminent way language plays an important role in this regard, for, although human beings acquire much learned behaviour by imitation, yet much is learned and acquired through language. The symbolic nature of language has a profound influence in cultural transmission, for, without language it would be impossible to transmit or receive information symbolically. It is through symbolic behaviour that man is able to transmit ways, goals, premises, values and a whole philosophy of life. It is only by learning that man is able to survive and cope with his physical, social and ideational environment.

2.1.7 Adaptive Quality of Culture

It is the very fact that culture is a response to life's problems that makes culture also adaptive. Any given situation or environmental condition is never static. It always depends on so many factors. Changes in these factors can always influence the culture, since a change in one factor can generate a chain reaction which definitely brings about the change on the given culture. As R. Piddington puts it, "Culture is essentially an adaptive mechanism, making possible the satisfaction of human needs, both biological

---

[14]MARC J. SWARTZ/ DAVID K. JORDAN, Culture: The Anthropological Perspective, University of Washington Press, p.154.

[15]Cf., LOUIS J. LUTZBETAK, The Church and Cultures, Divine Word Publications, Illinois, 1970, p. 78.

[16]C. GEERTZ, op. cit., p. 50.

and social".[17]

Some of the factors that can influence cultural adaptation can be temporal, ethical, religious, social or even political. In a special way, however, ecological factors exert profound influence on any given culture technologically, organisationally, and even conceptually. In any of these conditions, as E. B. Tylor confirms, "the institutions which can best hold their own in the world gradually supersede the less fit ones and . . . this incessant conflict determines the general resultant course of culture".[18]

2.1.8. Cultural Dynamism

It is often said that no one is an island. Man is always in need of the other. This contact with the others influences man very profoundly and leaves an impact on his culture. Apart from the adaptive factors highlighted above, man's contact with his fellowmen in other cultures is an important factor that generates a change in culture. This contact with other cultures can come about externally, for instance as a result of a conquest by another society, or even by the violent replacement of a society's rulers, or by colonisation, whereby another culture is positively brought into bear with and even made to suppress the already existing culture of the place. In all these cases, with the introduction of the new culture, the original culture is thereby forced to change. That is why culture is considered always dynamic and never static. The change can, however, be slow and gradual as in the case of cultural diffusion, although it can also be fast and drastic as in the case of military conquest or the violent replacement of a society's rulers. In a very special way, a contact between two societies with different cultural patterns influences culture changes in both societies. This type of change has much to do with diffusion or borrowing of cultural elements of one from the other, leading ultimately to a change in the original culture.

It is very essential to have this contact between cultures because, as observed by Roest Crollius, "through the contact with other cultures, man acquires a deeper understanding and firmer possession of his own culture, whereas, in his own culture he discovers the openness towards the values of other cultures".[19]

But if this cultural encounter is not to end up in a one-dimensional cultural assimilation, which ignores the riches of originality and results in the impoverishment or alienation of the partner culture, then it has to be dialectical, having immense value for both cultures in contact. As a matter of fact, "in and through the dialogue, the diversity of cultures, reveals itself as a synthesis of inalienable originality and communicable universality".[20] On

---

[17]RALPH PIDDINGTON, An Introduction to Social Anthropology, (2nd ed.), vol. 1, Edinburgh: Oliver & Boyd (1950) 1952, p. 219.

[18]E. B. TYLOR, op. cit., p. 62.

[19]A. ROEST CROLLIUS, "The Meaning of Culture in Theological Anthropology", in AA.VV., Inculturation: Its Meaning and Urgency, p. 61.

[20]Ibid., p. 62.

the other hand, a cultural monologue "would accept only one way of understanding cultural reality and measure all other cultural expressions according to the standard of this culture".[21] This is the case where people have, as it were, naturalised their culture, and have been completely enculturated. The tendency is then, to have a sort of fossilised notion of culture as something static and can never change, forgetting the simple fact that their common meanings and values are human products which are transmitted from one generation to the next. According to De Napoli,

> In a real sense the transmission to and the acquisition of the common meanings and values of a culture by a child is a type of brainwashing. It is precisely this aura of facticity which makes cultural changes such a difficult and . . . painful and disruptive process. [22]

This explains why it is sometimes difficult to effect a change in culture. The process of change which occurs when different cultural groups come into intensive contact is referred to as 'acculturation' - culture contact. In fact, it is the process of extensive borrowing in the context of superordinate - subordinate relations between societies. In contrast with diffusion, acculturation is as a result of some external pressure. Culture change through diffusion can be by direct contact, whereby elements of culture are first taken up by neighbouring societies and then gradually disseminated; or by intermediate contact, whereby a third party carry a cultural trait from one society to a receptive society. There can also be stimulus diffusion, whereby a society is stimulated into developing its local equivalent of a cultural element. Culture change by diffusion, however, is never automatic but always selective - adapting a particular cultural trait to its own traditions.[23]

Change of attitudes and behaviour of a society can affect a culture change. Such a change could even be in the autodynamic nature of the social and cultural system or, as suggested by Herskovits, it can even be in the "reinterpretation of the cultural elements whereby old meanings are ascribed new elements or new values change the cultural significance of the old forms".[24]

2.1.9 The Factor of Cultural Constraint

Cultural Constraint is a factor which arises from the fact that every

---

[21]D. TRACY, "Ethnic Pluralism and Systematic Theology: Reflections", in A. M. GREELY & G. BAUM, eds., "Ethnicity", in Concilium, n. 101, New York 1977, pp 91 - 99.

[22]MARIA DE LA CRUZ AYMES et al., Effective Inculturation and Ethnic Identity, Pontifical Gregorian University, Rome, 1987, p. 75.

[23]Cf., R. EMBER-MELVIN EMBER, op.cit., pp. 296 - 312.

[24]MELVILLE J. HERSKOVITS, Cultural Anthropology, New York, 1955, Knopf., p. 492.

society has its ideal cultural patterns, which are ideas of how people should behave and comport themselves in particular situations. And, as Emile Durkheim stressed, culture is something external to an individual, yet exerts a profound coercive influence on the individual.[25] That is why the individual is so much constrained to live according to the standards of the society one belongs. Any attempt by an individual to oppose this standard is always met by a societal reaction and even at times in certain societies it can take the form of ostracism or social isolation. There can also be an indirect constraint as results when one is subjected to societal ridicule for behaving in a way contrary to the societal standards.

2.2 Dimensions of Culture

Culture has been referred to as an 'integrated system of learned behaviour'. The term 'integrated' points to the multi-dimensional aspects embodying the existential environment of man. That is why culture is not just made up of one element. From the various definitions of culture seen above, one observes that culture is a complex concept, having much to do with such patterns as economics, childbearing, life-cycle, social organisation, politics, religion, art, play, etc. For clarity purposes it is essential to take a cursory glance at some of these component elements.

2.2.1 Religion

In search of self-realisation, man is confronted with the ultimate questions of the meaning of his life, its final significance and purpose. To get at the answers to these questions, one is opened up to an entirely other domain - the world of the sacred and the spiritual. This experience exposes man to the conviction that the visible world must necessarily have something to do with the spiritual universe. In the midst of his anxiety and dismay issuing from his visible world, man finds solace from his attachment to this other universe. It is this world of the sacred that gives him sense of direction, restores confidence in him, which in turn, leads him through acts and sentiments of submission and dependence, to develop a strong relationship with the Absolute governing this world of the universe, who is generally referred to as God. This attitude of awe, sentiment, submission, and acts of worship is what we call religion. Therefore, religion

> . . . signifies a unified system of beliefs and practices, individual and communal, in which man seeks salvation . . . through relation to a transcendent power (of some kind), and in which life is experienced as increased, unified, and given meaning

---

[25]EMILE DURKHEIM, The Rules of Sociological Method, Trans. by Sarah A. Soloway and John H. Müller, ed. Georg E. E. Catlin, (8th ed.), New York : Free Press, 1938, p. 3.

through union with this sacred reality.[26]

Seen from a sociological and functional point of view, religion

... answered to the problems of meaning at the point where
human knowledge faltered. It provided a relationship with the
beyond when human relationships no longer offered security
and when human control over environing conditions failed. By
its cognitive and emotional aspects, religion provided an overall
sense of direction and meaning to human life, and afforded the
mechanism for an adjustment to aspects of the human situation
beyond human control.[27]

It is for this reason that religion plays a fundamental role in culture. Religion
is one of culture's protective forms which mitigates the fears and
aggressions in individuals and societies since it consists of "an array of
beliefs and attitudes which help to defend us against vexing doubts,
anxieties and aggressions in individuals and societies".[28] Therefore, as a
central element in culture, religion "provides form and direction to human
thought, feeling, and action. It stabilizes human orientations, values,
aspirations and ego-ideals".[29]

In very simple societies, where man has an integrated vision of life
and world view, even such features as climate, illness and life are all
permeated by a deep spiritual sense. Especially in such simpler cultures,
religion can be considered as the fundamental cultural base and point of
departure, through which man tries to influence the spiritual world, and the
point from where he takes his bearings in his efforts to direct and control
his environment. Religion and culture necessarily coexist, for, while men
"must live in relationship with two incompatible and heterogenous realms of
experience; they must maintain relations with both the ultimate and the
mundane".[30]

Just as man has no single universally accepted way of coping with
his environment, so also differs man's approach to his God and his attitudes
to this God. That is why one finds as many forms of religion as there are
peoples and cultures.

---

[26]RICHARD VILADESAU, Answering for Faith, Paulist Press, New York
/Mahwah, 1987, pp. 75 - 76.

[27]THOMAS F. O'DEA, The Sociology of Religion, Prentice-Hall, Inc.,
Englewood Cliffs, New Jersey, 1966, p. 98.

[28]Ibid., p. 113.

[29]Ibid., p. 116

[30]Ibid.

2.2.2 Social Elements and Group Stratification

The fact that no man can exist alone demands necessarily a coexistence with others. Since everyone behaves differently from others, and since a standard pattern or code of conduct ought to be shared for a mutual coexistence, there exists in every society a standard of mutual relationships. This standard is connected to and interpenetrated by the psychology of any given people. The framework by which the communication gap and relationship between all within a given culture is measured is known as the social structure. The social structure of any culture is the relationship framework of its people, how they are classified, and how they interrelate. Social structure has much to do with the interwoven connections of the various categories, groups, classes, statuses of people in a given culture.

The behaviour of any individual in a society is determined greatly by the status symbol of that society, as well as the expectations and cultural demands of the society from the individual. This presupposes that every society has a predetermined framework of social participation of the individual in the society. One measures the interrelationship of the members of the society on this framework. If a society is an organised group of people who have learnt to aggregate together,[31] then it is imperative that the society should have its specific mode of classifying, categorising, and organising its members. It is through this classification that individuals are assigned their roles. Ralph Linton clarifies this point:

> The members of such a society are united by a multitude of common interests and a strong consciousness of kind based upon personal acquaintance and personal interaction. They stand as a unit against outsiders and divide the activities necessary to the well-being of the group among themselves according to a definite pattern. This pattern assures that all members of the group shall both contribute services and receive benefits.[32]

It is through the social structure that groups are internally organised. To enhance this, the individuals in the society are classified into age or sex categories, in order to enable each person participate in culture. This classification is prompted by the fact that males and females have differing potentialities at various age levels. There are seven basic categories of such classification in any culture, namely:- infant, boy, girl, adult - male and female, old - male and female. It is from this framework that each society

---

[31]"Every society from the primitive band to the modern state is really an organised aggregate of smaller organised groups. Thus the band is a configuration of family, friendship and work groupings, the tribe a configuration of bands, the state, in its simpler forms, a configuration of tribes which have been brought together by conquest or confederation, and so forth." - RALPH LINTON, op. cit., pp. 38-39.

[32]Ibid., pp. 37-38.

ascribes cultural roles to its members.

The existence of this stable framework of references, which stipulate the societal groupings, classifications of individuals and the categories in which they belong, dictate the participation of an individual in his culture.

2.2.3 Political Aspects of Culture

All societies have ways of organising themselves. It is the fact that people associate and interrelate with one another in the society, and must coexist mutually that necessitates further the organisation of the society in such a way that all exist in peace and harmony. Therefore every society has means of social control. Through the political administration authoritative decisions for the benefit of the society are arrived at and implemented. Through political organisation each society is able to maintain good relationship both within and outside the society. By means of the political elements troubles and disputes are prevented or resolved. Each society has always a system by which it deals with lawbreakers as well as social conflicts in general. What is referred to as political elements in any culture are the ways and means through which societal decisions are taken, social order is created and maintained, as well as social disorder is brought under control. This is a very important structure of any society - ranging from small to large communities such as bands, villages, towns, cities to multi-local groups such as districts or regions, entire nations, or even groups of nations.

2.2.4 Rites of Passage

Life is regarded and considered very precious in all cultures. Not only is life treasured, it is preserved, protected, nurtured, culturally celebrated and ritually insured. What is referred to in this work as 'Rites os Passage' is a category of rituals that mark and accompany the passage of an individual through the successive transitional and crises moments in one's life cycle, from one stage to another over time, from one role or social position to another. Through rituals the biological facts of birth, growth, reproduction and death are integrated with the human and cultural experiences. Biological factors dictate the fundamentals of our experience - birth, reproduction and death. But the ways in which these imperatives are manipulated and modified are dictated by one's culture. Rites of Passage try to concretise the fact that humans are not only naturally born as men and women, nor merely procreate and die, but they are culturally made what they are through ceremonies and rituals. Even though by birth one is male or female, yet through the rites of passage a society culturally defines and makes them man and woman, adult, husband or wife etc. Every human society has cultural rituals that not only solemnise and celebrate the various moments, but also serve the function of ensuring a continuity of societal ideals, and furnishing the individuals with a societal confidence and solidarity in the assumption of roles and functions in the society.

2.3   Psychological Presuppositions

To speak of anthropological presuppositions in inculturation may not constitute any wonder since the subjects discussed have an immediate anthropological bearing.   But when one speaks of psychological presuppositions in inculturation it may sound a bit suspicious since its connection is not immediately evident.   However, seeing that the topic has much to do with behaviour patterns and attitudes, which are specifically psychological concerns, it becomes clear and understandable.   Jean Piaget once remarked: "If we want to form men and women, nothing will fit us so well for the task as to study the laws that govern their formation".[33] Inculturation, which aims at making the Christian message permeate a people's way of life and mentality, must necessarily have to do with personality formation, learning processes, and the integration of the ideals of one's life.   These concern the field of psychology.   One must take note of the research findings and psychoanalytical conclusions in these areas. One has also to take account of certain sociological factors of the human personality.   Culture presupposes a society made up of individuals who share cultural patterns, are circumscribed within an environment, and have their proper personality traits and peculiarities.   Underlying the presuppositions is the conviction and a recognition of a fundamental basic fact that

> . . . all individuals are born by mothers; that everybody was once a child; that people and peoples begin in their nurseries; and that society consists of generations in the process of developing from children into parents, destined to absorb the historical changes of their lifetimes and to continue to make history for their descendants.[34]

In the following presuppositions, one's attention is drawn to the basic facts of an individual, circumscribed within an environment, and who, in order to arrive at maturity, undergoes several stages of development, has specific ways of acquiring the behaviour patterns of his society.   A treatment of these questions will be of immense help in any inculturation work.   Let us begin with the most fundamental of all.

2.3.1. **The Dynamics of Personality Development**

In order to locate the various strategic moments and pressure points for influencing the awareness of an individual, it is necessary to take cognizance of the various stages of the development of an individual.   One's interest in this section is simply to recognise and take into consideration in

---

[33]JEAN PIAGET, The Moral Judgement of the Child, The Free Press, New York, 1965, p. 9.

[34]ERIK H. ERIKSON, Identity: Youth and Crises, Faber and Faber, London, 1983, p. 45.

this work some psychological conclusions and findings on the development of individuals, and the features that characterise these developments. It is supposed that knowing the pressure points and utilising them in a new type of enculturative process, which would present to the individual a cultural pattern already integrated and animated by the christian values, would definitely lead to a change-oriented future in the commitment of an individual. This means that one can effect a change through the pressure points in the developmental stages. The stages of development, especially the earliest stages, are very important in one's life because "it is then that the basic attitudes toward life are formed".[35]

While there is a general agreement that the development of the human personality is graduated into stages, there are divergent views about the specific stages among psychologists. Freud regards personality development to have virtually been completed by about the age of six; while Piaget and Kohlberg gave the stages an epistemological focus. They see the stages from a cognitive point of view. However, Erikson and Levinson view the developmental stages as a life-long process, hence, they stretch the stages to cover the life-span of an individual. There are yet some who completely reject the idea of developmental stages, and rather prefer to focus their attention on the goals of personality development. For the purposes of this work, one prefers to lean more on the developmental stages elaborated by Erikson in his book titled, "Identity and the Life Cycle". Our choice of Erikson is for many reasons. The most important is the fact that since we are making a proposal for the inculturation of the rites of passage, which is a life-long programme, the developmental stages would suit and best highlight the points at stake in each successive stage of life. Eriksonian stages try to relate biological maturation with changes in social role as well as coordinate both with an account of person's conscious and unconscious psychic modes of adaptation. Besides, Erikson's stages have been clinically attested to and are a refined experience of Freudian psychoanalysis. Erikson's stages seem to be widely accepted. Fowler summarises our reasons for the preference of the Eriksonian stages thus:

> In sum, Erikson's eras and crises provide a helpful guide to what Sheehy calls "predictable crises" of the life cycle. From those crises of trust, autonomy, initiative, and so forth, which are reasonably correlated with maturation and age, represent life challenges with which all persons must deal. As a part of their coping, in their adaptation, faith forms, functions, and is changed. . . . Erikson has helped us in many ways to focus on the **functional** aspect of faith, the expected existential issues with which it must help people cope at whatever structural stage across the life cycle.[36]

---

[35]C. J. VAN der POEL, <u>The Search for Human Values</u>, Paulist Press, New York, 1971, p. 130.

[36]JAMES W. FOWLER, <u>Stages of Faith</u>, Harper & Row, San Francisco, 1976, p. 109.

According to Erikson, personality can be said to develop

> . . . according to steps predetermined in the human organism's readiness to be driven toward, to be aware of, and to interact with, a widening social radius, beginning with the dim image of a mother and ending with mankind, or at any rate that segment of mankind which "counts" in the particular individual's life.[37]

Within his structure, Erikson divided the developmental stages into eight. The personality development is governed by what he calls the epigenetic principle, which states that "anything that grows has a ground plan, and that out of this ground plan the parts arise, each part having its time of special ascendancy, until all parts have arisen to form a functioning whole".[38] Although the life that takes off at the embryonic stage as the foetus is the basis on which the future personality is constructed, and therefore, is very important. However, lack of reliable data of this stage makes it imperative to begin the first stage of development only at birth. So the first stage of development falls within the range of the moment of birth up till the first year. This is called the oral-sensory stage. As soon as a baby is born, it obeys immediately the bio-physiological laws of development, which generates and follows a succession of the unfolding of the infant's potentialities for significant interaction with those around him. During this stage, the child is receptive in many respects. This is the period when the child refers everything that comes around it into the mouth. Just as it is overwhelmingly in need of food, so also it is eager to 'take-in' whatever stimulates its eyes and other senses. Erikson therefore rightly refers to this stage as the 'incorporative stage', since the child is practically receptive to whatever it is offered.[39]

According to Erikson, it is already at this moment that the human infant meets up with the basic modalities of his culture[40], and this takes the form of "getting what is given" and in learning to get somebody to do for him what is wished. By this means a mutuality of relaxation is developed, which is important for the first experience of friendly relationship. It is recommended that at this stage, the infant's senses should be fed with stimuli and food in proper intensity and at the right time.

The later part of this first stage is characterised by a sharpening focusing ability and a more sensitive and localised hearing as well as the development of the teeth on the physical level. One observes at this stage, a tendency to incorporate, appropriate and observe more actively and a psychological increasing development of awareness in the child as a person. The overall importance of this stage lies in the creation in the child of the sense of trust, which, according to Erikson, "forms the basis in the child for

---

[37]ERIK H. ERIKSON, op. cit., p. 54.

[38]Ibid., p. 53.

[39]Ibid., p. 59.

[40]Ibid., p.160.

a sense of identity which will later combine a sense of being 'all right', of being oneself and of becoming what other people trust one will become".[41] It is very important here to note that the religious stand of the parents of a child has much to do with the reinforcement of the child's basic trust in trustworthiness of the world.

The second stage is the Anal-muscular stage. This falls within the second and the third year. At this stage, the child develops better formed stool, and is able to coordinate his muscular system. Characterising this stage is the development of autonomy or its antithesis - shame. The sense of autonomy is achieved by a continued consolidation of the sense of trust already created. This sense of autonomy is fostered by "a handling of the small individual which expresses a sense of rightful dignity and lawful independence of the part of the parents and which gives him the confident expectation that the kind of autonomy fostered in childhood will not be frustrated later".[42] This demands, in order to be safeguarded, a corresponding maintenance of autonomy and self reliance in the parents.

The third stage is the 'locomotor-genital' stage. This is between the ages of four and five. To characterise this stage is the development of movement, a perfection of language capability, and a consequent development of imaginative ability. The end product of this stage is the development of a sense of initiative or its critical alternative - sense of guilt. At this stage, the child is able to understand, and, since it has already an access to language, it can even ask questions about things. This stage involves a tremendous and sudden widening of his mental, emotional and social horizons.[43] During this stage, in the words of Erikson,

> He is ready to visualize himself as being as big as the perambulating grown-ups. He begins to make comparison and is apt to develop untiring curiosity about differences in sizes in general, and sexual differences in particular. He tries to comprehend possible future roles, or at any rate to understand what roles are worth imitating.[44]

With learning getting more pronounced, a sense of initiative is developed, and it is this which is the basis for a future sense of ambition and independence. It is noteworthy here that it is at this juncture that the conscience is developed, which is the cornerstone of morality.

On the relevance of this stage to Faith, Fowler remarks that this is the "imitative phase in which the child can be powerfully and permanently influenced by examples, moods, actions, of the visible faith of primally

---

[41]Ibid., p. 65.

[42]Ibid., p. 76.

[43]G. R. LOWE, The Growth of Personality, Penguin Books Ltd., England, 1972, p. 91.

[44]ERIK H. ERIKSON, Identity and the Life Cycle, W. W. Norton & Company, New York, 1979, p. 79.

related adults".[45]

The next stage is a longer one and stretches from the fifth to the thirteenth year. It is called the latency stage by Erikson. It is, properly speaking, the school age period, and that is why it is strongly characterised by both formal and informal education and learning, depending on whether the environment is a literate or preliterate one. As Erikson observed, this is socially a most decisive stage. Through cooperation with others one learns to do things and develops a sense of industry, and experiences a division of labour. The social value of this stage is described by Lowe thus,

> The achievement of trust, autonomy and initiative necessarily involve the child with increasing number of other people. By going to school, however, his social sphere is extended tremendously. He begins to interact not merely with parents but with teachers, and other adults, not merely with brothers and sisters but with other children of his own age.[46]

With reference to faith, in this stage the person begins to take on for him or herself stories, beliefs and observances that symbolise belonging to his or her community. "Such beliefs, moral rules, and attitudes are taken literally. Stories become a great means of transmitting values".[47]

Then comes the storming stage of puberty or adolescence - the pivotal point of Eriksonian scheme. This is the stage when an individual is primarily concerned with efforts at consolidating his social roles. It is at this stage also that personal and social values, interpersonal relationships and boundaries of all sorts are gradually confirmed and clarified, especially in group discussions and get-together of peers.[48] The adolescent tries to re-define everything and everybody in his world at this time; makes a revision and re-evaluation of all already acquired childhood identifications, and re-establishes his sense of continuity and identity. For Lowe,

> it is a period in which identity is gradually reintegrated, in a turbulent and largely externalised process of recapitulation. That is, as the adolescent searches for models and clear boundaries he is simultaneously reworking all his earlier crises and identifications.[49]

This tallies with what Erikson refers to as the 'ego synthesis'.[50] At this

---

[45]JAMES W. FOWLER, Stages of Faith, Harper & Row, San Francisco, 1981, p. 133.

[46]G. LOWE, op. cit., p. 128.

[47]JAMES W. FOWLER, op. cit., p. 149.

[48]Cf., G. LOWE, op. cit., p. 158.

[49]Ibid., p. 183.

[50]Cf., E. H. ERIKSON, op. cit., p. 94.

period, the adolescent tries to ensure that his ways are in consonance with the standards of the society. That is why one seeks for cultural recognition. Erikson observes that the ego identity of the adolescent "gains real strength only from whole hearted and consistent recognition of real accomplishment, that is, achievement that has meaning in their culture".[51] It is no wonder, then, that rites of initiation are generally held within this period in various cultures.

With reference to faith, Fowler would see the period as one characterised by 'Synthetic-Conventional Faith'. It is this type of faith that provides a coherent orientation in the midst of the complex and diverse range of involvements of the adolescent. At this juncture faith ought to synthesise values and information, and provide a basis for identity and outlook.[52]

After the adolescent come the three stages of adulthood. In the young adulthood, which starts from the twenties up to late thirties, one gets to the point when life really begins. Life for Erikson would mean "work or study for a specified care, sociability with the other sex, and in time, marriage and a family of one's own".[53] It is at this stage that one is confronted with the question of making choices - of vocation, of life partner and the shaping of personal and vocational dreams. One is completely taken up by building up a life structure on which to depend till old age. As an adult one begins to take seriously one's responsibility for commitments, lifestyles, beliefs, and attitudes. It is also at this juncture that one confronts the unavoidable tensions of: individuality versus social belonging; self actualization versus group survival.

There is the adulthood proper which is the stage that lasts from the forties to mid-sixties. This stage is generally characterised by generativity or stagnation which is its crisis alternative. One is at this period preoccupied with the creation and guidance of the next generation. This is a very salient and reflexive stage. One tries to reshape, reclaim or consolidate the past. This stage signals a beginning of the enjoyment of the fruits of earlier efforts, in terms of increasing security, comfort and influence.

Finally comes the Maturity Stage or Old age. This monopolises the last period of one's existence. It is called the integrity stage, although it can also, on the contrary, result in a crisis of despair. It is the culmination point of all personality development. This is the moment of looking back with nostalgia at life, which is fast coming to an end. Within this period, one simply supervises, and delegates one's authority and responsibilities.

Following up these stages, one is greatly enriched by the various values characterising each of the stages of development. The earliest stages furnish us with very important and indispensable moments for influencing an individual. One can rightly conclude that the seeds of personality development are sown at the very earliest periods of life, although personality formation is not limited or confined only to these stages,

---

[51]Ibid., p. 95.

[52]Cf., J. W. FOWLER, op. cit., p. 172.

[53]E. H. ERIKSON, op. cit., p. 101.

but stretch up through the adolescent to the adult stage when it is stabilised and considered as mature. It is very significant and noteworthy that the foundations of all the values which characterise the adult personality are constructed at the very beginning of the individual.[54] It is noticed also that in each stage there is always a continuity and a carry-over from the previous stages to the next in a cumulative manner.

From this survey, one pinpoints the earliest childhood stages culminating in the adolescent period as the most important pressure points for any valuable and long lasting influence of the adult personality. One recommends the utilisation of such pressure moments mostly for the inculturation of the faith. This is because during these stages, internalisation is made by the growing individual. This internalisation is very strong and remain operative throughout life. One ends this survey, then, by asking if the enculturation process in the developmental stages of an individual cannot be tapped and influenced to utilise the internalisation of the early stages of life for a construction of a future oriented deeper commitment in the individual.

2.3.2 Childhood Internalisation and Character Formation

When one realises that no aspect of any culture is genetically inherited, but that rather culture is transmitted to an individual in the process of enculturation, which necessarily demands the internalisation of values, then, the necessity of treating childhood internalisation in this work becomes evident and urgent. By internalisation one understands the in-taking of "some aspects of the external world into one's private mental life and having that internal representation of the external world exert an influence over one's thoughts and behaviour".[55] This can take the form of identification, which is psychoanalytically considered as the mechanism by which the superego of self-regulating moral code, is initially established in the child.

The period of childhood, as has already been seen above, is generally regarded as the most important stage in the formation of personality. So many psychoanalysts show special interest and pay attention to childhood stages of life because it is in childhood that most fundamental traits of the personality are established. In fact, psychoanalysis traces back to childhood stages the origins of certain drives and crises which are detected in the adult stages. The importance shown by parents in child-training is based on the fact highlighted by Aloy Nwabeke when he remarked that "the childhood period, though very short in the life of man, is the most vital; the formation got at this period is lasting and rewarding".[56]

---

[54]At least the origins of faith in the individual is traced to the development of the sense of trust in the young child (cf., ERIK H. ERIKSON, op. cit., pp. 66-67).

[55]Concise Encyclopedia of Psychology, Abridged ed. 1987, v.s. "Internalisation" by W. Samuel.

[56]ALOYSIUS I.A.N. NWABEKE, Liturgical-Catechetical Formation of Children in the light of Patristic Practice and Second Vatican Council Reform,

Childhood phase of life is also very important for anthropologists on account of the fact that culture is transmitted from generation to generation through the training of children. For this reason, child-raising is considered as one of the fundamental aspects of any culture. The childhood is recognised as the period when "the most intense projection of the world takes place".[57] In reference to the precious nature of the moment in the life of man, Lidz remarks,

> . . . these are the months when the foundations are laid, not only for future emotional stability, but also for basic though global character traits and for intellectual development. No part of life experience will be as solidly incorporated in the individual, become so irrevocably a part of a person, as infancy.[58]

In comparison to the other phases it is even regarded as the most important.[59] From all the references above, one concludes that it is within this period that the seeds of an integrated life of an individual is sown.

With reference to culture, the childhood period signals the inception of the process of enculturation and socialisation of the individual. As already seen above, enculturation is the process of the transmission of cultural patterns to an individual.[60] Both enculturation and socialisation are, however, carried out at the early stages of life. The family is the primary agent of both processes. It is through these processes that the child is introduced into

> the prescribed, permitted, and proscribed values of the society and the acceptable and unacceptable means of achieving such goals. . . . Family value systems, role definitions, and patterns of interrelationships . . .

Rome, 1986. This remark is taken from the cover-page.

[57]New Catholic Encyclopedia, v.s. "Personality".

[58]THEODORE LIDZ, The Person, Basic Books, Inc., New York, 1983, p. 124.

[59]"Le fase più importante del processo inculturativo è, però, quella che si attua nei primi anni di esistenza dell'individuo, anni durante i quali si struttura la personalità di base e si interiorizzano i valori fondamentali della cultura". - (FILIPPO DI GIACOMO, Lezioni di Antropologia Culturale, Teresianum, Roma, 1987, p. 38)

[60]Enculturation and socialisation are not the same. While socialisation concerns teaching the child the basic roles and institutions of the society through transactions between family members, enculturation deals with that which is transmitted symbolically from generation to generation. (Cf., T. LIDZ, op. cit., pp. 59-60).

as well as led into

> the acquisition of the major techniques of adaptation . . . not
> inherited genetically but are assimilated as part of the cultural
> heritage . . . such as status hierarchies, religious beliefs and
> ethics that are accepted as divine commands or axiomatically
> as the only proper way of doing things, and are defended by
> various taboos.[61]

The impact which enculturation has on the behaviour and personality of the
individual is so deep and lasting as Luzbetak reveals:

> From early childhood - in fact from the day one is born - one
> is drilled to conform to recognised ways. Companions and
> elders take great pains to teach the individual what is 'practical',
> 'useful', 'correct', 'true', 'polite', and 'disciplined'. The individual
> is punished and ridiculed for parting from approved ways,
> praised and rewarded for proper and correct behaviour -a
> training that at least intermittently continues till death.[62]

Enculturation is carried out not only by the family but by the entire human
environment that have an influence on the individual. This ranges from
parents and siblings, extending to kin and relations, teachers, friends and
peers, and in fact the whole community. Parents achieve this by what they
generally model, teach, and reward, but also by the child-rearing styles or
techniques they employ in their roles as parents. It ought to be noted that
in some societies, child-training is the method by which a group's basic ways
of organising experience is transmitted. Hence there can be a uniformity in
childhood experience in an area. Therefore, since parents have a common
culture and shared ideas on child-rearing with others, then, as some authors
conclude, "all the members of a fairly stable group . . . will have had similar
experiences in childhood. Parents with a common culture teach their
children much the same things".[63]

The process of enculturation commonly takes the form of instruction
which can be formal or informal or both. Enculturation has two major
aspects as Grunlan explains: "(1) the informal, which some call 'child
training' and in some senses precedes and in the other senses runs

---

[61]Ibid.; "Alcuni autori propongono - 'inculturazione' o 'socializzazione' per
indicare come 'integrazione sociale dell'individuo' l'intero svolgimento del
processo che si realizza nella rete di rapporti dinamici che l'individuo contrae
con il proprio ambiente sociale ed ecologico e in virtù dei quali struttura il
proprio 'patrimonio culturale e individuale" - FILIPPO Di GIACOMO, Ibid.

[62]L. J. LUZBETAK, op. cit., p. 77.

[63]MARC J. SWARTZ & DAVID K. JORDAN, op. cit., p. 154.

concurrently with (2) the formal, more commonly termed 'education'".[64] Early enough in the process of enculturation, bombarded with images, impressions, ideas and cultural values, the child takes in all these in the manner of a photographic camera. From the developmental characteristics of the oral stage which we have seen above, we know that the sensitive organs of the child already function very actively even though they lack the sharpening quality. It is essential here to recall to mind some fundamental epistemological principles of Thomas Aquinas, which would help to clarify the basis for the internalisation. It is apodictically established that:

a) It is impossible for our intellect in its present state of being joined to a body capable of receiving impressions, actually to understand anything without turning to sense images.[65]

b) Species stored up in the possible intellect remain there in a habitual way when the intellect is not actually understanding. Thus, in order for us actually to understand, a mere storing of species is not sufficient we must also use them, and indeed in accord with the things of which they are images, which are natures existing in particular.[66]

c) Lastly, the intellect can know forms which exist individually in corporeal matter by abstraction from the individual matter, represented by sense images.[67]

From these epistemological axioms one holds as certain the fact that children gather all the information with which they are stimulated for future operation. Man relies on his store of knowledge for all his actions, since every knowledge exists in order to be expressed at the opportune time.

Besides, the Piagetian theory on Child's Cognitive development certifies that even at the early stages of a child, there exists in the child an ability to perform intellectual operations, even though this evolves in a progressive but complex manner as the child progresses in growth. In any case, there is no doubt that between the ages of four and five, formal thinking is already stabilised.[68]

On the basis of these two references, it is certain that during the enculturative process, especially at the early stages of life, the experiences, impressions, values, and cultural patterns are internalised. Internalisation is a powerful feature in enculturation such that some authors as Hoebel emphasise this internalisation aspect in their definition of enculturation. For instance, Hoebel thinks of enculturation as "both a conscious and unconscious conditioning process whereby man as child and adult, achieve

---

[64]S. A. GRUNLAN & M. K. MAYERS, Cultural Anthropology, Akademie Books, Michigan, 1988, p. 73.

[65]ST.THOMAS, Summa Theologiae, 1a. 84, 7.

[66]Ibid., 1a. 84,8.

[67]Ibid., 1a. 85, 1.

[68]Cf., J. PIAGET & B. INHELDER, The Psychology of the Child, Basic Books, 1969, p. 5; (cf., also Encyclopedia of Educational Research, 5th ed., v.s. "Cognitive Development", by Francis J. Di Vesta).

competence in his culture, internalises his culture, and becomes thoroughly enculturated".[69] In internalisation, the dreams and expectations as well as the rules and requirements of the society are taken in, so to speak. Lidz expatiates this:

> Children internalise some of their parents ways as their own ways of living their lives . . . and in the process take on some societal directives. Some parental directives . . . are taken as a reference system of what behaviour is prescribed, permitted or proscribed which we term the super ego directives. That is, some behaviourial standards are internalised as part of a person's basic ways of thinking, and some continue to be experienced as externally imposed standards to which a person conforms in order to remain at peace with the self, very much as the child had conformed with parental wishes and edicts.[70]

It is the internalisation that forms the basis for the identity formation and this, to a very great extent, touches upon one's character as an individual. Once the internalisation has taken root in the child, it becomes very difficult to interfere with or go against them.[71] There is so much in common between the workings of these internalised values and the role of conscience in man. Some people even tend to identify the two[72], as Van der Poel remarks: "Though this psychic function has a great resemblance with our understanding of conscience, it may not be equated with it unqualifiedly." But he observes that

---

[69]E. A. HOEBEL, Anthropology: The Study of Man, McGraw, New York, 1972, p. 40.

[70]T. LIDZ, op. cit., p. 251. For Freud, "the superego is the internalization of all the restrictions to which the ego must bow. It is forced upon the child ('von aussen aufgenötigt') by the critical influence of the patents, and later, by that of professional educators, and of what to the early Freud was a vague multitude of fellow men ('die unbestimmte Menge der Genossen') making up the 'milieu' and 'public opinion'(Freud, 1914). Quoted in ERIK H. ERIKSON, Identity and Life Cycle, p. 19.

[71]"Una volta che il 'super-ego' è stato accettato mediante una attitudine emotiva composta di paura, di rispetto ed amore l'individuo ha assimilato in pieno la cultura morale della sua società, che inibisce molti dei suoi impulsi delinquenziali, non solo in vista di premi o sanzioni che può ricevere dagli altri, ma per timore della disapprovazione del 'super-ego' stesso, che suscita nel suo intimo il doloroso senso della colpevolezza e del rimorso." (FILIPPO DI GIACOMO, op. cit., p. 40).

[72]"In relazione all'ideologia che a seconda delle culture è stata inculcata nel corso del processo di inculturazione, il 'super-ego' può essere classificato con la 'voce di Dio', la 'coscienza', i 'comandamenti della società', il 'bene di tutti', la 'volontà della maggioranza'. ecc.". - Ibid.

The super ego and the ego ideal are a residue of the child's earliest awareness of his total dependency on his parents and others. . . . Thus the superego is to large extent a super-imposed parental authority which the person has internalised. This same authority keeps exercising its coercion even without physical presence.[73]

From the point of view of the compelling influence of the internalised values on the attitude of the individual, one is inclined to think that Freud was right in stating that:

Mankind never lives completely in the present; the ideologies of the super-ego perpetuate the past, the traditions of the race and the people, which yield but slowly to the influence of the present and to new development, and so long as they work through the super-ego, play an important part in man's life.[74]

To sum up, it is clearly evident that an intervention with inculturation even at the early stages of life will definitely interfere with and influence the establishment of the ego-ideal and the super-ego. Without this interference, the inherited ego ideals of the community will be internalised. This, as we have seen, has its coercive and moral force, which guides and controls every individual. Once this is internalised and integrated with the conscience in an individual, it becomes an uphill task to adjust it, since it is always obeyed and complied with. One proposes, then, a stepping-in at these moments of internalisation with inculturation. This would ensure that the seeds and values of a culture, animated by and integrated with Christian values, are internalised and thereby become points of reference in the subsequent behaviour of the individual as the internalised super-egos do.

Besides, the character of an individual is not something formed overnight and from nowhere. It takes its roots from the childhood internalised values. What happens at the adolescent period is only a final fixation and synthesis of all former identifications. If what is internalised is the seed of a culture animated by christian faith, no doubt, one's character and identity would be greatly influenced by these values in living a committed life of faith when it is stabilised.

In order to understand more clearly how and why individuals are greatly affected by their culture, we shall have to see the following subsequent sections dealing with the influences on the individual.

2.3.3 Culture and the Individual in the Society

The concept of culture necessarily implies two other concepts - the

---

[73]C. J. VAN DER POEL, op. cit., p. 129.

[74]FREUD, New Introductory Lectures of Psychoanalysis, Lecture 31: The Anatomy of the Mental Personality, New York: Norton, 1933, pp.95-96. (Quoted in ERIK.H ERIKSON, Identity and the Life Cycle, p. 159.)

individual and the society. A single individual does not share cultural patterns. It takes a group of individuals within a society to share a pattern of life. But the concepts of the individual and the society, being the components of the concept of culture, at the same time, give an impression of a diametrical opposition to each other, so that it becomes essential to distinguish and establish the relationship between them. Reinhold Niebuhr made an observation of this apparent contradiction in the two terms when he remarked that,

> The community is the frustration as well as the realisation of individual life. Its collective egoism is an offence to the individual's conscience; its institutional injustices negate the ideal of justice, and such brotherhood as it achieves is limited by ethnic and geographic boundaries.[75]

It is, therefore, necessary to see the relationship between them.

The term 'individual' is translated from the Greek 'atomon', meaning 'what is not divided'.[76] It means a single human being distinct from every other, and, as it were, ontologically complete in himself, and cannot be identified with anything else. Every individual is a unique, irreplaceable, incommunicable being, different from every other. One's individuality is rooted in egoism, which is characterised by a subjectivity which allows entrance to no one except in confidence and intimacy. Even when an entrance into this subjectivity is gained, there remains still in the individual an inaccessible and inexpressible domain. This is the inwardness which constitutes the core of one's individuality. Reflecting on the immense potentialities found in the individuality of man, and seeing them as the source of one's worth, dignity and respect, John Macquarrie remarked:

> So each human being is a unique irreplaceable centre of freedom and creativity, engaged in his or her task of fashioning a unique human life-story. At the same time, each one has his unique givens and his unique situation, and these constitute, as it were, the raw material of the life-story and also the limits to what is possible for that human being.[77]

One's individuality is revealed when one sets himself to know his culture. It is the individuality which receives the culture, as Mary Goodman explains: ". . . the individual child is not merely an empty vessel to be filled nor a

---

[75]REINHOLD NIEBUHR, The Nature and Destiny of Man, Nisbet 1941-3, vol. 11, p. 320. (Quoted in JOHN MACQUARRIE, In Search of Humanity, SCM Press Ltd., London, 1982, p. 92.)

[76]The New Catholic Encyclopedia, ed.1981, s.v. "Individual".

[77]JOHN MACQUARRIE, op. cit., p. 85.

largely passive receiver of culture. His individuality is apparent from birth".[78]
However impressive the concept of the individual may be, equally striking is the essential sociality of the individual. Luzbetak defined society as "a permanently organised aggregate of persons sharing a common way of life and group consciousness".[79] Although an individual is ontologically unique, independent, and irreplaceable, yet, through birth, one is launched into the world, helpless, and as it were, a no-body except for the equipment of bio-psychic structures and potentialities.[80] From birth it becomes glaringly clear that for one to exist and survive, other individuals must necessarily have much to do with the individual.[81] Anatomically, physiologically, and psychologically, each human being is from beginning oriented towards a relation with another. The fact of being born into the family structure confirms this. The family is the smallest unit of any society. Therefore, being a member of the family means already forming part of a society. Lidz highlights the social structure of the family. According to him,

> The family constitutes the fundamental social unit of virtually every society: it forms a grouping of individuals that the society treats as an entity; it helps stabilize a society by creating a network of kinship systems; . . . and it provides roles, status, motivation, and incentives that affect the relationships between individuals and the society.[82]

Finding oneself within the society, an individual is constantly influenced by the members of the society, especially in the process of enculturation. As observed by Goodman,

> Whatever the nature of his society the individual moves through a complicated web of interpersonal relationships. Each relationship involves communication and interdependence. Some relationships are important for personal security. An important part of enculturation is learning the patterned expectations associated with particular relationships. . . . All

---

[78]MARY ELLEN GOODMAN, The Individual and Culture, The Dorsey Press, Homewood, Illinois, 1967, p. 128.

[79]L. J. LUZBETAK, op. cit., p. 111.

[80]". . . human infants are born with a dual heritage, . . . They have a biological inheritance that is transmitted through the genes from generation to generation, and a cultural heritage into which they grow and which they must assimilate to become persons". (THEODORE LIDZ, The Person, p. 11)

[81]Ralph Linton pointed this out when he wrote: "The individual is so completely dependent upon others during infancy that he cannot survive without eliciting response from them". (RALPH LINTON, The Cultural Background of Personality, p. 6.)

[82]THEODORE LIDZ, The Person, p. 51.

through his life he will be affected by other persons whom he encounters in patterned relationships, and he in turn will affect them.[83]

It is through other individuals that one is introduced into the ways of life of the society. Concretely, then, a society is an organised and systematised aggregate of individuals sharing the same environment and behaviourial pattern referred to as culture. Although society and culture are not identical concepts, they are however interdependent. Society refers to people and their social organisation, while culture refers to their acquired way of life.[84] The society has worked out the patterns of life as responses to the existential problems of their environment.

The individual is circumscribed within an environment where social and cultural forces affect the individual. It is from the constant interaction between the individual and these social and cultural influences that the individual's personality evolves. Hence the individual can be considered as limited by these societal influences, and therefore, does not enjoy absolute freedom as the concept would demand. The question, then, arises as to which should take precedence - the individual or the society? In answering this question, one has to take note of some essential facts clearly outlined by Linton. One of these is the fact that "the society rather than the individual has the significant unit in . . . species struggle for survival". Another fact is that societies "persist far beyond the life span of any one individual". Also societies perpetuate themselves and survive by making use of the individuals who are assigned roles to play for the life of the society.[85] People are born into the society, live and die, while the society remains interminably through successive generations, even if under new conditions. Considering these basic facts, Macquarrie tries to answer the question. He holds that

> . . . perhaps it would be no more correct to say that society is prior to the individual in an ontological as distinct from a chronological sense, than to say that the individual is prior to society. Both the social and the individual poles seem equally original in the being of man, and their tension is there from the beginning as one of the factors contributing to the dynamics of human life.[86]

This definitely goes to prove that between the individual, his society and culture, there exists a reciprocal pull and interaction. This generates a tension between what existentialists refer to as authentic and unauthentic

---

[83]MARY ELLEN GOODMAN, op. cit., p. 102.

[84]Cf., STEPHEN A. GRUNLAN & MARVIN K. MAYERS, Cultural Anthropology, p. 40.

[85]Cf., RALPH LINTON, op. cit., pp. 10f.

[86]JOHN MACQUARRIE, op. cit., p. 85.

existence.[87] The role and preoccupation of the individual is how to maintain an equilibrium and balance these socio-cultural forces. While one tries to satisfy oneself and live an authentic existence, there is the other problem of adapting to the restrictions from the culture and society. It is this vacillating situation of the individual that Howell reflected when he observed that,

> In its ontological development . . . the human organism is faced with the problem of adapting itself on the one hand to the restrictions imposed by the particular cultural forms and on the other hand to achieving satisfaction for its instinctual impulses.
> . . . The enculturational process, . . . exerts a regulatory function on the course of their interaction.[88]

So, while counter-cultural attitudes and behaviour of the individual threatens the integrity of the society, the individual, on the other hand, is compelled to cultural conformity by the coercive nature of social and cultural constraints. It is interesting to note with Lucien Richard that "humans are involved in webs of significance that they themselves have spin, since the inherited culture forms the individual's identity, which through enculturation process, evolves by internalising the society's self-understanding, self-image and valuing".[89] This dialectical relationship is further beautifully described by Herbert Mead, whom Thomas Groome paraphrased thus:

> Having externalized ourselves into culture and society, and culture and society having taken on a life of their own, the empowerment and limitations of that world are now taken back into our consciousness as our own. The possibilities and parameters that our social/cultural context appears to offer become our own perception of our possibilities and parameters. In other words, the objectified culture and society created by us and our predecessors become internalized as the basis of our

---

[87]Martin Heidegger regards as unauthentic existence the acceptance "in our day-to-day life , all the standards, the beliefs and prejudices of the society in which we find ourselves. . . . in every detail of our lives failing to distinguish ourselves from the mass", while grasping that "human reality is characterised by the fact that each human being is , uniquely, himself and no one else, and that each of us has his own possibilities to fulfil", and that "our concern with the world, instead of being a mere concern to do as people in general do, . . . can become authentic concern, to fulfil our real potentiality in the world". (MARY WARNOCK, Existentialism, Oxford University Press, Oxford, 1986, p. 55)

[88]HALLOWEL, 1949, p. 318, (quoted in MARY E. GOODMAN, op. cit., p. 129).

[89]LUCIEN RICHARD et al., eds., Vatican II: The Unfinished Agenda, Paulist Press, New York/Mahwah, p. 106. It is the culture in which a child is raised that moulds its personality. (cf., T. LIDZ, op. cit., p. 13)

own self-identity.[90]

From this relationship, one understands clearly the difficulties which the individual experiences when faced by a situation that demands a going-against the internalised patterns of behaviour of his society. This is our major concern. Briefly, it is the problem which surfaces by the fact that the individual, because he is a part of the society, finds himself pulled to the opposite direction by the constraining forces of the society. Surely, the individual is not an automaton, or a 'helpless slave' of his culture. Definitely one retains one's free-will in spite of all these forces. One has only to remember that culture remains "potential guides" for the behaviour of the individual and ways for solving human problems of the individual. The ways of culture are not the only possible ways open to an individual. Hence, as Luzbetak remarked, "the individual can and does part from standard and approved ways. Man is moulded by his culture and pressured by it, but not chained to it".[91] It is the same point that Ralph Linton emphasises as he writes:

> No matter how carefully the individual has been trained or how successful his conditioning has been, he remains a distinct organism with his own needs and with capacities for independent thought, feeling and action. Moreover, he retains a considerable degree of individuality. His integration into society and culture goes no deeper than his learned responses, and although in the adult these include the greater part of what we call the personality, there is still a good deal of the individual left over.[92]

It is on account of this that one can, at times, go against one's cultural ways. It is rather the consequences of the cultural coercive pressures that force individuals to conform to the cultural ways. The cultural constraints of a society is drilled into the individual and internalised in the process of enculturation. As some authors confirm,

> This expectation of external punishment will incline the individual to conform to shared understandings just as the internally based punishment in individuals with guilt oriented superegos will. The externally based source of punishment is found in individuals with a shame oriented superegos". Both types of superegos provide the moral force that plays a pervasive role

---

[90]THOMAS GROOME, Christian Religious Education, Harper & Row Ltd., 1980, p. 112.

[91]L. J. LUZBETAK, op. cit., p. 78.

[92]RALPH LINTON, op. cit., pp. 14-15.

in motivating cultural conformity in all societies.[93]

It is only when the individual plays his roles in accordance with the systematized societal patterns that one feels fulfilled. On the other hand, "the ability to integrate into a single configuration elements of behaviour some of which serve to meet individual needs, others to satisfy social necessities, and to learn and transmit such configurations as wholes is the thing that makes human societies possible".[94]

So, society exists for the common good of individuals, but uses the individual to survive. Even if its systematised patterns of life are subject to change, and really do change, they, however, remain permanent and enduring.

2.3.4 **Influences on the Individual**

From above, it is seen that the individual, in spite of his individuality is necessarily defined as one in relation. This is on account of so many factors which compel him to coexist and need the attention and support of others. In taking his place in the society, the individual is exposed to so many influences in the course of his life. These influences begin right from the infantile period and continue throughout life. While one's physical and human environments exert a lot of influences on the individual, one also influences so many others in the society. It would interest this work to take note of these influences which affect the character, belief and actions of an individual in a manner that the individual cannot freely act on his own. Most of these influences in a big way characterise one's personality, and determine one's existential attitudes. At times, some of the influences are so strong that it becomes difficult for one to tow an independent line of action that could be completely independent of any influences. Since one discusses the apparent non-committal existential attitude of the Igbo Christian to the Faith, which arises much out of the environmental situation with its multiple social and cultural factors, which influence the individual, one considers it important to expose some of these psychological influences as a preamble to any attempts at salvaging the situation.

In the course of one's life, one is not only influenced by biological factors, which are responsible for the physique, intelligence and the intensity of the drives that motivate one's personality. There are other influences coming from the environment, family, society and culture. As Ralph Linton points out:

> Between the natural environment and the individual there is always interposed a human environment which is vastly more significant. This human environment consists of an organised group of other individuals, that is, a society, and of a particular

---

[93]MARC J. SWARTZ & DAVID K. JORDAN, Culture, University of Washington Press, Chicago, pp. 144-145.

[94]RALPH LINTON, op. cit., p. 16.

way of life which is characteristic of this group, that is a culture. It is the individual's interaction with these which is responsible for the formation of most of his behaviour patterns, even his deep-seated emotional responses.[95]

First and foremost, one's environment contributes in shaping one's personality. One's upbringing is greatly conditioned by the surrounding environment. It makes a big difference if one is brought up in either a civilised, or peasant or agricultural environment. One is so much limited by one's environment. The human infant is born preadapted to an "average expectable environment". The individual is not born as a "tabula rasa, but rather with unique inherited characteristics which will influence the adult personality".[96] This receptacle accepts whatever environment one is born into. As Erikson explains, "it is the subtle and complex 'milieu' which permits a human baby not only to survive but also to develop his potentialities for growth and uniqueness".[97]

In the preliminary stages of one's development, the environment furnishes the experiences which determine the resultant behaviour of an individual. Knowing and understanding one's environment gives a clue to understanding one's behaviour, for, the environment, as Linton observes, "is indispensable for the understanding both of individual personalities and of personality in general".[98] From the point of view of the human environment, right from the maternal womb, the foetus is exposed to the direct physical influences from the mother. It is generally agreed by psychologists that the stresses and strain of the foetal environment has influences on the foetus. For instance, Gordon Lowe points out:

> The physical influences which play upon the infant during the pre-natal period may determine in crucial ways, what he will be like after he is born. For example, if the mother is over-exposed to X-ray radiation, or if she catches German measles, he may be born malformed.[99]

Lowe is not a lone voice here. The same confirmation is made by Lidz who writes,

> The emotional problems of the pregnant woman can affect the course of the pregnancy and the fetus. The baby's development does not start at birth but with conception. It is

---

[95]Ibid., p. 8.

[96]WILLIAM A. HAVILAND, Cultural Anthropology, Rinehart and Winston, New York, 1978, p. 41.

[97]ERIK H. ERIKSON, Identity and the Life Cycle, p. 162.

[98]R. LINTON, op. cit., p. 7.

[99]GORDON R. LOWE, The Growth of Personality, p. 3.

responsive to its fetal environment. If the mother bleeds seriously or if there is marked disturbance in her metabolic equilibrium, the fetus can develop an anomaly through interference with its maturation.[100]

So, as early as the foetal stage, an individual is subjected to various influences. For the infant, the influences are much, for,

the infant although by no means passive, is helplessly dependent of his ancestry, his biological heredity, and the particular environment in which he finds himself. If these are not good there is not much he can do about it. Infancy is a period in which things happen to us more than we happen to things.[101]

The childhood influences have much value, since it is within these earliest stages of life that most of the basic attitudes are formed, which attitudes, according to Van der Poel, "influence the individual's approach to and appreciation of himself and others, and thus greatly influence his inclination and his behaviour".[102] Correlating these childhood influences with the dimensions of faith, James Fowler referred to them as the influences of the imitative phase, through which the child can be powerfully and permanently influenced by examples, moods, actions and stories of the visible faith of primally related adults.[103] One notes alarmingly here that the religion of parents greatly influence the individual. Although the child is not fully conscious, yet these influences have so much to do with the later life as adults. They necessarily play a major role in the individual's moral judgement concerning his activities in the future.[104]

On a higher scale, the family forms the environmental base of the individual, especially at the early stages of development. Lidz points out that

Not only is the family the setting in which the child's personality development takes place, but the parents' personalities and interactions as well as the transactions of the family as a whole profoundly influence the child's development and who the child

---

[100]THEODORE LIDZ, op. cit., pp. 101-102. (For more details of the pre-natal influences on the foetus cf., Association for the Aid of Crippled Children, 1964; Corah, et al., 1965).

[101]G. LOWE, op. cit., p. 48.

[102]CORNELIUS J. VAN der POEL, The Search for Human Values, p. 130.

[103]Cf., JAMES W. FOWLER, Stages of Faith, p. 133.

[104]Cf., C. VAN der POEL, Ibid.

becomes. In a sense, the parents' ways and personalities enter into the child's makeup as much as do their genes.[105]

The identity of the individual is strictly to be defined by the parental influences to which one is subjected. Lidz regards these influences as 'most persistent' and sees their effect as very encompassing for the still unformed infant and small child. The influences would aim at integrating the family ways and the child's reactions to them in such a way that "they can be considered determinants of his or her constitutional make-up, difficult to differentiate from the genetic biological influences with which they interrelate".[106] Seeing the parental influences as fundamental, Lidz remarks that "all subsequent influences will modify those of the family, but they can never undo, or fully reshape these early core experiences".[107]

In a very special way, the mother's influence on the child is very predominant and all encompassing. It touches every aspect of life since the child is completely immersed in dependence on its mother for everything. It is even said that "the child's awareness and assessment of how good the world is will be largely determined by the kind of care and attention he receives from his mother".[108] Therefore, the family, as the primal group is influential in the development of the individual, even from the fact that it is the family that transmits to the individual the basic cultural pattern of the society. Although one can later in life, from association with others, differentiate and distinguish between the family influences and those of his peers and outside groups, and even be able to make adjustments, yet the parental influence remains operative throughout life. Hence Lowe is right in writing that

> . . . parental attitudes, whether pathological or benign, may be seen reverberating in their influence through several generations in a given family. Both the sins and virtues of the parents may be visited on the heads of the children even unto the third and fourth generation.[109]

On a yet wider scale, there are the societal and cultural influences, which, as has already been demonstrated above, exert their influence of the individual. As early as the young child leaves home for the school, not only is his social sphere extended, he also begins to get a wider dimension of influences. These come from the teachers, other adults, and peers and schoolmates. The influences from this wider group either strengthen the parental influences or modify them. In any case, in these influences, the

---

[105]THEODORE LIDZ, op. cit., p. 74.

[106]Ibid., p. 48.

[107]Ibid.

[108]G. LOWE, op. cit., p. 88.

[109]Ibid., p. 65.

child begins to experience, although in a miniature way, the very beginnings of the societal influences of a later life. From the interaction from this wider group, one gets prepared to adapt and conform to the society. As one grows to interact with the wider society, these miniature experiences get more stabilised. In interactions with the society, a sense of ethnic belonging is revealed. One's experience of this wider social group would definitely motivate a modification of the family influences.

Through the process of enculturation, the society's patterns of life are transmitted. These patterns of life - culture - influences one in two different ways. There are the influences derived from the culturally patterned behaviour of other individuals. These are experienced especially at the early stages of life. There are also the influences flowing from the experience by the individual of the patterns of behaviour characteristic of his society. These patterns serve as a model which will ultimately later in life determine one's personal responses to situations.[110] When the behaviourial patterns are internalised, they begin to operate as a moral force of the individual. Some authors point out that

> The individual often experiences the workings of these motives by feeling 'good' about doing something or trying to avoid 'feeling bad' for what he does or does not do. These motives are based in the individual's conscience or more accurately in the psychoanalytic sense, "superego" and their general effect is to influence the individual toward continuing to do what he learned from his parents early in life.[111]

One can then understand the vacillating attitude of one who took in the cultural values and internalised religious impressions in childhood. It becomes extremely difficult when one attempts to adopt new attitudes in life. Trying to give reasons for this, the same authors above explain that

> In his earliest years the individual is trained by loving parents, and he has learned what behaviour they think is good and what bad; he has also so identified with them . . . Every individual will have a set of things that has been taught are bad and good, but a 'core' of shared good things and bad things are, of course elements of culture, and in a society whose members have guilt oriented superegos or consciences peoples' anticipation of punishment from within ("pangs of conscience") will incline them to conform to these elements of culture.[112]

---

[110]"Culturally patterned behaviour directed towards the child may serve as a model for the development of some of his own behaviour patterns". (RALPH LINTON, op. cit., p. 91.)

[111]MARC J. SWARTZ & DAVID K. JORDAN, op. cit., p. 143.

[112]Ibid., p. 144. On the superego, Freud stated, ". . . the superego of the child is not really built up on the model of the parents, but on that of the parents' super-ego; it takes over the same content, it becomes the vehicle

Besides this internally based punishment consciousness, there is the societal external source of control already discussed above. All these factors constrain and influence the behaviour of the individual.

From above one can see that an individual can be variously influenced by so many factors, especially in the moments of internalisation; it has also been seen that these influences come as experiences which the individual makes and feels in his physical and human environments. One can conclude that if all the various environmental circumstances of an individual are taken note of, individuals can be variously influenced if the inculturation process touches upon the influencing environment of the individual.

2.3.5 **Personality Development of the Igbos**

Having surveyed the dynamics of personality development, it becomes necessary to refer this to the Igbo context. By speaking of the personality development of the Igbos, it does not mean that the Igbos do not share with the rest of humanity the developmental structure highlighted above. One simply intends to point out some specific differences which underlie the same developmental structure among the Igbos. While the Igbos share the general characteristics with others, there are some peculiarities which characterise their personality development.

Personality development among the Igbos is fundamentally based on the psychology of the Igbos. The western concept of the individual is very incomplete with reference to the Igbos, who, instead of an 'I' concept, have a 'we' concept in the definition of an individual. The Igbo is necessarily defined in terms of a communitarian belonging. Among the Igbos, one is, not simply because one exists, but rather, because one belongs to his community. This means that community psychology forms the basis of Igbo attitude to life. This characteristic is integrated with a sense of group consciousness, solidarity and communal responsibility. Instead of individual personality, then, what is highlighted is the community personality. One's personality is measured in terms of the community personality. One integrates one's attitudes, desires, values, and feelings with that of the community. Igbo community is based on the extended family system. As Aleke pointed out,

> Being reared from childhood within this mode of psycho-social disposition, where person-to-person interaction is not restricted, and above all, where the patterning of individual behaviours is channelled towards collectivistic dimensional attitude, one cannot be insulated from being the common candidate to the tenacious

---

of tradition and of all the age-long values which have been handed down in this way from generation to generation"(Freud, 1932). Quoted in E. H. ERIKSON, Identity and the Life Cycle, p. 159.

pre-dispositions of this community.[113]

When a child is born, therefore, it is introduced into the community made up of the nuclear and extended families. This is because every child is considered as a property of the whole community, for, as Mozia pinpoints, "a child is not referred to as 'my child' ('nwam') but as 'our child' ('nwa anyi'). This shows the child from the start that it belongs not only to the parents, but also to the entire community".[114] On account of this, the child is exposed to a bombardment of influences and impressions from this community. As the child grows up, it is fully aware that it belongs not only to its nuclear family, it grows up surrounded by the members of the extended family. The child sees itself

as a child of everyone in the household, where everyone shares in its education. Everyone within the environment is responsible and responsive to the maturity of the child. The child learns to appreciate its role as a member of its immediate and extended family, community. As a child of everyone, uncles, aunts, cousins, friends and neighbours, the child becomes conscious of its utter dependence on others as well as others on it.[115]

Right from childhood, one is already well integrated within the community and grows to maturity in the midst of this community spirit. It goes without saying, then, that the child receives its enculturation from his various interactions. It is interesting to note that among the Igbos, as early as possible, the child begins to participate in the world of the adults. Uchendu testifies to this, when he writes that

Igbo children grow up and participate in two worlds - the world of children and the world of adults. Igbo children take an active part in their parents' social and economic activities. They are literally everywhere. They are taken to the market, to the family or village tribunal, to funerals, to a feast, to the farm, to religious ceremonies. They help entertain their parents' guests. There are no children's parties which they are encouraged to dominate, nor are there parents' parties from which they are excluded. If there is a social or ritual ceremony

---

[113]CLETUS E. ALEKE, "Social Psychological Integration of Adolescent Personality into Adulthood in Igboland", (Ph.D Dissertation, Università Antoniana, Rome, 1978, p. 234).

[114]MICHAEL MOZIA, Solidarity in the Church, and Solidarity Among the Igbos of Nigeria, Rome, 1982, p. 237.

[115]R. NWEKE, An Optional Philosophy for a Nigerian Educational System, Università Antonianà, Rome, 1979, pp. 72-73.

going on in an Igbo village, everybody is welcome.[116]

This observation is a clear proof that Igbo children start early to be active observer participants. They get easily acquainted with the way of life of their community from the day-to-day experiences of the extended family. As they observe, they try to imitate what they see. Hence, Uchendu further notes that ". . . in their own world they dramatise adult roles and spend their leisure hours doing 'nursery' cooking, playing father and mother, holding 'play' markets and mock fights".[117] In effect this means that before one grows to the next chronological stage of development, one has already started to perform the subsequent personality roles expected of him. Transition can, therefore, be described as gradual and smooth. In the description of the smooth transition and continuity of personality development of young people in Samoa, Mead observed:

> From early childhood on, youngsters are involved in work tasks that have a meaningful connection to the work they will perform as adults. They are involved in the care of younger children, in the planting and harvesting of crops, and in the gathering and preparation of food. Their entrance into adult work is gradual and continuous, with work tasks structured so as to be graded to children's skills and intelligence. . . . By the time they have reached late adolescence . . . are well trained in the tasks they will need to perform as adults.[118]

This description vividly tallies with and represents the same situation among the Igbos, as can be testified from above. This life of imitation eventually leads them to early maturity, because by so doing, they anticipate their future roles as adults from their tender age. Generally speaking, Igbo children mature comparatively earlier than their counterparts in western culture. Of course, this early maturity of Igbo children is dependent on and motivated by and as a result of so many factors. Such factors could be, for instance, on account of one's position in the family; the number of children in the nuclear family; the occupation of parents; early contact with other grown-ups; and especially the living presence of elders in the child's environment, and so on. In this last case, it is believed that one shares the wealth of wisdom and experience of the elders.

Another important aspect in the growth structure of Igbo children is the fact that the sibling grown-up in the family help to bring up their little ones. This feature exposes the children very early to various experiences and interactions with other children. The siblings would take the children with them out to the village square, where they pass the time playing with

---

[116]V. C. UCHENDU, op. cit., p. 61.

[117]Ibid.

[118]MARGARET MEAD, Coming of Age in Samoa, Morrow, New York, 1928. (Quoted in L. STEINBERGER, Adolescence, Alfred A. Knopf, New York, 1985, p. 109).

their peer groups. Green made an observation of this feature among the Igbos and remarked:

> . . . to a considerable extent the children bring each other up, small ones looking after yet smaller in a manner strongly reminiscent of Stepney or Poplar . . . I have seen a little girl of about five or six carrying a newly born baby over her shoulder or sitting down and giving it water to drink. Later on children will take the baby out with them when they go to play or tend it while their parent go to market.[119]

This feature definitely enhances early maturity in the little ones. From these early outings, a lot of impressions are absorbed and experiences made. From a concrete example encountered during a catechism class in a parish, it is unbelievable as it is a fact that one of such infants brought to the class by its sibling sister, was able to reproduce all the prayers in the vernacular before the elder sister who brought her could do the same. It was really very amazing, but it proves what is said above.

With reference to enculturation, due to this early exposure, the Igbo child learns much of the standard way of life of the community very early. Enculturation takes the form of informal education, since generally speaking, the traditional environment is preliterate, although illiteracy is now fast disappearing with the multiplication of schools everywhere, even in the villages. However, the aims of the traditional education is to prepare one for life, and to be a functional member of the society, as well as to equip one to assume his traditional roles in the community. Right from the beginning, one is made to know that survival is the product of profuse sweat and hard work. That is why parents train their children to be tough. When there is a temptation to be over-indulgent on a child by its parents, the child is sent to a relation in the extended family, who would ensure a hard but thorough up-bringing for the child. It is, therefore, correct to say that "the raising of the children . . . was not an exclusive responsibility of the parents, but had to be done with the cooperation of the family relations in conformity with the African practice of the extended family".[120]

In the process of child training and enculturation, efforts are made to give the child an all-round training - physical, moral, spiritual, intellectual, and character. The entire community shares this responsibility, for, as A. Okeke explains,

> Everyone in the home, in the village, and in the community wanted the Igbo child to be sociable, truthful, brave, humble, have stamina and be of unreproachable conduct at all times. For this reason, everyone joined in correcting or praising any child whenever and wherever he failed or succeeded in showing

---

[119]M. M. GREEN, op. cit., p. 82.

[120]FESTUS C. OKAFOR, Africa at the Cross-Roads, Philosophical Approach to Education, Vantage Press Inc., New York, 1974, p. 74.

acceptable norms of behaviour.[121]

With special reference to this work, and from the ethical-religious point of view, a great part of the content of the informal instruction of the Igbo child, deals with the religious life of the people. This forms the central content of the traditional norms of the community enshrined in what is referred to as the 'Omenani'.[122] As Mozia hinted, even though he was more preoccupied with the solidarity dimensions,

> The child is made to learn certain traditional forms of rules and regulations contained in 'Omenani'. These include the participation in the socio-religious life and ceremonies of the community so that the spirit of cooperation and collaboration is gradually imparted to the child.[123]

It should be noted here that children are subjected to making a lot of internalisations of the various aspects of the people's cultic and religious practices. Besides, in the every-day life, a lot of experiential religious feed-ins are registered in the child. One should not forget that everyday life and activities among the Igbos are intergrated and punctuated with religion, and every aspect of the culture has religious undertones and reference. These impressions are internalised in the child. As the child passes to adolescence and adulthood, he is already acquainted in a very mature type of way with the 'rules of his trade'.

From the influx of influences surrounding one in the process of the Igbo personality formation, therefore, one is compelled to

> . . . unconsciously or consciously absorb into . . . inner self, primarily the ways of life, different personality idiosyncratic characteristics of individuals, modes of behaviour, values of the society as verified in individual tendencies and in turn the consequent externalisations of these factors in their various modes of structural behaviour.[124]

The resultant identifications in the individual is heterogenous in form. This means in effect that the Igbos "internalise not only personality idiosyncratic behaviours of their parents, the modulated values the nuclear family can pass on to them, but also those characteristics of the members in the

---

[121]F. C. OGBALU & E. N. EMENANJO, eds., Igbo Language and Culture, vol. 2, University Press Ltd., Ibadan, 1982, p. 18.

[122]An explanation of 'Omenani' has already been given in the treatment of the Igbo Morality in the second chapter above.

[123]M. MOZIA, op. cit., pp. 239-240.

[124]C. E. ALEKE, op. cit., p. 216.

society and the real values of the society in her uncounterfeited state".[125] These internalisations make their impact as motivating force and principles of operation later in the adulthood. They surely become a part and parcel of one's life, for, as Mozia points out,

> In whatever walks of life he later finds himself, he always has the early community life as a point of reference. In this way, the child passes through the process of maturation and, with an integrated personality, he is capable of participating fully in the unifying of any later community in which he might find himself.[126]

It is clear, then, that the Igbos have a sort of community based personality development. Unless an individual develops in this communitarian platform, one remains outside the societal consciousness of the Igbos. Inculturation, taking into account the other factors treated in this section, must also necessarily involve this group consciousness of the Igbos. Only in terms of this group consciousness can a meaningful integration be made between the animating christian principles and the cultural roots of the Igbos in a manner that would be really enduring.

2.3.6 Summary and Implications for Christian Inculturation

Briefly, one has considered in this chapter, the presuppositions of Inculturation. Since culture has so much to do with human behaviour in the society, it was deemed wise and necessary to take note of some cultural and psychological presuppositions, which have much to do with any inculturation. Among so many factors determining the behaviour of the individual are the internalised values, which act as the reference point for the individual's mode of life. It is seen that childhood internalisations greatly influence one. Since this work aims at making a proposal for inculturation among the Igbos, a look into the personality development of the Igbos was taken. This exposed a community type of psychology, which ought to be taken note of, for any fruitful inculturation among the Igbos.

From the psychological expositions above, it becomes very clear that for any inculturation of the Christian faith among the Igbos, the enculturative process of the Igbo people have to be necessarily and fruitfully utilised as a means of effecting a change in the modal personality structure. Any inroad into the people's culture, which ignores this silent but sure enculturative process is bound to meet with major, if not impassable obstacles. It also means that it is not to be seen as an overnight venture. Since it takes generations to realise and arrive at the cultural modal personality structure of any people, it is also to be expected that, for the inculturation of the faith to be effectively rubbed into the Igbo modal personality structure, years of active inculturative integrated enculturation is

---

[125]Ibid.

[126]M. MOZIA, op. cit., p. 238.

involved.

The communitarian psychology of the people in question is to be noted and inculturation should tow the line of this way of life for it to be successfully realised. Since the Igbos have a 'we' psychology, and the group integration of an individual is obligatory, for inculturation of the faith to be successful, it means that this group feeling and togetherness has to be tapped and necessarily seen as platforms to be used in order to succeed. The Faith has to assume this group background. This necessitates the employment of the traditional structure, without the traditional rituals. Any line of action in the inculturative process among the Igbos, in order to succeed, has to bear this "we" concept imprint. In fact, "whatever happens to the individual happens to the whole group, and whatever happens to the whole group happens to the individual. The individual can only say: 'I am, because we are; and since we are, therefore I am'".[127] It is to this quality that Mbiti refers when on a general level he further explains:

> In traditional life, the individual does not and cannot exist alone except corporately. . . . He is simply part of the whole. The community must therefore make, create or produce the individual; for the individual depends on the corporate group. Physical birth is not enough; the child must go through rites of incorporation so that it becomes fully integrated into the entire society. These rites continue throughout the physical life of the person, during which the individual passes from one stage of corporate existence to another.[128]

Christian inculturation among the Igbos should build on this communitarian mentality, otherwise it remains on the periphery of the people's conscious wave length. It is for this reason that one intends to explore the possibilities of communitarian structurisation of the Faith among the Igbos in the subsequent sections of this work that treats of the chosen aspects of the Culture. The "We" philosophy seems even to be advantageous, since any success in this direction would have enormous impact on the whole traditional community. This can also lead to a communitarian declaration for Christianity.

The influence groups of the Igbo include not only the nuclear family, but stretches to the extended family, the tribe and the community at large. It is this big group that make the "We". An approach of dialogue can effectively influence these agents.

The early participation of the Igbo children in the adult life is a clear indication that the early stages of the Igbo child is a necessary stage in gaining access to the "we" psychology of the adult Igbo. Early participation of children in the adult life is of course not exclusive only to the Igbos. One observes it in some other cultures, but one argues here that with the group

---

[127] JOHN S MBITI, African Religions and Philosophy, Heinemann, London, 1969, pp.108-109

[128] Ibid.

88

psychology of the Igbos, it is a factor that can profitably and advantageously be employed in ushering in an authentically inculturated faith for the future generation. When the various influence agents surrounding the individual are themselves influenced, these would set the transformation in motion.

CHAPTER 3

3   **CHRISTIAN ATTITUDE TO CULTURE**

If the incarnation of the faith within a given culture is to be authentic, it has to be an action of the Church.   The Church, although primarily preoccupied with the spiritual domain, is necessarily bound up with the temporal, since it is made of human beings who have a history, tradition and, therefore, are necessarily bound to a culture.   The Church is expected to lead people from their anthropologically bound situation in life up to God. This is where the relationship between the Church and Culture comes in. It is, therefore, essential here to expose the attitude of the Church to culture in general, both in the past and leading up to the present.

Since this work intends to raise some fundamental questions on the relationship between Christianity and Igbo Culture, with a mind to establish the specific role awaiting Christianity in Igbo Culture, it is of paramount importance to expose the unique and indispensable role of Christ in Cultures, as well as the attitude of Christianity to Cultures.   Since the Christianity in Igboland is a part of the universal Church of Jesus Christ, it must necessarily have to look into the past and see what the attitude of Christ and the Church has been with reference to Cultures.   This would serve as a solid base in setting about any proposals in the area of Inculturation.

3.1   **Christ and Culture**

Christ is the unique and fundamental message of God to all people. The message is simply that, at the fullness of time, the Word of God was made flesh, and dwelt among men.   He dwelt among men in order to show men the way to the Truth that leads to Life, since Christ is the Way, the Truth and the Life (Jn 14:6).   The Word became man in order that "they (all men) may have life, and have it abundantly" (Jn 10:10).   And of all the names in the world given to men, this is the only one by which we can be saved (Acts 4:12).   It is on account of this that "every knee should bow, and every tongue confess that he is Lord to the glory of God" (Phil. 2:10-11). Christ is the true light that enlightens all (Jn 1:9-10).   He is the redeemer of the world, who, coming into the world, identifies Himself with all men,

> for by his incarnation, the Son of God has united himself . . .
> with every man.   He worked with human hands, he thought
> with a human mind, acted by human choice, and loved with a
> human heart . . . he has truly been made one of us, like us in
> all things but sin.[1]

---

[1]JOHN PAUL II, Redemptor Hominis, Encyclical, 4th March 1979, no. 8.

Christ is the revealer of God to man, and the revealer of man to man - the ideal for man. Pope John Paul II teaches:

> In Christ and through Christ God has revealed himself fully to mankind and has definitely drawn close to it; at the same time, in Christ, and through Christ man has acquired full awareness of his dignity, of the heights to which he is raised, of the surpassing worth of his own humanity, and of the meaning of his existence.[2]

Christ came to liberate man from all the shackles that had held him in bondage, for

> . . . we see Christ as the one who brings man freedom based on truth, frees man from what curtails, diminishes and as it were breaks off this freedom at its root, in man's soul, his heart and his conscience.[3]

Christ is the ". . . key, the focal point and the goal of man, as well as of all human history".[4] He is the divinised humanity, the perfect man, the model which God had in mind when He created man in his image and likeness.[5] Christ, being the centrality and the end of both history and man, is he, in, with, and for whom all was willed and created.[6] All history and the whole of creation find their origin and end in him.[7] Even the very sense of man, the nucleus of his personality, and the ultimate reason of his dignity stand essentially in his being for, in, and with Christ.[8]

One finds in Christ the incarnation of the highest and universal values which belong to man, and to which man is directed - such values as: liberty, love, solidarity, true sense of religion, upliftment and rebellion against all that humiliates man. For man who is in dismay and has lost his sense of

---

[2]Ibid., no. 11.2

[3]Ibid., no. 12.2

[4]VATICAN II, Gaudium et Spes, no. 10.

[5]S. RAPONI,"L'immagine-somiglianza nei Padri", in Temi di Antropologia Teologica, Teresianum, Roma, 1981, p. 313.

[6]CARLO LAUDAZI, "L'uomo nel Rapporto con Dio", Punti nella Facoltà Teologica, Teresianum, 1986, p. 4.

[7]Ibid., p. 72.

[8]G. GOZZELINO, "Vocazione e destino dell'uomo in Cristo", p. 72, quoted in C. LAUDAZI, op. cit., p. 69.

direction, Christ is the only hope of orientation.[9] Christ is the very one, who, having been lifted up, draws all men to himself, so that as head of all, he may reconcile all things through him and for him - (Col 1:20). Hence Christ is God's message to all cultures, and the sign of God's universal love for humanity.[10]

The singular and unique place of Christ shines out glaringly clear from the highlights above. One can, therefore, rightly claim that

> there is one salvation, one way of salvation, one saviour of the world, and that is the eschatological salvation valid for all through the one who came that all might find life, who died that the world might be reconciled, who was raised that hope might live for the victory of God, and the restitution of all things in him.[11]

On the attitude of Christ to Culture, from certain utterances of Christ especially in his attack against the practices of the Pharisees, who hold tenaciously to the traditions of the elders, while abandoning the commandments of God, one may have the impression that Christ is opposed to culture. But it should not be forgotten that Christ was rather more preoccupied with drawing attention away from the externalism of the pharisees to the inner conversion of man. However, examples abound in the Gospels of Christ's active participation in the Jewish culture.[12] The fact that Christ participated fully in the culture of the Jews leaves no doubts as to the relationship of Christ to cultures. But just as Christ transformed the Jewish traditional celebrations, giving them authentic christian character, so is the Church expected today to carry on this transformation of Cultures in such a way that all cultural traditions find their ultimate destination and orientation in Christ. In order to identify with each culture in its historical context, "Christ takes them up, purifies them, and fulfils them in order to take them to their eschatological goal, so that God may be all in all (I Cor 15)".[13]

From this unique and indispensable role of Christ in cultures by virtue of his Incarnation, being made flesh in each culture and thus feeling at home, Christianity, which is the continuation and the prolongation of this

---

[9]BRUNO MORICONI, "Gesu di Nazareth, Paradigma dell'uomo", Lecture Notes, Teresianum, pp. 11-30.

[10]VATICAN II, Nostra Aetate, no. 4

[11]CARL E. BRAATEN, "The Uniqueness & Universality of Christ", in Mission Trends no. 5, p. 87

[12]Christ participated in the Jewish Purification Rites at the Presentation in the Temple, at the Jewish Feasts of Passover, Unleavened Bread, etc. Cf., Lk 2:22-24; Jn 5:1; 6:4; 7:10; 12:1; 13:1

[13]PIETRO ROSSANO, "Christ's Lordship and Religious Pluralism", in Mission Trends, no. 5, p. 34

Incarnation of Christ, finds no other option than to be motivated by the same incarnational principle of Christ in the midst of cultures. That is why Christianity must become part of society "for the same motive which led Christ to bind himself . . . to the definite social and cultural conditions of those human beings, among whom he dwelt".[14] It is only in this way that Christianity may succeed in making Christian life "a principle that animates, directs and unifies the culture, transforming and remaking it so as to bring about 'a new creation'".[15]

3.2   **The Magisterium and Culture in general**

The very first traces of what can even be referred to as attempts at inculturation is definitely the circumstances of the first Council of Jerusalem, during which the nascent Church tried to confront directly the problem of the spread of the faith to non-Jewish peoples. The decisions of this Council is certainly the first formal statements of the early Church in reference to other non-Jewish cultures.[16]

After this Council, there does not seem to have been any other formal statements at the time, except that from his writings, St Paul seems to have made prolific use of the cultural circumstances of the areas he evangelised, to preach the Gospel. In the Greek speaking areas he employed the use of the people's thought patterns to transmit his message. This example of St. Paul paved the way for the Apologists and the Fathers, who later had to transmit the message of the Gospel through the legitimate use of greek philosophic concepts and symbols.

Going through the ecclesiastical archives, it is very interesting and consoling to discover that the idea of the incarnation of the faith in cultures has occupied a significant place in the priority of the Popes at least from the time of Pope Benedict XV up to our time. This has always received a great attention from the Popes in their prophetic ministry, so much that some encyclicals have been specifically devoted to this idea. The Popes see the incarnation of the faith as the ultimate purpose of all evangelisation, and therefore, consider it a fundamental ministry of the Church. In the encyclical, _Evangelii Praecones_, Pope Pius XII proclaims:

> . . . the ultimate goal of Missionary endeavour . . . is to establish the Church on sound foundations among non-Christian peoples, and place it under its own native hierarchy.[17]

---

[14]VATICAN II, Ad Gentes, no. 10

[15]PEDRO ARRUPE, "On Inculturation", A Letter to the whole Society, Rome, 14th May 1978, Cur. Gen. 78/5, pp. 1-2

[16]Cf., Acts 15: 1 - 11, 22 -29.

[17]PIUS XII, _Evangelii Praecones_, A. A. S., 1951, p. 507

Also, on the aims of the Church in missionary strategy, the Pontiff, in one of his letters clearly states that

> The Church's aim is not the domination of peoples or the gaining of temporal dominions. She is eager only to bring the supernatural light of faith to all peoples; and to promote the interest of civilisation and culture, and fraternal concord among nations.[18]

The Popes, therefore, anxious to ensure the accomplishment of this important ministry of the church, have bequeathed to the Church various encyclicals enunciating the norms, principles and guidelines, which should serve as a basis for evangelisation in this direction. A highlight of some of these guidelines will be of immense help in establishing a solid base for the major interest of this work.

As a fundamental prerequisite for any incarnational work, it has been the teaching and desire of the Church that indigenous clergy be trained, since it really belongs to them to carry out the incarnational work of the Gospel in their land. This was one of the most important points emphasised by Pope Benedict XV, who, understanding the value of the native clergy, remarked:

> Linked to his compatriots, as he is by the bonds of origin, character, feelings and inclinations, the indigenous priest possesses exceptional opportunities for introducing the faith to their minds, and is endowed with powers of persuasion far superior to those of any other man. It thus frequently happens that he has access where a foreign priest could not set foot.[19]

With the same aim in mind, Pope John XXIII instructed that Seminary training of priests should be geared towards this incarnational orientation. He taught :

> It should also be aimed at sharpening the students's mind, so as to enable them to form a true estimate of the cultural traditions of their own homelands, . . . and to discern the special points of contact which exist between these systems and the Christian religion.[20]

As a follow-up to the need for native clergy, the Popes express the right attitudes and the function which any incarnational work calls for, with regard to the existing cultures of peoples. They advocate respect, discernment of the positive elements of the culture in question, which would ultimately be engrafted and incorporated within the christian faith. Of course the

---

[18]PIUS XII, Epist. Perlibenti equidem, A. A. S., 1950, p. 727

[19]BENEDICT XV, Maximum Illud, A. A. S., 1919, p. 445

[20]JOHN XXIII, Princeps Pastorum, A. A. S., 1959, p. 843

engrafting would be after a serious critical evaluation. It is the mind of the Popes that whatever is tainted in any way has to be purified. Pope Pius XII categorically stressed this point in <u>Evangelii Praecones</u> thus :

> The Church from the beginning down to our time has always followed this wise practice: let not the Gospel, on being introduced into any new land, destroy or extinguish whatever its people possess that is naturally good, just or beautiful. For the Church, when she calls people to a higher culture and a better way of life . . . does not act like one who recklessly cuts down and uproots a thriving forest. No, she grafts a good scion upon the wild stock so that it may bear a crop of more delicious fruit.[21]

On the purifying and transforming function, the same Pontiff clarifies what the Church had hitherto done.

> . . . after freeing them from error and all contamination, she has perfected and completed them . . . made her own the native art and culture . . . . She has carefully encouraged them . . . to a point of aesthetic perfection. By no means has she repressed native customs and traditions but has given them a certain religious significance, she has transformed their feast days . . . to celebrate mysteries of the faith.[22]

On the attitude and disposition demanded for this function, Pope Paul VI advocates that the "transposition has to be done with the discernment, seriousness, respect and competence which the matter calls for" in the various fields concerned.[23]

Hence it has been the teaching of the Popes that "whatever there is in the native custom that is not inseparably bound up with superstition and error" is to be recognised and used by the Church. They have always given cultures a kind treatment, consideration and preservation.[24]

The mind and attitude of the Popes has been re-echoed in the documents of the Vatican II, a veritable testament and point of reference for the Church in the modern times. One finds in <u>Lumen Gentium</u> and also repeated in <u>Ad Gentes</u> the accommodating attitude towards cultures. Whatever is good or true in cultures is considered to be "a preparation for the Gospel", hence,

> whatever good is found sown in the minds and hearts of men or in the rites and customs of peoples, these are not only

---

[21]PIUS XII, <u>op.cit.</u>, p. 521ff.

[22]<u>Ibid.</u>, p. 522

[23]PAUL VI, <u>Evangelii Nuntiandi</u>, Encyclical, 8th Dec. 1975, no. 63

[24]Cf., A. A. S., 1939, p. 429

preserved from destruction, but are purified, raised up, and perfected for the glory of God . . . [25]

The negative aspects of cultures are purged and restored.

On the role and expected attitude of Christians towards the customs and traditions of their homeland, the Vatican Fathers clearly state that Christians must identify with the culture, bearing witness to Christ in their culture. They should share and participate in their social and cultural life, since they are members of their society.[26] In what one may consider as an important manifestation of the readiness of the Church for Inculturation, the Council declares,

> they must give expression to this newness of life in their own society and culture and in a manner that is in keeping with the traditions of their own land. They must be familiar with this culture, they must purify and guard it, they must develop it . . . they must perfect it in Christ, so that the faith of Christ and the life of the Church will not be something foreign to the society in which they live, but will begin to transform and permeate it.[27]

This, in effect, means that the local Church is to borrow from the customs, traditions, wisdom, teaching, arts, and sciences of their people.[28]

It is expected in any incarnational transplantation of the faith that the Christian principles should permeate the cultural structure of the people, so that while they assume their inalienable identity, they yet adhere to the universality of the Church which can only be one. With reference to these two aspects, Paul VI clarifies:

> In the mind of the Lord, the Church is universal by vocation and mission, but when she puts down her roots in a variety of cultural, social and human terrains, she takes on different external expressions and appearances in each part of the world.[29]

But very meticulous in order to safeguard the two dimensions, the same Pontiff sounds a serious note of caution:

> Evangelisation loses much of its force and effectiveness if it does not take into consideration the actual people to whom it

---

[25]VATICAN II, Lumen Gentium, no. 17; Ad Gentes, no. 9

[26]VATICAN II, Ad Gentes, no. 11

[27]Ibid., no. 21

[28]Ibid., no 22

[29]PAUL VI, op.cit., no. 62

is addressed, if it does not use their language, their signs and symbols, if it does not answer the question they ask, and if it does not have an impact on their concrete life. But . . . evangelisation risks losing its power and disappearing altogether if one empties or adulterates its content . . . if, . . . one sacrifices this reality and destroys the unity without which there is no universality, . . . [30]

Hence, the faith, while taking a cultural root in any land, should not lose its grips on the universal source.

With direct and specific reference to the attitude of the Church to African Cultures in general, Paul VI, in his assessment and recommendations, which are automatically to be seen as principles, expressed that

while these values which have been handed down ought to be respected as a cultural legacy from the past, . . . it is sometimes necessary to know how to discriminate: to assess critically and eliminate those deceptive goods which will bring about a lowering of the human ideal, and to accept those values that are sound and beneficial. . .

Continuing, the Pontiff extols the culture thus,

The Church views with great respect the moral and religious values of the African tradition . . . because she sees them as providential, as the basis for spreading the Gospel . . . and beginning the establishment of the new society in Christ. [31]

In his address at the closing session of the Symposium of African Bishops in Kampala, the same Pontiff categorically declared:

. . . you may, and you must, have an African Christianity. Indeed you possess human values and characteristic forms of culture which can rise up to perfection such as to find in Christianity, and for Christianity, a true superior fullness, and prove to be capable of a richness of expression all its own and genuinely African. [32]

Also John Paul II in his visit to Nigeria, made a similar appraisal of the culture, and recommended that the good and beautiful aspect of the culture has to be recognised by the Church, while a purifying work ought to be done on the obnoxious elements. On a positive note the Pontiff said among other things:

---

[30]Ibid., no. 63

[31]PAUL VI, Africae Terrarum, no. 13

[32]Idem, Address in Kampala, A. A. S., 1969, p. 577

The Catholic people . . . have the opportunity . . . to give a corporate witness to the Gospel of Jesus in the culture in which they live. They have the power to bring the Gospel into the very heart of their culture, into the fabric of their everyday lives.[33]

Briefly, the Christian attitude to Culture has been positive with a sincere desire to utilise the positive elements of any given Culture in constructing a solid base for the flowering of the Christian faith. The Church regards the positive elements of any culture as a fertile preparation for the Gospel. From the observation of the elements of Igbo Culture, certain positive elements shine out.

3.3   **Igbo Cultural Potentials for Christianity**

An author, generally speaking of Africa, once remarked,

The African, however, should be grateful for being blessed with a basically sound, enduring religious and moral tradition. Its belief-system and cultural practices are, praeparationes Evangelii, or suitable material for Gospel proclamation.[34]

Also, at the conclusion of their Plenary Business Meeting in Nairobi, the AMECEA Bishops jointly remarked,

We Africans are a religious people. We have our own values. Without these values no ideology can offer an adequate and lasting reason for respecting one another . . . Our own African and religious values are the rock foundation on which our society must be built. These are the values that our society must reflect in its policies, its public morality and on its daily life.[35]

From the outline of Igbo culture, one cannot but be tempted to re-echo and apply the same remarks above with reference to the religion and culture of the Igbos. It is, however, clear that both positive and negative elements are found in the culture. While there are many potentials that are very fertile in enhancing and consolidating the faith, since they can be considered as a preparation for the Gospel, there are many other negative aspects, which

---

[33]JOHN PAUL II, Address to Bishops in Lagos, A. A. S., 1982, p. 615

[34]CHUKWUDUM B. OKOLO, "Traditional African and Christian Values", in AFER, Vol. 29, No. 2, 1987, p. 91.

[35]Some highlights of the AMECEA Business Meeting, AFER, Vol. 24, No. 5, Oct. 1982, p. 261.

stand as obstacles to the faith and are obnoxious to authentic human existence.

Our intention in going through the elements of Igbo culture is to furnish a panoramic view for a discovery of possible fertile cultural base for Christianity. One can classify the potentials latent in Igbo Culture into three main groups. There are purely positive potentials, which ought to be fully recognised by Christianity and recommended without doubts. These include some elements in the social and political traditional set-up. Others include the linguistic, recreational, associational elements, as well as solidarity spirit, nomenclature, moral standard, sense of the sacred, and Igbo concept of the Supreme God.[36] These would definitely boost the Faith if fully tapped.

Then, there are some potentials, which, on account of their traditional value, are so important to be ignored or neglected. These elements, however, are intertwined with rituals and superstitious practices, that they cannot be recommended for christians without first being refined and purified. Such potentials are the ancestral allegiance, age-grades, village daughters' union, title-taking, rites of passage, and traditional healing means and medicines. Since no syncretism is to be entertained, a thorough analysis, sorting out, and purification work in inculturation is called for.

Lastly, there are some entirely negative aspects, such as false worship, belief in charms, and superstition, witchcraft, reincarnation, preponderance of fear rather than love in religion, negative attitudes towards twins and childlessness, diseases, insufficient stress on individual responsibility as regards sin and punishment; polygamy, harmful medicines, vengeance, hatred for enemies etc.[37] These aspects should be done away with, for their inhuman nature.

It is in reference to the positive and quasi positive cultural values that the Holy Father Pope Paul VI remarked:

> Indeed, you possess human values and characteristic forms of culture which can rise up to perfection such as to find in Christianity, and for Christianity, a true superior fullness, and prove to be capable of a richness of expression all its own, and genuinely African.[38]

---

[36] A more detailed list of the positive aspects of the traditional religion is enumerated during the Seminar on the New Era of Evangelization in Nigeria to include: "Belief in God, spirits(good and bad), life-after-death, immortality to some extent, helping the dead, belief in the sacred, sacrifice, prayer, shrines, confession of sins and expiation, participation in sacrificial meals, organized worship, religious feasts and months, reward or punishment after death, forces above man, strong community aspect of religion, and the priesthood. - Cf., New Era of Evangelization, Proceedings of the National Seminar on New Era of Evangelization, 1 - 3 May 1984, p. 75

[37] Cf. Ibid., p. 76.

[38] POPE PAUL VI, An Address at the closing session of the Symposium of African Bishops, in Kampala, Uganda, 31 July 1969.

It is our firm conviction that Christianity would find in these discovered potentials a solid base for homely christian practice. This is possible only if the faith is engrafted within their cultural framework, in which the Igbo christians would feel at home, and which continues to influence them. With this possibility, the Igbo Christian, propelled by culturally oriented christian principles, would live his life convincingly without feeling alienated from his fatherland. The discovered potentials are a fertile field, which would pave a way for such convictions. If the potentials are, on the other hand, ignored and not tapped, the effect would not be far from the remarks of Ignatius Zvarevashe, who, speaking of the overall effect in Africa, said:

> . . . the majority of African Christians will continue to live a double life and the faith will remain foreign to them. Consequently, Christianity or the faith will have failed to touch and perfect . . . African Culture.[39]

3.4   Christian Attitude to Igbo Culture

Having made an evaluation of Igbo Culture in the preceding section, one is now able to reflect on not only the roles and attitudes which Christianity ought to play, but also the roles which it has actually played in the past with reference to Igbo Culture. Earlier the unique and indispensable role of Christ in cultures as well as the attitude of Christianity to cultures have been adequately highlighted. This serves as the measuring yardstick and the guiding principle when viewing such relationship with any concrete culture. It ought to be borne in mind that christianity has already lived for more than a hundred years among the Igbos. One is in a privileged position, then, today to look back at the actual situation of the meeting of Christianity with Igbo Culture, within the framework and guidance of the ideals and principles mentioned above.

3.4.1 Expected Roles of Christianity in Igbo culture

In the preceding section, some categorisation has been made in the evaluation of the cultural potentials. Some elements in Igbo culture have been discovered to be good and beautiful. One should expect that these

---

[39]IGNATIUS M. ZVAREVASHE, "The Problem of Ancestors and Inculturation", in <u>AFER</u>, Vol. 29, No. 4, August 1987, pp.242ff.

elements should be recognised as a solid base on which to build on. The complicated but important elements, as one expects, should naturally prove difficult, and, therefore, demand a thorough but careful study and purification. The third group of cultural elements that are so obnoxious and inhuman should naturally attract a straightforward rejection and destruction.

The scope of this work is more of a conscientization, and as such, allows no room for the single treatment of the elements. One's ultimate aim, however, is to single out one or two areas and deal with them in a detailed type of way. It is on account of this that one here makes only a sort of general indication of the proper attitude called for in situating the faith on the elements.

3.4.1.1   Positive and Dialectical Role

We have seen that such elements as the linguistic elements, the social structure, Igbo Nomenclature, Recreational elements, Igbo moral standard, traditional political framework, associations, hospitality, concept of the Supreme God, and deep sense of the sacred, fall within the good and beautiful elements of the culture. Their positive value arises from the fact that they have no obstacles whatsoever, as well as from the strategic value they have among the Igbos. Christianity is expected to employ these elements for the purpose of internalising the faith.

The linguistic elements, for instance, provide such features as proverbs, folklore, and poetic symbols in conveying important values. It is noteworthy that any serious discussion among the Igbos, that is bereft of these linguistic features is considered unimportant, equivalent in value only with children's rabbles. It would be very wonderful for Christianity to enunciate the christian doctrines making adequate use of the linguistic features. This would be a vivid expression of the doctrines within the categories of thought of the Igbos. The various dogmas of the faith would have a big chance if they were to be transmitted by means of the linguistic elements. It should be noted that this element serves a pedagogical purpose.

The Igbo social structure, with a strong family base is a wonderful strategy to utilise. Concerning this Basden had to remark:

> . . . a Missionary has unique opportunities of becoming acquainted with village life, for, from the very nature of things the soundest policy is for him to live in the closest communion with the people whom he seeks to influence.[40]

The social structure furnishes one with easy access into the life of the people. Even the village squares - 'ilos' as they are called, are the rallying points for the people, hence they can be profitably employed, counting on the structural and psychological influences of such places on the people. Would these squares not serve as catechism centres, since people would not be lacking there at any time of the day. The use of such traditional

---

[40]G. T. BASDEN, Among the Ibos of Nigeria, p. 45

contexts could have overwhelming influence on the people, and dispose them to feel at home with the faith. It is important to note the importance and significance of these contexts for the traditional community. All very important matters and decisions are discussed in these places. Consciousness of this in citing the Christian community centres is expected to yield maximum dividend.

The extended family structure and its interaction are favourable to the growth of the faith in quality and quantity. Tapping this community spirit and the sense of solidarity of the people is an asset for Christianity. Within this milieu christian charity could flourish, since in actual fact, the Igbo sense of solidarity is nothing but being a brother's keeper. Group cohesion is greatly facilitated in this structure. Practising the faith in such a context could serve as veritable imitation of the first century christian communities. That is why it is to be seen as devastating the idea of trying to dismantle this family unifying structure. Uprooting anybody from this traditional structure would be tantamount to alienating the one from his home as well as from the very nerve centre of his social life, his culture.

It has been seen that there is no distinction between the Igbo concept of the Supreme Being and the Christian idea of God as the supreme Being. The only aspect that is lacking is the trinitarian mystery, but then, the belief in the deities and spirits is already a predisposition to accepting the Trinitarian doctrine. The Igbos are already in tune with the mysterious world. Hence, the Igbo sense of the sacred should be a rich potential which Christianity should recognise in building up the spiritual life of the Igbo Christians. If the sense and respect of the sacred found in Igbo traditional religion is to be focused on the christian mysteries and especially on the sacramental presence, its effect on christian practice would be immense.

One notes with pride that the Igbo Nomenclature is not haphazardly given. They are primarily expressions of the divine attributes, hence they are theological. What could be more divine than names expressing divine attributes? These expressions are merged with the peculiar historical records of the family. Employing such names as baptismal names would not only be singing the praises and glory of God, but would even promote the consciousness of the divine-human relationship and interaction within the family.

The political sector with its structure has been shown as the most strategic area in the traditional life of the Igbos. It is a fact that one who has no active voice in the community, cannot but be considered and regarded as a second class citizen. If the Igbo christian should have nothing to do with the village administration, they automatically would have no say in their traditional community. This ends up in being alienated. If the Igbo christian is not allowed to take the titles of the land, his membership of the age-grades viewed negatively, cannot take part in the masquerade society, and when he gets old cannot, as a result, assume the headship of the community on account of the allied implications, then the Igbo christian can be thought of as passive and completely alienated from his land, having no possibility of influencing the community in any way whatsoever. As has been explained above, these administrative arms of the traditional community are the policy makers, whose decisions are final and binding on all. Whoever makes the laws of any land, command the population. One would expect that Christianity ought to clear the obstacles in the political elements through a dialogue with this system, and make it possible for christians to enter into these strategic arms of the community. It is there that christians are expected to apply the christian principles and act as leaven within the community. Through dialogue these arms could be purified, and thereby christians are enabled to assume their rightful place and roles, for,

> . . . although they are first of all citizens of the Kingdom of God and members of his great family, do not for all that cease to be citizens of their earthly fatherland.[41]

The same attitude of dialogue and purification is expected of Christianity with regard to the recreational elements. Festivals, music and dancing play very important roles in any culture, and besides, are very strong means of communitarian psychology and solidarity. Christianity should try to make it conducive for Igbo christians to join their kit and kin in these moments of enjoyment and relaxation. Even though, false worship, use of charms, and superstition at times characterise these aspects, yet purification of these through a dialogue, could have lasting effects. One would not expect an attitude of segregation, which would only succeed in keeping off christians from these exercises. It must be accepted that if christians are kept off these community celebrations, they are, as it were, psychologically knocked off, since inwardly they feel a strong natural attraction to mix up with their kit and kin. One should also remember that commensalism manifests a symbol of unity and love. Christianity is expected to uphold this symbol within any community rather than destroy it. It is all the more so among Igbo communities, where staying together in every aspect of life is a distinguishing factor and imperative.

Still on the value of the recreational elements, one would think that it ought to be an enrichment of the christian Liturgy if the common native musical airs are employed in liturgical celebrations. We have noted above the much influence which music plays on Igbos as a whole. Christianity ought to utilise maximally this influence of music. It would not suffice to offer only a translation of the western musical tones and airs in Igbo language, since they are unnatural to the people, and are, therefore, very mechanical. Any such translations would always lack "the living and soul-stirring effect engendered by the native songs".[42] It is this effect that forces an author to remark:

> Anyone who has had the privilege of witnessing at close quarters the inherent vitality and artful expressivity of African Music dreams of the time when this music will be given its full right and recognition, its opportunity of reforming and recreating

---

[41]POPE PIUS XII, Evangelii Praecones, A. A. S., 1951, pp. 523ff.

[42]G. T. BASDEN, Among the Ibos of Nigeria, p. 192.

the worship and the services of Christian Church in Africa.[43]

Christianity should see in the high moral standard of the Igbos a good disposition and preparation for the complementary function of christian morality. The many taboos and prohibitions in Igbo Morality are simply practical conclusions of the contents of christian morality. Christianity ought to recognise and perfect some of these.

3.4.1.2   **Corrective and Substitutive Role**

Such elements exposed in the Culture, which are intertwined with so many false worship and superstition demand from Christianity a thorough purification work. Purification is essential, because, inasmuch as these elements are not intrinsically bad, yet they are surrounded by so many superstitious practices and rituals which thereby render them contaminated and incompatible with the faith. These elements ought not be ignored by Christianity, since they play very important roles in the traditional system. In order to sieve out the superstitious elements, a distinction has to be made to find out the essential aspects of the element in question. It is in reference to such distinctions that Bishop M. U. Eneja writes,

> As in feasts and celebrations, our ancestors had good reasons for establishing these . . . . These reasons or objectives one may call the 'soul' . . . The externals or emblems are just signs of this internal, grave, substantial reason.[44]

This reason or intention for establishing a practice, is essential and at times laudable. Hence it is not this aspect that needs a purification or purging. It is the rituals surrounding these practices which ought to be replaced by christian rituals. As the same Bishop further observes,

> According to the faith of the traditional religionists, idols and charms are of help. Therefore they surround the rites for titles, engagements, feasts, etc. with sacrifices, libations, charms, etc. It is this aspect that needs much purification. Sometimes a good part or the whole ceremony has to be omitted. If necessary a replacement may be made.[45]

The purification would consist in the removal of non-essential superstitious aspects and practices, and supplying christian rituals in their stead. Hence

---

[43]H. WEMAN, "African Folkmusic in Christian Churches in Africa", A Paper to "All-Africa Conference of Churches, Nairobi/Kenya" for Liturgy and Church Music in Africa, 1974.

[44]BISHOP M. U. ENEJA, My Involvement in Evangelisation, Lenten Pastoral, Enugu Diocese, 1984, p. 24.

[45]Idem, On Fire For Christ, Lenten Pastoral, 1985, p. 20.

the Bishop recommends:

> Since the 'soul' (the objective) of these . . . which is embedded
> in the body (superstition) is good, the Christian removes the
> body - superstition and replaces it with another body - christian
> practice. It is not surprising that our ancestors had to bury
> these good ideas in superstition since they are thoroughly
> religious people.[46]

By this method Christianity guarantees the cultural orientation for christians. So, the expected role of Christianity here is to discover the essential and fundamental objective for the practice in question, which is always good, and, then, build a solid faith and rituals on this base. This demands an intensive and critical study of the elements, in order to expose both the good nerve centres of the elements and the superstitious parts that should be substituted.

There remains yet another dimension of the supposed role of Christianity in Igbo culture. Some inhuman practices have been also exposed in the culture. One would expect Christianity to fight for and put an end to such inhuman practices in the traditional system as human sacrifices, throwing away of twins, dedicating human beings to certain idols and shrines, abandonment and throwing away of people suffering from such diseases as leprosy and small-pox. The early Missionaries in Igboland seem to have devoted their attention to this aspect, as our evaluation of their ministry would reveal. The laudable role in this regard remain indelible and evergreen. They had to search for, recover, restore and rehabilitate such people. Christianity has so much of a dismantling role to play. The negatively inclined practices should be made to disappear.

3.4.1.3   Extraordinary Role

Christianity must play another role in Igbo culture. Such values which are glaringly lacking in Igbo culture, and which distinguish christianity from other religions have to be supplied. Although Igbos are very friendly, and their hospitality unparalleled, yet, the Igbo has a profound hatred for his enemy. Vengeance and 'lex talionis'[47] is their guiding code of conduct with regard to enemies. It is expected that Christianity should impart and teach the virtues of forgiveness and charity towards enemies in Igbo culture.

In the situation where the subjection of women obtains (and there are really many of such cases in the Igbo traditional system), it belongs to Christianity to redress this degradation of women, demonstrating the equality of all God's children.

---

[46]Idem, My Involvement in Evangelisation, p. 23.

[47]Cf. Ex. 21:24.   In fact, there is an Igbo proverb that says: "Emem, mbolu". That means: If I am wronged, I will revenge. This is however, opposed to the regulations in Lv. 19:18, which is also expressed in Jb. 31:29.

One sees a gap in this regard in Igbo culture, and it belongs to Christianity to supply the missing virtues.   Briefly, one would say that it is expected of Christianity to play the role which was summarised by the Seminar on the New Era of Evangelisation thus:

> Our attitude towards traditional religionists should be openness to receive, dialogue, incarnate, purify, redeem, adopt, adapt, and reject what is harmful to the evangelisation and true conversion. The evangelizer must not forget that christianity is supernatural and that it is not an evolution of traditional religion, though elements of traditional religion can help and should help in the evangelization process.[48]

This role of Christianity ought to be considered as very important and, therefore, urgent.   If Christianity makes use of the positive elements for the consolidation of the faith - engrafting and incarnating christian principles within the cultural framework of the Igbos, there will be a strong hope of a lasting christianity in Igboland.

3.4.2 Evaluation of the first century experience of Christianity in Igboland

For a mature analysis and evaluation, in order to give a balanced judgement of the first century missionary experience of Christianity in Igboland, it is essential to highlight some aspects of the Missionary ventures that have characterised these years.

One of the events in history that followed the great ethnological studies and discoveries was the Missionary movements. Following directly the green light and the urge arising from the colonisation of various lands, there began the Missionary Religious Congregations that produced men of very sterling missionary spirits, who, leaving their families, homelands, and countries, like the biblical Abram, made their ways into those unknown lands. It is such missionary movements that made it possible to open up Christianity in places like China, Japan, India, and, in fact, Igboland. As the Missionaries went, they were accompanied by special support and encouragement from their homelands, but also by guiding principles from the Ecclesiastical authorities, stipulating the right code of conduct for the missionaries in foreign lands. One of such guidelines are the Instructions issued by the Propaganda Fide in 1622, which got inserted into the Constitutions of the various Missionary Congregations. Some lines of this Instruction read thus:

> In no way spend any effort nor present any argument to change their rites, their customs, and their way of life unless these are flagrantly opposed to religion and good morals. For

---

[48]CATHOLIC SECRETARIAT OF NIGERIA, New Era of Evangelisation, p. 77.

what is more absurd than to bring France or Spain or Italy or any other part of Europe to China? It is not these that you should bring but the faith which does not spurn or reject any people's rites and customs, unless they are depraved, but on the contrary try to keep them, - admire and praise what deserves to be respected.[49]

This instruction of the Sacred Congregation serves, then, as the yardstick for measuring the success or failure of any missionary venture.

Through Missionary expeditions, so many Christian groups and Religious Congregations found their way into the frontiers of Igboland. It is interesting to note that the first group to arrive in Igboland were the Anglican Missions, who, through the cooperation of the British colonial movements and settlement in Igboland, occupied the very heart of Igboland. The Anglican Mission was established in Onitsha as far back as 1857.[50] It was only after about several decades that the first Catholic Missionaries arrived on the River Niger in 1885. They were the Society of African Missions, who settled on the West bank of the Niger; and the Holy Ghost Fathers, who occupied the Eastern part. With their arrival, began the first stage of the adventurous enterprise of the missionary strategy in Igboland. No sooner had they settled down, than they set themselves to till the ground for the planting of the seed of Christianity.

The first decades witnessed little achievements as they had to face the problems of rivalry and antagonism from their Protestant counterparts, who, as one would expect, being the first to occupy the place, got alarmed by the arrival of the Catholic groups, and therefore had to sit up. They had all the more to sit up as the Catholic Missionaries began immediately to gain grounds in spite of their coming later. As Ekechi remarked, "there is no question that the coming of the Catholic Missionaries had seriously shaken the security of the Protestants and especially of the Church Missionary Society."[51] On the whole, both parties suffered the inability to penetrate into the mainland of the Igbos.

It was only after the colonial occupation of Igboland in 1905 that the Missionaries utilised the colonial administrative centres as stations, and were, thus able to penetrate into the interior. The initial obstacles notwithstanding, the pioneer Catholic Missionaries in a short time made a nice impression of, and captivated the Igbo people. They employed many methods to win converts. These methods include the rescuing and buying over of slaves; the care of the sick and the destitutes; the distribution of charity; and most especially, through the establishment of schools. Of course, it is understandable that they made a quick progress, since people were quick

---

[49]"Instructio Vicariorum Apostolicorum ad Regna Synarum Tonchini et Cocinnae Proficiscentium", in Collectanea Sacrae Congregationis de Propaganda Fide, I, Rome, 1907, p. 130.

[50]E. ISICHEI, A History of the Igbo People, p. 160.

[51]F. K. EKECHI, Missionary Enterprise and Rivalry in Igboland, 1857 - 1914, Frank Cass, London, 1972, pp. 75-76.

in identifying with the Missionaries, whom they consider to be good to them, and who protected them and were interested in their welfare. Therefore, while in the first half of the century, both christian denominations had about one thousand baptised christians, in the second half, a great change has taken place. For instance, in 1921, of about a population of four million Igbos at the time, a total of 284,835 were already christians, and out of this number, 26,499 were catholics, being the largest single denomination then. By 1931, the number of Catholics have increased to 94,049.[52] The reason for this was not far to seek, for

> churches and schools were thronged, especially when it was known that a missionary could protect his adherents against the ruthless warrant chiefs, who became agents of the new regime, and that schooling gave them immunity from forced labour.[53]

It is even testified to by Isichei that the missionaries tended to lean on the side of Christians in local disputes, even when, as it sometimes happened, the christians were wrong.[54] Another testimony of the captivating influence of the Catholic Missionaries comes even from a protestant, who, as a result of this, and in an alarming manner, called on his fellow protestants to sit up. This protestant wrote:

> The Roman Catholics have made education an evangelical tool and they are succeeding. The Roman Catholics . . . succeed because of personal touch. Their priests are very approachable. They play with children in the streets and visit the poorest houses in order to make converts. Mothers bring their children, children bring their brothers and sisters to their beloved Church.[55]

Such a remark gets a re-echo from Ekechi, who also observed that the Missionaries

> . . . appeared to many local people as a different kind of whiteman : a kind who came for the welfare of the people. This is vitally important . . . in order to understand the aspect of the eventual mass movement towards the Roman catholic

---

[52]Cf., J. P. JORDAN, Bishop Shanahan of Southern Nigeria, repr., 1971, Dublin.

[53]E. METU, God and Man in African Religion, p. 169.

[54]E. ISICHEI, op. cit., p., 167.

[55]E. O. ENEM, "What are we Anglicans Doing?", A Lecture at Diobu, Port Harcourt, Eastern Nigeria, 1950, pp. 3-5.

church at the turn of the century.[56]

It is essential at this juncture, to remark that before the advent of the early Missionaries, certain evil practices existed in Igboland, such as the banishment and throwing away and a consequent abandonment of certain categories of people who suffer from such awful diseases as small-pox, leprosy etc. These diseases were considered as abomination. There were also the abandonment and throwing away of twin babies, because twins are considered as abnormal.[57] There was also the practice of human ritual sacrifices at the burial of great Chiefs, and traces of cannibalism. It was the Missionaries who put a stop to all these practices by rescuing such victims, and providing succour and medicare to them, and building orphanages and leprosy clinics for these. This accounts for the coinage of the name 'Ukamaka', (which means 'the Church is good, kind, merciful, and helpful), which people gave to their children. Such a name is an eloquent testimony of the appreciation of the Igbos for the roles of the early Missionaries. It is credit to the Missionaries that mothers gave such names to their children. Incidentally these rescued victims became the first christians ultimately. Isichei expatiates:

> . . . the bulk of the first Christian converts were drawn from the poor, the needy and the rejected: the mothers of twins, women accused of witchcraft, those suffering from diseases such as leprosy which were seen as abominable. Finding little satisfaction in the world around them, they turned to Christianity with a single-minded devotion which astonished all who beheld it.[58]

Of course there were also some wealthy and prestigious chiefs who were converted, manifesting a great spirit of sacrifice and total abandonment especially at that moment. An example at hand was the famous Chief Idigo of Aguleri, whose conversion was described by a missionary thus:

> . . . such a conversion deserves to be described as a miracle of grace, because it meant dismissing extra wives, thus breaking up normal home-life, and surrendering much of one's social standing, thus denying oneself many of the joys of public life, and of course it involved an uproar in the wide and elastic

---

[56]F. K. EKECHI, Ibid.

[57]"The birth of twins was regarded as a great calamity. The mother was isolated and the children were destroyed. The navel cords were not severed. It was believed that human beings should propagate their species by single births. For a woman to bear more than one child at a time was regarded as degrading humanity to the level of beasts." V. C. UCHENDU, op. cit., p. 58.

[58]E. ISICHEI, op. cit., p. 162.

circle that made up an Igbo family.[59]

Talking of education in the missionary strategies in Igboland, the image that immediately comes to mind is that of no other than Bishop Shanahan, who more than any other, laid the foundation of Christianity in Igboland. The Church today in Igboland is seen as the veritable fruits of his ingenuity. Motivated by his wide concept of education which aimed at training people not only to read the Bible in the vernacular, but also with an orientation to personal improvement spiritually and materially, Bishop Shanahan made education his principal strategy, which "endeared his school to the people, and made him enjoy great patronage from, and partnership with, the then colonial administration."[60] On account of his educational policy and strategy, Bishop Shanahan is described as a 'masterly strategist' who

> . . . recognised and exploited to the full the two salient factors
> of the early colonial situation: the Igbo people's thirst for
> education of the one hand, and the colonial government's need
> for educated African personnel, on the other hand.[61]

Ekechi also makes an appraisal of the educational strategy of the Missionaries, remarking that "for Catholics, education was not merely as a tool to spread their Christianity, but also as a means of ensuring Catholic ascendency, because good education would help the young men to earn a good living in the country".[62] Consequently, by 1920 the Holy Ghost Missionaries had 559 primary schools, with a total population of 33,737 pupils; twelve years later, it had risen to 1,386 schools and churches. But there were negative effects as well, because, as the Missionaries got devoted to the schools, gradually they lost contact and close touch with the people, which characterised their early beginning. On account of this distance from the people, an access to the language of the people was lost. This signalled also the closure of the gates to the people's culture. This was to have adverse consequences for the Church in Igboland.

Beside education, the Missionaries employed yet another method in maintaining their converts. They tried to create an entirely new cultural environment for their converts. The intention of the Missionaries was to build Christianity on a completely new non-cultural foundation. Father Jordan himself, one of the Missionaries, explains the rationale of this method,

> The idea was to form a christian village centred around the
> Church and Father's house. According as people embraced

---

[59]J. P. JORDAN, op. cit., p. 63.

[60]A. O. MAKOZI & G. J. A. OJO, eds., History of the Catholic Church in Nigeria, Macmillan Nig., 1982, p. 42.

[61]E. ISICHEI, op. cit., p. 172.

[62]F. K. EKECHI, op. cit., pp. 116-117.

the true faith they were induced to build a hut for themselves in the village and thus to cut themselves off as far as possible from pagan influences. These influences were certainly considerable, because everything in native life from cradle to the grave bore the stamp of false worship . . .[63]

With this method, the christians were separated and segregated from their kit and kin who were traditionalists, in order not to be ensnared into traditional religious practices. This strategy, however succeeded in estranging the Christians from their traditional culture, and thereby paved a way for the consequences which one observes among christians in Igboland today.

Generally speaking, after a century of missionary ventures in Igboland, it gives a great joy to look back and see the fruits of the efforts of these pioneer Missionaries, who virtually spent all and were themselves practically spent, to plant the seed of Christianity. Invariably most of them lost their lives in Igboland. It is frightening indeed to go through the long list in the necrology of the early Missionaries. One need not be told of the concomitant difficulties and that were the lot of these Missionaries. Would it be enough to talk only of the permanent separation which they suffered, such as separation from their homes, families, country, and friends? At times, such separation was for life, since many never returned home. Or would one forget the entirely different climatic conditions under which they worked, being exposed to tropical diseases and sicknesses? Sometimes they had to ply routes in the seas and local waters and roads which were never followed in history, with its consequences. Would one forget the poor diet which they were naturally compelled to as well as a completely different environment and social situations from their homes? There remains the most difficult aspect which is the language factor. It still remains an enigma how they were able to communicate with the people especially at the initial stages. Despite the language they were able to establish a link with the people. It must not be forgotten that they were treated in some places with so many prejudicial hostilities by the people out of the provocations arising from the slave trade experiences.

Today, after all these difficulties, one looks back to discover that through these efforts and sacrifices, the faith they planted has not only germinated, but has also grown into a quasi adult Christianity at least externally. There is an evidence of this growth in the ever-increasing number of the baptised, the confirmed and the married; the parishes and dioceses; booming vocations to the priesthood and religious life; the church organizations, religious societies and confraternities, educational and social institutions. Taking a quasi roll-call in terms of growth of the ventures of the early Missionaries, Bishop Nwedo highlights the first century as the

. . . period that sees our Provincial Major Seminary, Bigard Memorial Seminary grow to be the biggest of its kind in the world; period that witnesses the tremendous growth in number of the children of the Catholic Church in our territory, the period

---

[63]J. P. JORDAN, op. cit., pp. 27-28.

that has given us hundreds of native priests, given to Bishop Shanahan's former Prefecture 16 Dioceses, 13 indigenous Bishops, two Archbishops, and 2 Cardinals.[64]

Paying a glowing tribute to the early Missionaries, he flamboyantly remarked,

They have played their part very well, have prepared the ground, planted the crops, tended them, and seen them yield rich harvest. Look around and see: how beautiful the fruit of their labour! The strong communities of solid catholics all over our Country, the many exemplary Christian families which form the bulwark of Catholicism in our Province, and from which as from a good garden, blossom beautiful flowers of vocation to the Priesthood and Religious life; the numerous lay organisations in which men and women, old and young, boys and girls actively exercise their faith or fulfil their proper share of the mandate "Go teach".[65]

No mean tribute is paid to the Missionaries when Basden in a similar manner remarked that their faithful ministry "has left an indelible impression upon the hearts of the people." For him, the Missionaries

laboured to build up the Church of God in this part of Ibo-land, adding their quota of living stones, whether few or many, to the sacred edifice, until, their work accomplished, they entered into rest, or were transferred to other spheres of service.[66]

In his own estimate of the first century activity of the Missionaries, Uchendu writes,

In terms of the number of converts, the missionary activity in southern Nigeria must be described as very successful. Statistical information is not necessary to convince an observer that this region is now overwhelmingly, if only nominally Christian.[67]

The Church and the people of Igboland will ever remain grateful to the early Missionaries for the indelible mark they have left in the history of Christianity in Igboland.

At this juncture, it is appropriate to make an evaluation of the above

---

[64]ANTHONY G. NWEDO, Centenary Celebration in Eastern Nigeria 1885 - 1985, Homily delivered at Onitsha on 7th Dec. 1985.

[65]Ibid.

[66]G. T. BASDEN, Among the Ibos of Nigeria, p. 296.

[67]V. C. UCHENDU, "Missionary Problems in Nigerian Society", in Practical Anthropology, vol. 11, no. 3, (May-June 1964), p. 109.

highlighted Christian encounter with Igbo culture for the past century in order to understand the reasons for any possible proposals as to the functions which Christianity ought to take up as a challenge in Igbo culture.

A critical analysis of the first century experience of Christianity in Igboland reveals a fundamental missing gap in the faith - culture dialogue. As Ukpong rightly observed,

> A careful analysis of the situation reveals that the observed acts of syncretism among African Christians is not so much a sign of lack of Christian commitment as an expression of the fact that Christianity, as transmitted to the African, has not been made to respond fully to his culturally based religious aspirations.[68]

This is because,

> . . . Man reflects on divine truths from a certain cultural standpoint. The fruits of such reflection formulated as theology necessarily bear the imprint of that culture. Culture must, therefore, be seen as an inseparable part of any theological system.[69]

It is, therefore, a very big mistake which frightens one even to the point of asking questions on how far the arduous toils of the apostolate of these long years would last. Questions of far-reaching anthropological implications are now being raised. Bearing in mind the guidelines already enunciated above from the Sacred Congregation of the Propagation of Faith, as well as the teaching of the Popes on this matter, our first attention is drawn to the dislodging influence which the missionary venture has had on the cultural life of the Igbo Christians, such that it can rightly be claimed that the Igbo Christians find themselves suspended between two worlds, without having a base in any of them. Isichei speaks of this dualistic and ambiguous life of the Igbo Christian thus:

> The extent of the Christianisation of Igboland is a question of depth and sincerity, as well as of numbers. The first generation of Igbo Christians often displayed an apparent contradiction - on the one hand they were enthusiastic and fervent Christians, but, on the other, they frequently embraced practices which the Churches condemned. Many became polygamists or defied the Church's embargoes on title-taking, or consulted diviners or wore charms in time of trouble.[70]

This weak point in the life of Igbo Christians furnishes a reason for the

---

[68]JUSTIN UKPONG, "The Emergence of African Theological Theologies", Theological Studies, 45 (1984), p. 510

[69]Ibid., p. 511.

[70]E. ISICHEI, A History of the Igbo People, p. 183.

criticism made by Mullan some decades ago. He observed,

> The Church has been planted in Africa, but its roots in its new
> soil are not strong. The reasons for this is not far to seek.
> Christianity to the African is revolutionary. It completely alters
> his attitude, not only to his religion, in its social and personal
> aspects, but also to the structure of his society and to his
> relations with his community. It draws him away from the
> society which hitherto was his support, and he feels rotten . .
> . So in time of stress he slips back to seek security in the old
> patterns of life.[71]

In any evangelisation work, interculturation is a factor that ought to
be acknowledged as an interaction having consequences for both cultures
involved, yet, one must be careful in this process so that the 'importation
of cultural elements should never be so overwhelming as to alienate people
from their original culture'.[72] Taking note of this fact, one reviews in pains
the attempts by the missionaries to deculturise their converts. The
missionaries had a plan to disorientate their converts culturally, with the
effect that being culturally uprooted, their cultural centre of life would no
more hold. Tearing people away from their cultural surroundings is nothing
but alienating them from their home. This is exactly what the missionaries
did, as one them, Father Jordan testifies:

> As people embraced the true faith they were induced to build
> a hut for themselves in the village and thus cut themselves off
> as far as possible from pagan influences.[73]

Anything that connects them to the culture of their people were completely
negatively viewed as sinful. That is why Igboaja sharply remarked:

> Missionaries lost their patience and resorted to an elimination
> method. They aimed at erasing, obliterating, phasing out
> whatever existed before their arrival. They termed them pagan,
> devilish, and idol-worship. Everything was condemned: burial
> ceremonies (ikwa ozu nkwa n'abo), masquerading (iti mmanwu),
> dancing (igba egwu), local cosmetics (igbu uli,. . .), title-taking
> (ichi ozo, ime oha, etc.), outings (ipu afia, iwa-na-ogbo etc.).[74]

Deploring the encouragements given to the early Christians by the

---

[71]J. MULLAN, The Catholic Church in Modern Africa, Geoffrey Chapman,
London, 1965, p. 24.

[72]Cf. AYLWARD SHORTER, Toward A Theology of Inculturation, Orbis
Books, Maryknoll, New York, 1988, p. 63.

[73]J. P. JORDAN, op. cit., p. 38.

[74]E. U. IGBOAJA, "From Uka Fada to Uka Anyi", A Centenary
Celebration Lecture, Enugu Diocese, 1985, p. 3.

missionaries to crush the pagans who were their kit and kin, the same Igboaja gives a vivid picture of the cultural clash between the missionaries and the traditional way of life. The converts were ordered to

> . . . clear the bush (Ajofia); clear the traditional places of worship of our forefathers, fight the masquerades, defile sacred places and objects, flout taboos, expose traditional secrets and the mysteries like the masquerades (Ika mmanwu), condemn local title, and indeed fight against everything that has something to do with the modus vivendi of the people. Not just a people a century old, but a people whose origin dates as far back as research history can go . . . [75]

Igboaja is not alone in the report of the cultural destructive tendency of the missionaries. Basden as well testifies to it as he remarks:

> The result is a complete upheaval of the political, economical and social affairs of the country. Every native institution has been shaken in its foundations and, at the present rate of progress, a great many of the most interesting facts concerning the primitive customs of the people will soon be matters of history and tradition only. [76]

It is no wonder, then, why Chinua Achebe, summing up the general feeling and pathetic sentiments of the Igbo people in the face of this cultural devastation and destructive tendency, sadly writes in his classical novel: "He has put a knife on the things that held us together and we have fallen apart". [77]

In his x-ray of the changing scene consequent on the culture contact and the conflict that characterised that era, another scholar writes:

> Christianity . . . confronted the traditional people with a radical alternative. It was a blow at the heart of the traditional system - the religious order which sanctioned and protected its ideological assumptions . . . initially, the attack of the Christians on the traditional religion opened the flood gates to the overwhelming changes that were to follow . . . . The impact of the new religion was devastating, for it affected the most fundamental and therefore the most cohesive factors in the traditional system. [78]

---

[75]Ibid.

[76]G. T. BASDEN, Among the Ibos of Nigeria, p. 20.

[77]CHINUA ACHEBE, Things Fall Apart, Heinemann Educational Books Ltd., London, 1958, pp. 124-125.

[78]E. OBIECHINA, Culture, Tradition and Society in the West African Novels, African Studies Series, pp. 228-229.

As one would expect,

> . . . with time, most of the shrines began to crumble, traditional
> feasts were neglected and associations which brought the
> young and the old together became obsolete. Traditional religion
> is fast becoming the preserve of an aging minority who live in
> the countryside.[79]

Perhaps a more disturbing observation is that made by the Bishops
of Igboland in testimony of the shallowness of the faith of Igbo Christians.
They observed:

> A settled spiritual allegiance is not yet a realised fact in the
> Christian life of our many converts. Most of our Catholics do
> not find any incompatibility in plural belonging . . . . Easily,
> airily, they slide out of one skin into another or rather by some
> miracle peculiar to themselves they comfortably wear both skins
> at once.[80]

All these are very strong pointers to the fact that either 'the change from
traditional religion to Christianity was so sudden that they hardly had the
time to reflect on their beliefs or adjust to their new way of life',[81] or, as
Ukpong would see it, 'Christianity has been presented to them as a set of
principles and not as a way of life; for, to become a way of life for Africans,
Christianity must be made relevant to and expressive of the way they live
and think'.[82] The fact that such aspects as divination, fortune telling and
medicine-making are today on the increase and have even christians as their
patronisers, raises a serious question as to the depth of conversion effected
in these years.

It is very necessary here to observe that from all these criticisms, the
fundamental problem is that of acculturation and transculturation. One
cannot deny the fact that at the first contact of christianity with Igbo culture,
accepting the faith meant accepting the missionaries' culture and way of
life.[83] Therefore instead of the gradual insertion of the christian faith within

---

[79]E. I. METUH, God and Man in African Religion, pp. 172-173.

[80]CATHOLIC BISHOPS OF ONITSHA ECCLESIASTICAL PROVINCE, Put
Out Into Deep Water, Pastoral Letter, 1985, pp. 11-12.

[81]E. I. METUH, God and Man in African Religion, p. 170.

[82]JUSTIN UKPONG, op. cit., p. 520

[83]"In so far as one preaches the gospel as it has been developed within
one's own culture, one is preaching not only the gospel but also one's own
culture. In so far as one is preaching one's own culture, one is asking
others not only to accept the gospel but also renounce their own culture and
accept one's own."-B. LONERGAN, Method in Theology, London: Darton,

the cultural base of the people, or paving the way for a cultural diffusion of christian principles, there was more of the external pressure on the people to adopt a new way of life. Some of these criticisms above testify that there were strong attempts at deculturisation and detribalization of the converts, and destruction of traditional values. One can say that there was more of cultural conversion to a new cultural allegiance, all in the name of evangelisation. It was an attempt to effect a culture change by people, who, as foreigners, remain outside the system to be changed. There was no entrance at all into the people's culture to see if anything good can come out of it. It is no wonder then, that the result is, on the one hand, alienation of the converts in their homeland, and on the other, a lack of an integrated and personalised christian life. It has to be acknowledged, as some authors point out, that

> . . . change is almost always initiated by someone within the cultural community. Even though the idea may have been sparked by contact with another culture, it still must be introduced from within to be accepted. The alternative to this scheme is change forced upon a people through superior might, whether moral or physical. This is the sort of change that missions have often been responsible for, and that resulted in such unfortunate reaction.[84]

The case of Igbo Christianity is exactly this alternative referred to.

Judging from these important revelations and criticisms, one hesitates in paying a glowing tribute to the missionaries in their christian ventures in Igboland within the past century. One tends to blame them for this glaring loophole in their strategy. Arinze, however, cautions against such an attitude, since the missionaries had their own limitations. According to him,

> It is not right in 1985 to blame the missionaries of Africa for not carrying out profound inculturation in 1885. The missionaries were of another culture and language, often the climate was difficult for them and the studies we have today on different cultures were not available in those days. Missionaries were few in number, communication is much slower than it is today. A proof of the difficulty of inculturation is that even today there are still many problems that local bishops, priests and laity have not succeeded in resolving.[85]

In conclusion, one is only left with the present day challenges of re-

---

Longman & Todd, 1972, pp. 362-363.

[84]DALE W. KIETZMAN AND WILLIAM A. SMALLEY, "The Missionary's Role in Culture Change", in WILLIAM A. SMALLEY, ed., Readings in Missionary Anthropology, William Carey Library, California, 1978, p. 528.

[85]FRANCIS CARDINAL ARINZE, "Incarnation of the Gospel in Cultures", in Echo From Africa and other Continents, Jan. 1986, p. 5.

entering into the Igbo cultural potentials with the intention of recovering the firm, sound and non-repugnant cultural base on which to incarnate the christian faith.

3.5   Conclusion: Urgent Need for Inculturation in Igboland

So far, an attention has been focused on one basic fact. It has been an effort to trace a missing link in the foundations of Christianity in Igboland. After a century of existence, it should be said that Christianity has come of age in Igboland. But it is disheartening to discover that Christianity has, in all these years, remained on the periphery of people's lives. What makes it even worse is the fact that Igbo christians seem to live a double type of life in order to be able to accommodate both the christian and cultural demands.

A diagnosis reveals an initial fundamental mistake. There is a missing link between the faith and the culture of the land, on which framework Christianity would have sunk its roots. As a guide for the encounter between the Faith and Culture as well as to serve as a point of reference, an enquiry was made into the Christian fundamental attitude to any culture. The fact is that Christianity has always respected and recognised what is good and beautiful in cultures, and has always carried out a purification of whatever is tainted, thereby transforming them. This is the reason for pointing out the good values that ought to be utilised in salvaging and reconstructing the situation.

From the enquiry, without doubt, the obvious way out is no other than that of Inculturation, for, as Shorter remarks,

> One must start with the indigenous culture itself to discover what its authentic human values are, and how far these values are already christian values or can develop as seeds of the Gospel into christian values.[86]

When one applies the principles of the christian attitude to Igbo culture, possible indications for inculturation in Igbo culture are revealed. Any possible proposal in this regard in this work is intended to serve as a sample for inculturation among the Igbos. It has to be emphasised straightaway that one does not in any way advocate any syncretism between christianity and Igbo religion. The solution that comes to mind is that of undressing Christianity in Igboland of its foreign elements, in order to properly dress her in the real cultural garb of the Igbos. Christianity in Igboland has found itself in the phase, when missionaries have become culturally educated, and strive to present the person of Christ and his teaching in terms of the new culture, and perceive new insights into the christian faith. During this phase, according to Shorter,

---

[86]A. SHORTER, African Culture and the Christian Church, London: Geoffrey Chapman, 1973, p. 69.

Gradually the clumsy translations and approximations of their first efforts will be replaced by new images and new connections of ideas. Some of the imported cultural elements will fall away to be replaced by indigenous ones.[87]

Hence one is not proposing an Igbo Theology, but rather an Igbo perspective of Christian Theology. This would reveal an authentic Igbo face or version of the one Christian Theology. To achieve this, Sawyer warns,

. . . care must be taken to avoid syncretistic tendencies as well as a hollow Theology for Africa . . . . The answer lies in the rigorous pursuit of systematic Theology, based on a philosophical appraisal of the thought-forms of the African peoples.[88]

Therefore, while holding intact the fundamental christian elements, one tries to convey these in the cultural thought patterns of the Igbos, in such a way that the Igbos, taking off from their context and traditional structure, would see the christian teachings and values from their own natural perspective. This, in effect, boils down to and demands an urgent need for inculturation of the faith in Igboland.

The situation greatly poses a challenge to Christianity in Igboland. This challenge is equally urgent, since one sees the present stand and desire of the Igbos to return to the cultural roots as a golden opportunity to be tapped. If the Igbo christians are not guided and offered an answer in their present quest for return to the cultural roots, the consequence would be grave for the christian faith, since neo-paganism, which is already knocking on the door, would take the stage, and be standardised. Also the religious climate of the nation as a whole at this moment, coupled with both the economic and political strategies, are strong temptations for the Igbo christians to think of Islamic religion as an alternative and substitute. The Bishops of Igboland are aware of this urgency, hence Bishop Eneja remarks,

Especially at this period of our history, no one who loves this country can ignore the movements with regard to culture. This situation is mobile, delicate, serious. With care, intelligent examination, prudent handling much good would accrue from culture and customs. The exercise is replete with great promise for our people and the world.[89]

At the face of the enormity of this challenge for Christianity in Igboland, one tends to despair of success. But, realising the possibilities and the potentials at the disposal of Christianity in Igboland, one is greatly

---

[87]A. SHORTER, Towards a Theology of Inculturation, p. 63.

[88]HARRY SAWYER, "What is African Christian Theology?", Africa Theological Journal, 4, p. 19 (1971).

[89]M. U. ENEJA, On Fire for Christ, p. 18.

encouraged to be optimistic for a hopeful and brighter future for Christianity in Igboland. This hope is based on the fact that the Church in Igboland is comfortably equipped quantitatively as well as qualitatively with a nearly entire indigenous Episcopal Conference, averagely buoyant number of educated Clergy and Religious, as well as a responsive and active Laity, adequately versed in the allied studies demanded by the Inculturation work. Shorter rightly remarked that

> When evangelization begins to be placed in the hands of the indigenous Christians themselves, then the process is speeded up, and the whole cultural system should start to be enlivened from within. This is the beginning of inculturation properly so-called . . .[90]

The Church leaders are equally aware of the implications involved, hence they have unanimously accepted this challenge, remarking that "the task of the next century is to see that our Christians not only believe with their heads, but that they also become Christians to the marrow of their bones".[91] This is only possible through Inculturation. Igbo Christianity shares the same conviction with Wijngaards, who, speaking of African Christianity as a whole, remarks,

> The permanence of Christianity will stand or fall on the question whether it has become truly African: whether Africans have made christian ideas part of their own thinking, whether Africans feel that the Christian vision of life fulfils their own needs, whether the Christian world view has become part of truly African aspirations.[92]

It is the same conviction that spurs one on in going ahead in the search for the safe roots of Christianity in Igboland.

The next section intends to treat of the concept of Inculturation and the necessary prerequisites for a successful Inculturation work. This should serve to clarify and channel our thoughts and ideas in the subsequent sections.

---

[90]A. SHORTER, Towards a Theology of Inculturation, p. 63.

[91]Pastoral Letter of Onitsha Provincial Bishops, p. 13.

[92]JOHN WIJNGAARDS, African Events, August 1985.

CHAPTER 4

4   **INCULTURATION**

4.1   **Preamble**

After the diagnosis of the situation of Christianity in Igboland, it can be rightly admitted that what one finds is a sort of 'sandwich' Christianity, having a very flamboyant christian external features with an internal underlying cravings for fundamental cultural roots. Samuel Ruiz Garcia refers to the mere superimposition of a layer of Christianity as "sandwich religion", which according to him, "is the best possible 'culture medium' for the growth of religious syncretism".[1] The necessary alternative to this situation is Inculturation - "missionary work based on the principle of incarnation - a challenge both anthropologically and theologically".[2] That is why the question of Inculturation should be discussed at this juncture. It is essential to know what Inculturation is, and to establish the reasons and the guiding principles for Inculturation before one is able to talk of inculturation in the Rites of Passage.

From the almost over-flooded questions raised today in nearly all disciplines of Theology, one does not hesitate to see Inculturation of the Christian message as one of the 'signs of the time', of which Pope John XXIII talked. One can even go further to consider this as one of the most serious problems confronting the Church today. Many a time, references are made to the same fact by the use of so many terms. Such terms as 'adaptation', 'accommodation', 'indigenisation', 'incarnation', 'contextualization', 'enculturation', 'acculturation', 'interculturation', 'transculturation', even 'africanisation', have been variously utilised to refer to the same reality. At times, one talks of "Sitz im Leben" in theological and biblical circles. Although these terms all have their specific meanings, yet they have been mixed-up with the idea of Inculturation that it becomes very essential to clarify and sharpen our concepts, so as to offset the confusion arising from flippant use of all these terms.[3] Therefore the fundamental questions are: What is Inculturation? Why is Inculturation necessary? What principles guide any Inculturation work? Answers to these questions will serve as guides in making any proposals in inculturation.

---

[1]SAMUEL RUIZ GARCIA, "The Incarnation of the Church in Indigenous Cultures", in Missiology, vol. 1, no. 2, April 1973, p. 23.

[2]Ibid., p. 21.

[3]Cf., S. RAYAN, "Flesh of India's Flesh", Jeevadhara 6 (1976): 259.

4.2   The Motivations and Origins of Inculturation

The term "inculturation" is of a recent coinage semantically, although its reality and practice dates back to the very past.[4] Fundamentally speaking, the idea of inculturation relates two important facts - the Gospel Message and the human culture. It concerns the transmission of the divine message to man in his cultural situation. As such, this idea dates back to the first signs of God's self revelation to mankind even in Creation. The divine self-revelation in creation at the very beginning, by which a definite shape is given to the formless void - "tohuwabohu"[5] is already a sign of Inculturation. The act of creation, bringing the human culture into existence out of nothing, is the effect of God's decision to communicate Himself to humankind in space and time.[6] It must be remembered that God's unique plan of self-revelation in creation is founded on and projected towards Christ as the centre of salvation.[7] Hence God's election and interaction with the people of Israel in the Old Testament are steps leading up to the ultimate self unveiling of God in the Incarnation of Christ. The manifestation of God to man, as the record of Revelation testifies, is always made within the spatial, temporal and cultural conditions of man.[8] Therefore, issuing from the Incarnation as the source, have flowed all inculturational tendencies, both before and after, up to the present.[9] Evangelisation is the transmission of

---

[4]"While inculturation is a word which became current in circles concerned with evangelization only after 1975, yet the reality of inculturation has been with the Church from the very beginning . . ." Lucien Richard, "Mission and Inculturation: The Church in the World", in Lucien Richard, et al., eds., Vatican II: The Unfinished Agenda, Paulist Press, New York/Mahwah, p. 105.

[5]Cf., GERHARD von RAD, Genesis, SCM Press Ltd., 1972, pp.49-51.

[6]"L'idea biblica di creazione da Dio punta verso lo stabilimento di una nuova relazione del mondo e dell'uomo con Dio, relazione invisibile agli occhi della carne e solo visibile alla fede". ARMINDO VAZ, Per una Antropologia dell' Antico Testamento, Appunti nella Facoltà Teologica, Teresianum, Rome, 1987-88, p. 39.

[7]"Cristo ... è il piano di Dio; la creazione, in tutto il suo lungo arco, fino al totale compimento, altro non è che la proiezione e l'attuazione permanente di "Cristo". CARLO LAUDAZI, L'uomo nel Rapporto con Dio, Appunti nella Facoltà Teologica, Teresianum, 1986, p. 5.

[8]"L'uomo è nell'orizzonte di Dio solo perché Dio ha scelto l'orizzonte della forma umana come termine del suo rivelarsi definitivo". Ibid., p. 4.

[9]"Da Abramo, si potrebbe dire, fino a Giovanni Paolo II, la parola di Dio si è inculturata nella storia rivolgendosi a uomini di cultura diversa ed ha assunto le forme culturali del tempo in cui è risuonata." P. Rossano, "Il Vangelo verso le culture e le religioni", in AA.VV., Portare Cristo all'uomo, vol. 1, Studia Urbaniana, 22, Università Urbaniana, Roma, 1985, p. 73.

the Incarnation to all people of various cultural backgrounds. All theological discussions have been only honest efforts to make God's message be plausible, clearer and acceptable to people of all ages and different cultural backgrounds. As pointed out in Gaudium et Spes,

> . . . the Church has existed through the centuries in varying circumstances and has utilized the resources of different cultures in its preaching to spread and explain the message of Christ, to examine and understand it more deeply, and to express it more perfectly in the liturgy and in various aspects of the life of the faithful.[10]

These indications only point to the reality of Inculturation, since, as a term, its origin is only of a very recent past. In theological circles, the various terms outlined above, were interchangeably employed in reference to matters of Inculturation.

As motivations for the coinage of the term in question, the Vatican II made profuse use of such terms as "adaptation", and even "incarnation" in reference to the admission into the liturgy of some traditional and cultural elements.[11] In Ad Gentes, the Church talks of "implanting itself among all these groups in the same way that Christ by his Incarnation committed himself to the particular social and cultural circumstances of the men among who he lived".[12] Spelling out still the dimensions of the mission of the Church, the Council expressly said,

> The effect of her work is that whatever good is found sown in the minds and hearts of men or in the rites and customs of peoples, these not only are preserved from destruction, but are purified, raised up, and perfected for the glory of God, ... [13]

The same idea is here being conveyed. Going further, the idea is reinforced when Christians are said to have the obligation "to give expression to this newness of life in their own society and culture and in a manner that is in keeping with the traditions of their own land".[14] Also, since the process has a relation to the process of the Incarnation, the local Churches are asked "to borrow from the customs, traditions, wisdom, teaching, . . . of their people everything which could be used to praise God".[15]

Apart from these pointers, more challenging motivations come from the teachings and addresses of the recent Popes. While Pope John XXIII

---

[10]Vatican II, Gaudium et Spes, no. 58.

[11]cf., Vatican II, Sacrosanctum Concilium, nos.38-40, 65.

[12]Id., Ad Gentes, no. 10.

[13]Id., Lumen Gentium, no. 17.

[14]Vatican II, Ad Gentes, no. 21.

[15]Ibid., no. 22.

talked of up-dating the Christian Message[16], for which reason the Vatican II was convened, Paul VI dwelt at large with enunciating principles and guidelines for evangelisation work today. In the encyclical devoted to evangelisation the Pope said many things about inculturation without using the term. The Pope pointed out the intimate relationship between the Christian Message and human cultures, streamlining the dynamics and interaction that should be taken into account in any evangelising work. The Pope encouraged inculturation saying:

> The split between the Gospel and Culture is without a doubt the drama of our time . . . Therefore every effort must be made to ensure a full evangelisation of culture, or more correctly of cultures. They have to be regenerated by an encounter with the Gospel.[17]

He further spoke of "assimilating the essence of the Gospel message . . . into the language that . . . people understand . . . ". (Language is here to be anthropologically and culturally understood).[18]

In what may be referred to as an inspiration for the use of the term "Africanisation", Pope Paul VI in Kampala charged the African Bishops with the idea of inculturation when he said: "You may and you must have an African Christianity".[19] In the same vein, Pope John Paul II, addressing the Kenyan Bishops in Nairobi, this time employing other terms, said:

> The acculturation or inculturation which you rightly promote will truly be a reflection of the incarnation of the word, when culture transformed and regenerated by the Gospel, brings forth from its own living tradition original expressions of Christian life, celebration and thought.[20]

One can observe from all these various indications, a new approach channelled towards evangelisation. It is these indications that have ultimately led to such new vocabularies in Mission Theology as "enculturation", "acculturation", and "inculturation" - the first two terms being

---

[16]cf., JOHN XXIII, Message to Humanity, Oct. 1962.

[17]PAUL VI, Apostolic Exhortation, Evangelii Nuntiandi, 8 Dec. 1975, AAS LXVIII (1976), no. 20.

[18]Ibid.

[19]Id., Address at the Closing Session of the Symposium of African Bishops, in Kampala, 31 July 1969.

[20]JOHN PAUL II, African Addresses, Editrice Missionaria Italiana, Bologna, 1981, p 178.

formerly purely anthropological terms.[21] But it must also be acknowledged that other factors contributed to the development of the concept of Inculturation. As Joseph P. Fitzpatrick observes, such other factors include "the understanding of culture which the social sciences have provided in recent decades, the appearance in relatively short time of many new nations, 'the increasing awareness of personal identity and culture,' the rivalry between conflicting ideologies, and the advance of technology".[22]

4.3 **Previous Terminologies and Meanings**

Having made inroads into the conjectures surrounding the term in question, one returns on a serious note to the nagging question: what is inculturation? Being a new word, there is not yet a generally accepted definition. So, one has to rely on and consider the indications above in assigning a meaning to inculturation. With these as guide, an examination of these terms above would help to project the authentic meaning to be given to inculturation.

It is interesting to note that most of the terms associated with the concept of inculturation are anthropological by origin, but have been given theological and missiological orientation. For instance, adaptation, interculturation, enculturation, acculturation, transculturation, and even accommodation are fundamentally terms of cultural anthropology. In theological and missionary circles, they acquire a new meaning and dimension, along with their original meanings. For instance, 'adaptation' anthropologically, is the process whereby a population establishes means of existing and surviving in a specific environment.[23] Its acquired meaning in theological and missionary circles portray it as an adjustment process whereby a selection of certain rites and customs are made, purified and inserted within apparently similar Christian rituals in order to meet up with the cultural requirements of an area.[24] 'Accommodation' has also a similar meaning even though Luzbetak defined it as "the respectful, prudent, scientifically and theologically sound adjustment of the Church to the native

---

[21]cf., LUCIEN RICHARD, "Mission and Inculturation: The Church in the World", in LUCIEN RICHARD, et al., eds., Vatican II : The Unfinished Agenda, Paulist Press, New York, p. 93.

[22]JOSEPH P. FITZPATRICK, One Church Many Cultures, Sheed & Ward, p. 190.

[23]CONRAD P. KOTTAK, Cultural Anthropology, Random House Inc., New York, 1975, p. 371.

[24]J. M. WALIGGO, et al., Inculturation: Its Meaning and Urgency, St. Paul Publications, Africa, 1986, p.11. Cf., ANSCAR J. CHUPUNGCO, Cultural Adaptation of the Liturgy, Paulist Press, New York, 1982, p. 48.

culture in attitude, outward behaviour, and practical apostolic approach".[25] 'Indigenisation' is a "quest for cultural revival, not only in the secular but also in the religious domain". It is defined by Nzomiwu as "an attempt to take more seriously a people's cultural background in discussing and imparting religious beliefs, commitments and attitudes".[26] Indigenisation has a restricted meaning projecting the necessity of promoting native personnel for playing leadership roles in the local Church, and seen as very good means for carrying out authentic adaptations. 'Enculturation' is a technical term in cultural anthropology which indicates the learning experience by which an individual is initiated and grows into his culture, and thereby acquires a culture. Herskovits defined it as "the aspects of the learning experience which mark off man from other creatures, and by means of which, initially, and in later life, he achieves competence in his culture".[27] 'Acculturation', on the other hand, refers to the phenomenon which results when groups of individuals having different cultures come into continuous first-hand contact, with subsequent change in the original culture patterns of either or both groups.[28] In liturgical circles, there is what is referred to as 'liturgical acculturation' which is the "process whereby cultural elements which are compatible with the Roman liturgy are incorporated into it either as substitutes or illustration of euchological and ritual elements of the Roman rite".[29] 'Transculturation' and 'interculturation' are purely cultural concepts. While 'transculturation' means the transference of cultural traits, symbols, meanings, patterns, values, or institutions of a specific culture to almost all other cultures,[30] 'interculturation' is the interdependence of cultures for mutual enrichment. 'Contextualization' is a term demanding a knowledge of the real situation; it is an effort to adapt the Gospel message to the man of today in a "dynamic, and convincing way - taking into account the human concrete situation". Ukpong refers this term to "all endeavour aimed at making the Christian message relevant to the local context".[31] It is therefore to be seen as a communicational exigency, and as such, cannot be equated to inculturation which is something more than communication. Then, there is the term 'africanisation' which sounds a bit parochial. When used in

[25]LOUIS J. LUZBETAK, The Church and Cultures, William Carey Library, California, 1970, p. 341.

[26]J. P. C. NZOMIWU, "The African Church and Indigenisation Question: An Igbo Experience", in Afer, Vol.28, no.5, (Oct.1988), p. 324.

[27] M. J. HERSHOVITS, Man and His Works, New York 1952, p. 39.

[28]Quoted by L. LUZBETAK, op. cit., p. 214.

[29]ANSCAR J. CHUPUNGCO, Cultural Adaptation of the Liturgy, Paulist Press, New York/Ramsey, 1982, p. 81.

[30]MARCELLO DE CARVALHO AZEVEDO, Inculturation and the Challenges of Modernity, Gregorian University, Rome, 1982, pp. 7-8.

[31]JUSTIN S. UKPONG, "Contextualizing Theological Education in West Africa: Focus on subjects", in CHIEA Vol.3, no.3, Sept.1987, p. 60.

reference to Christianity, it means incarnating Christianity within the African culture. It may serve to refer to Inculturation, as, for instance, when the Pope referred to it, to mean 'making Christianity to be truly African in a way that it becomes a part of their thinking and way of life', which requires, to be realised, in the words of the Holy Father, "that . . . African souls become imbued to its depths with the secret charism of Christianity, so that these charisma may then overflow freely, in beauty and wisdom, in the true African manner".[32]   However, this term limits inculturation only to the African continent. Also the term carries with it the false and dangerous connotation of a crave for everything african. Finally, the term 'incarnation' is borrowed from the mystery of the Incarnation. It aims at applying the principle of incarnation to evangelisation process, which means that the Church has to "implant itself among all peoples in the same way that Christ by his incarnation committed himself to the particular social and cultural circumstances of the men among whom he lived".[33]

4.4   **What is Inculturation?**

It has already been remarked that inculturation has so much to do with evangelisation of cultures. It is essential, then, to compare the meanings of these various terms with the concept of evangelisation. This will help to eliminate the irrelevant terms.   Pope Paul VI defined evangelisation to mean "affecting the standards by which people make judgements, their prevailing values, their interests and thought patterns, the things that move them to action and their models of human living".[34]   This means, in other words, "the intimate transformation of authentic cultural values through their integration in Christianity".[35]   With this meaning as a guide, one observes that most of the terms fall short of the essential elements.   Indigenisation, in as much as it is one of the best means of effecting adaptation, has a very restricted meaning. It, however, remains a means of effecting the objective. Adaptation and accommodation give the impression of an external, and therefore, superficial tolerance of culture. The terms lack that intimate relationship which should exist between the two values in contact.[36]   Enculturation, however, seem to be an important

---

[32]PAUL VI, Address to the African Bishops, in Kampala.

[33]Vatican II, Ad Gentes, no. 10.

[34]PAUL VI, Evangelii Nuntiandi, no. 19.

[35]LUCIEN RICHARD, op. cit., p. 103

[36]The Bishops observed: ". . . inculturation is different from a simple external adaptation, because it means the intimate transformation of authentic cultural values through their integration in Christianity in the various human cultures".   THE EXTRAORDINARY SYNOD OF BISHOPS 1985, Message to the People of God, St. Paul's Editions, Boston, 1985, p. 63.

concept to be considered and employed in inculturation. Since it is a gateway into a culture, and lasts the whole life-span of an individual, it ought to be utilised in inculturation. It should play an assisting role. However, it ought to be noted that, while enculturation deals with the insertion of an individual into his culture, inculturation concerns the insertion of christianity into the culture. Christianity is supranational; it is not, and cannot be identified with a culture. That is why acculturation cannot stand for inculturation. Transculturation and interculturation are simply irrelevant.

One is ultimately left with the term 'incarnation'. It seems to have a meaning that even overrides inculturation, since inculturation only tries to approximate the idea of the Incarnation. If evangelisation is an effort to realize by expansion in space and time the fruits of the Incarnation, the Incarnation cannot but be seen as the origin and model of all evangelisation. In Church's documents the Incarnation appears as the primary motivation and pattern for inculturation.[37] For this reason, the title of this work bears the term 'incarnation' instead of 'inculturation'. It is, however, necessary to draw attention to a possible danger of the use of this term, a danger which Lucien Richard also points out. He observes:

> . . . the main reason for hesitation in using the incarnation as a model is that the incarnation applies to the relation between the human and the divine, while inculturation applies to the passage of culture into culture.[38]

Apart from this danger, one is more inclined to see with Rayan who remarked that

> Some would reserve the word 'incarnation' for the basic mystery and insist on clarity and distinction of ideas. Others find incarnation the aptest language and symbol for understanding and expressing reality as seen by Christian faith. We take incarnation, both word and thing, sign and reality, seriously in all its rich and endless resonances.[39]

Hence, one uses inculturation and incarnation interchangeably in this work to mean the same thing. In whatever way one sees it, inculturation is supposed to make the Christian message go deep into the roots of culture in order to provoke a radical reaction in the culture. In fact, it should be a reciprocal action in the sense of "the donation of the cultural values to the Christian faith so that Christianity is deeply rooted in those values, and the

---

[37]Cf., Vatican II, Ad Gentes, no. 10; Lumen Gentium, no. 13.

[38]LUCIEN RICHARD, op.cit., p. 109.

[39]S. RAYAN, Ibid.

regeneration of the cultural values by the Christian values".[40] Taking all that have been said into account, what could be seen as inculturation?

4.5   Definition of Inculturation

Inculturation seems to have acquired a wide publicity during the 32nd General Congregation of the Society of Jesus in 1974 - 1975. It appeared in their decrees after this meeting.[41] In an explicit letter from the Superior General of the Jesuits of 14th May 1978, the Jesuits were charged with the work of Inculturation. In this letter, inculturation is described as the

> . . . efforts which fulfil the Church through the incarnation of the Gospel message and values to take form and in terms of every culture, in such a way that the faith and Christian life of every local Church are inserted into their cultural framework in a very intimate and profound manner as possible.[42]

As a follow-up, A. R. Crollius attempts a definition, bringing out the fundamental function of the Gospel values in the culture in which it is inserted, thus:

> The inculturation of the Church is the integration of the Christian experience of a local Church into the culture of its people, in such a way that this experience not only expresses itself in elements of this culture, but becomes a force that animates, orients and innovates this culture so as to create a new unity and communion, not only within the culture in question but also as an enrichment of the Church universal.[43]

In both of these descriptions, the essential elements of inculturation are mentioned: the insertion of the Gospel message into a culture, the receptacle being the cultural roots; this is in order that the message germinates in the roots for a new fruit - the innovation of the culture. In the same vein, Elobuike Uzukwu thinks of inculturation as:

---

[40]EUGENE E. AZORJI, Some Recurrent Problems of Christian Inculturation in Nigeria with Special Reference to the Igbo People, Università Urbaniana, Rome, 1988, p. 34.

[41]Cf., 4th, 5th & 6th Decrees of the 32nd General Congregation of the Society of Jesus held 1974-75.

[42]PEDRO ARRUPE, "Letter on Inculturation", Rome, 1978. The translation is mine, and made from the Italian version, in PIME 24, Marzo 1982, p. 89.

[43]J. M. WALIGGO et al., op. cit., p. 43.

Christ incarnating in a certain culture to bring out a new way
of life. That new life emerges from the Good News and
culture, it animates and transforms the people into the new
People of God in that particular culture.[44]

Another author, yet emphasising the aspect of the intimate relationship, tries
to define inculturation as "the dynamic relation between the Christian
message and culture or cultures; an insertion of the christian life into a
culture; an on-going process of reciprocal and critical interaction and
assimilation between them".[45] There is another definition by William Reiser
which points at another aspect to be taken care of in inculturation -
faithfulness to the essentials of the christian faith. He defined inculturation
as "the process of a deep, sympathetic adaptation to and appropriation of
a local cultural setting in which the church finds itself in a way that does not
compromise its basic faith in Christ".[46]

In a manner that brings out more vividly the operative force of the
Gospel message in the use of the cultural potentials of any culture, Joseph
Cardinal Tomko defined inculturation as:

. . . the profound insertion of the Gospel in the very heart of
the determinate culture, so that the fertile seed of the faith can
germinate, develop and fructify, according to the potentiality and
peculiar character of that culture.[47]

Although all these definitions are positive enough for acceptance, yet,
for the purposes of this work, one would think of inculturation as the
profound insertion of the Gospel message and Christian values into the very
cultural roots of a people in such a way that Christianity, having incarnated
and thus feels at home among the people, now acts like leaven from the
cultural roots, utilises the cultural potentials, sprouts, develops and
transforms the people's way of life so as to take their place as authentic
branches of the Church Universal.

Concretely for the Igbos, inculturation would mean the bringing of the
Gospel values into the nerve centre of the Igbos. This would be in no other
place than the cultural roots, which, for the Igbos, operate like very sensitive

---

[44]E. E. UZUKWU, Church and Inculturation, Pacific College Press, Obosi,
1985, p. 26.

[45]MARCELLO DE CARVALHO AZEVEDO, op. cit, p. 11.

[46]WILLIAM REISER, "Inculturation and Doctrinal Development", Heythrop
Journal 22 (1981) 135, quoted in LUCIEN RICHARD, op. cit., p. 105.

[47]JOSEPH CARDINAL TOMKO, "Inculturation and African Marriage",
Afer 28, no.3/4 (June/August 1986), p. 155.

transmitting wave-lengths.[48] It means bringing Christianity into the cultural framework, so that the traditional community understands, appreciates and accepts christianity through their traditional and normal mode of thought and life. With the internalisation of the Christian values within their cultural roots, the same values become the operative seeds in the authentic transformation of the cultural life of the Igbos. This would make the Igbos feel every inch permeated by the Christian values, thereby identifying the reality of Christ in their everyday life's experiences. When the Igbos see Christianity being expressed through their traditional signs and symbols, they cannot but be provoked in a radical way into a transformation which would be manifested in every aspect of life, due to their integrated vision of life. When the Igbo feels in every aspect imbued with christian values, and these values seen as their motivating influence and source of animation, dictating the tempo of their life by making use of their cultural system and framework, then, and only then, can Christianity in Igboland be said to be inculturated.

Since the treatment of inculturation as such in this work is for a functional exigency, one is limited only to the very relevant aspects of inculturation. Let us therefore, turn attention to the scope and reasons for inculturation.

4.6   **The Scope of Inculturation**

In order to establish the reasons for Inculturation, it is essential to know the scope and dimensions of Inculturation. Inculturation is usually mentioned in relation to missionary territories and contexts. This gives the impression that it is a concern of areas where missionary work is still in progress, or where the Christian message has not yet been announced. It is no wonder, then, that the term evolved in missionary circles and discussions. When the Vatican II made provisions for the adaptation of the liturgy, an explicit mention and reference was made to the mission lands.[49] This would mean that Inculturation concerns such areas as Africa, Asia and Latin America, where evangelisation work had been wrongly carried out, and where there exists glaring evidence of the lack of integration of the faith with the cultural background. All along, it is assumed that, since some areas in western countries have already been evangelised, and therefore, being regarded as Christian areas, they are thought to have no need for Inculturation. But today, after the devastating and corrosive effects and

---

[48]"Culture, in relation to a people, can be compared to a radio and its 'frequency'. And just as a radio picks up every sound which is attuned to its frequency perfectly and with ease, and transmits the same clearly and strongly, so also can a people absorb the christian message and make it a part of themselves, provided this message is properly brought to them through the radio frequency of their culture." (PAUL C. EKOWA, This quotation is taken from the presentation of the thesis "The Background of Igbo Catholicism: A Historical Survey", on 28 April 1989).

[49]Cf., Vatican II, Sacrosanctum concilium, no.40.

influences which Modernism and secularisation with their related tendencies have had on these so-called christian lands, fresh and very serious questions are being raised, which establish the fact, rightly observed by Azevedo, that "these cultures cannot be responsibly considered as Christian any more. Most of the meanings, values, and current patterns that underlie their social practice and their symbolic level are certainly not in accordance with the meaning and values of the Gospel".[50] Consequently, Arrupe concludes,

> It is clear that the need for inculturation is universal. Until a few years ago one might have thought it was the concern only of countries or continents that were different from those in which the Gospel was assumed to have been inculturated for centuries. But the galloping pace of change in these latter areas . . . persuades us that there is need of a new and continuous inculturation of the faith everywhere if we want the gospel message to reach modern man and the new 'subcultural' groups. It would be a dangerous error to deny that these areas need a re-inculturation of the faith.[51]

So, then, the scope and need for inculturation is not limited to mission lands alone but is felt everywhere. However, seeing that today so many cultures are fast disappearing on account of urbanisation and modernising influences, a further question crops up: Inculturation into what? Into a culture that is disappearing, or an emerging culture, the forms of which are still only vaguely seen? In answer to this question, and with particular reference to Igbo culture, it must be recognised, as Azorji also pointed out, that "there is continuity and discontinuity of Igbo traditional beliefs - a continuity that has presented a burden to the authentic Christian inculturation, and a discontinuity that has betrayed our cultural identity and personality".[52] Besides, Chupungco draws attention to the fact that

> Adaptation does not mean returning to primitive or discarded ways. But neither does it mean futuristic approach or assumption of cultural forms that are still in the process of being assimilated. Adaptation refers to firmly established values and traditions which have shaped for many generations the religious, family, social and national life of the people. . . . it must seek stable cultural elements which the people can identify as their own.[53]

Therefore, the resultant culture for inculturation cannot but be the present-

---

[50]MARCELLO DE CARVALHO AZEVEDO, op. cit., p. 29.

[51]PEDRO ARRUPE, "Letter on Inculturation", Rome 1978, p. 2

[52]EUGENE E. AZORJI, op. cit., p. 38.

[53]ANSCAR J. CHUPUNGCO, op. cit., p. 77.

day culture. It has to be the cumulative culture of the society of today, standing at the cross-roads of the ancestral past, of colonial and neo-colonial history and of modern era. With reference to Africa, "it is this modern African person who seeks to cling to the person of Christ, not his ancestors. This means that any attempt at inculturation must take into account the real situation in which the African Christian lives".[54]

4.7   **Reasons for Inculturation**

Since the need for Inculturation is universally felt, one can adduce the following as the necessitating reasons:-
a)   The strongest and the most fundamental reason for Inculturation is the Incarnation of Christ. As Christ incarnated himself within the Jewish cultural background even to the point of anonymity of life[55], so the Church is expected to incarnate in every people and cultural background without being identified with any culture. This is because the Church is the prolongation in time and space of the same Incarnation of the Word of God. Inculturation is "a theological imperative arising from incarnational exigency".[56] It is not an option. The Church is aware of this fact, hence it is stated that the fundamental reason is for the Church to be able to "offer all men the mystery of salvation".[57] In realisation that Inculturation is an exigency of evangelisation, which is 'indispensable and urgent', Pope Paul VI emphasised:

> Evangelisation loses much of its force and effectiveness if it does not take into consideration the actual people to whom it is addressed, if it does not use their language, their signs and symbols, if it does not answer the questions they ask, and if it does not have an impact on their concrete life.[58]

b)   The Church evangelises culture because through it man achieves true and full humanity.[59] The Gospel message is addressed to the culture proper to each age. It must be recognised, as Ekwunife points out, that the only way to live one's life meaningfully in its manifold relationships is in and

---

[54]BILL KNIPE, "Inculturation in Africa" in Missi, December 1985, no. 476, p. 1.

[55]Cf., BRUNO MORICONI, "L'uomo Gesù di Nazareth", in AA.VV., Temi di Antropologia Teologica, Teresianum, Roma, 1981, p. 675.

[56]ANSCAR CHUPUNGCO, op. cit., p. 59.

[57]VATICAN II, Ad Gentes, no. 10.

[58]PAUL VI, Evangelii Nuntiandi, no.63.

[59]VATICAN II, Gaudium et Spes; no. 53.

through one's particular culture.[60]

c)   Besides, faith is a gift of God that demands a human response. Although faith is not culture, yet it demands inculturation in order to be expressed. Man responds to this faith by living the faith within his proper cultural context, and in the forms proper to his culture. If this faith is presented to him outside his cultural framework, the faith remains external. The obvious effect of this is lack of a commitment.

d)   Inculturation would make Christians feel at home and be permeated to the marrow by Christian values and ideals. To highlight this sense of feeling at home of Christians within their culture, A. Crollius writes:

> Thus, the purpose of inculturation is not to salvage a traditional culture, but rather to render present in the galloping process of change which affects all cultures the light and the life of the Gospel, so that each culture may become a worthy "habitat" of God's pilgrim people - a tent rather than a fortress - and an irradiating light that adds to the splendour of the entire cosmos.[61]

While inculturation would make Christians feel at home in their proper culture, the resultant effect is that Christianity ceases to be alien, but rather launches its roots deeply among any people.

e)   In his address to the College of Cardinals, Pope Paul VI enunciated another strong reason for inculturation. He said,

> The conditions of the society in which we live oblige all of us therefore to revise methods, to seek by every means to study how we can bring the Christian message that modern man can find the answer to his questions and the energy for his commitment of human solidarity.[62]

The conditions of the society which the Holy Father talks about is no other than the modern scientific mentality, which, in the words of Bishop Onaiyekan, "calls for an appropriate theological language, just as the diversity of cultures within the Church requires different formulations if all men are to hear the preaching about the marvels of God each in his own

---

[60]A. EKWUNIFE, "African Culture: A Definition", in CHIEA, Vol. 3, no. 3 (Sept.1987), p. 14.

[61]A. R. CROLLIUS, "Inculturation: Newness and Ongoing Process", in J. M. WALIGGO et al., op. cit., p. 65.

[62]PAUL VI, Evangelii Nuntiandi, no. 3, (a quotation of Address to the College of Cardinals, (22 June 1973), AAS 65 (1973) 383).

language. Cf. Acts, 2:11".[63] This is the dominant influence of modern societies called "secularism".[64]

f)   Another important reason for inculturation is to relax the strained tensions created by a lack of dialogue between Christianity and various cultures in various areas in the work of evangelisation.[65]

g)   The revival of traditional religion under the umbrella of culture in so many areas today in spite of all the modern negative influences, seriously acts as a pointer to the need for inculturation. It must be understood that religion is a very important, if not the central element, in culture. Its influence in any culture is immense.[66]

From all these reasons above, one agrees with the Holy Father that inculturation is indispensable and, therefore, urgent.

4.8   **Guiding Principles for Inculturation**

Except for its newness as a term, the practice of inculturation had existed in the Church since its origin. The first concrete problem that confronted the early Church, which led to the holding of the first Council of Jerusalem, and which opened the gates of Christianity to non-Jews, was a case of inculturation. It was also the question of inculturation when the Church had to be enfleshed in Hellenic linguistic framework in order to explain and formulate the doctrines of the faith and gain a foothold in Hellenistic lands. The history of the church reveals a lot of adaptational tendencies that have crystallised today into what is today referred to in liturgy as the Western Christian rituals. The underlying principle in all these tendencies and adaptations have been derived from the mystery of the Incarnation, even though at times substitutive and assimilative methods were employed. The mystery of the Incarnation, which is the source and reason

---

[63]JOHN ONAIYEKAN, "Why a New Era of Evangelization", in New Era of Evangelization, Seminar Proceedings on New Era of Evangelization organised by the Catholic Bishops Conference of Nigeria, 1-3 May 1984, p. 45.

[64]Cf. J. P. FITZPATRICK, op. cit., p. 181.

[65]In Igboland, such tensions exist between christian values and the traditional cultural values such as: polygamy, initiation rites, funeral rites, marriage rites, title-taking, oaths, osu, birth rites, with-craft, etc. Cf.,New Era of Evangelisation, p. 83.

[66]"Oggi, tuttavia, si pone particolare attenzione alle culture, perché appare con più chiarezza il nesso che unisce gli uomini con le culture in cui vivono e respirano . . . nessun soggetto umano potrebbe vivere e operare stando in opposizione con la cultura della società a cui appartiene". P ROSSANO, "Il Vangelo verso le culture e le religioni", in AA.VV.,Portare Cristo all'uomo, vol. 1, Studia Urbaniana, 22, Università Urbaniana, Roma, 1985, p. 73.

for all inculturation must also provide the guiding principle for carrying out the inculturation of the Christian faith in any culture. The same mode by which Christ entered the historical-cultural reality of a particular people, establishes the mode by which the Church continues this Incarnation into the various cultures in which it finds itself.[67]

By the Incarnation Christ became one of humanity in everything except sin (cf. Heb. 2:14-18; 4:15). Christ's identification with humanity even to the point of anonymity is an incontestable pillar of the dogma of the Incarnation.[68] As Eugene Hillman puts it:

> So Jesus of Nazareth is not a disguise used by God, not a human outer garment covering the divinity, not something foreign or extrinsic to what we are. He really is one of us, like ourselves in our everyday experience of life, circumscribed by the particularity of time, place, ethnicity and culture, while thinking, acting and loving with a human mind, will and heart.[69]

Any inculturation should, therefore, operate in this same manner. Taking off from the Incarnation, the mission of the Church is rightly taken to be the evangelisation of all cultures. In the principles enunciated in Evangelii Nuntiandi, the safeguard of the essentials of the Christian Faith and the necessary relationship between the local Churches and the Church Universal stand out very clear. The Pope pointed out that the individual Churches

> . . . have the task of assimilating the essence of the Gospel and of transposing it without the slightest betrayal of its essential truth . . .

He continued,

> But on the other hand evangelisation risks losing its power and disappearing altogether if one empties or adulterates its contents under the pretext of translating it, . . . one sacrifices this reality and destroys the unity without which there is no universality, out of a wish to adapt a universal reality to a local situation.[70]

---

[67]Cf. Vatican II, Ad Gentes, no.10.

[68]"Egli non è vissuto in un mondo irreale, ha realmente condiviso il mondo dell'uomo fino a chiudersi nell'anonimato di una vita che scorre al ritmo di un martello che batte e d'una sega che stride." BRUNO MORICONI, "L'uomo Gesù di Nazareth", in AA.VV., Temi di Antropologia Teologica, Teresianum, Roma, 1981, p. 675.

[69]EUGENE HILLMAN, "Missionary Approaches to African Cultures Today", in AFER, Vol. 22, no. 6 (Dec. 1980), p. 343.

[70]PAUL VI, Evangelii Nuntiandi, no. 63

These two points are to be specially taken note of in any inculturation. This means that, while inculturation would not be a superficial tacking-on of the Faith, but rather a penetration of the totality of culture,

> . . . it must not lose the universality of the Faith, but must be an expression of the essence of the faith in a particular cultural style, thus avoiding secession or helpless isolation, but conscious of the unity it shares with the variety of other cultural manifestations of the Faith.[71]

To safeguard this, therefore, the Church enunciated in <u>Sacrosanctum Concilium</u>, procedures for carrying out adaptations. It involves a thorough study with sympathy of the given culture by experts. The legitimate ecclesiastical authorities would recommend a proposal to the Holy See for approval. Before any approval, the Holy See grants a permission for experimentation of the proposal for some time. And then, finally comes the approval.[72] From this ecclesiastical stipulation emerge some points.

To carry out inculturation a deep knowledge and understanding of the faith is called for. If the essential doctrines of the faith would not be sacrificed, one ought to have a clear and distinct ideas of the fundamentals of the Christian Faith. It does not suffice just to have a common knowledge. It demands an expertise knowledge.

Moreover, a thorough study of the culture in question is of paramount importance. Since inculturation would deal with the permeation of the Christian message into the kernel of culture in order to animate it, a haphazard treatment of the culture is bound to remain on the periphery and can only yield a superficial fruit if any at all. It equally demands an expertise venture to penetrate the roots of any culture, being as it were so complex. In this aspect it would be ideal to enlist the active participation of men and women born and brought up in a culture. In many a culture, a penetration into the cultural roots is often not possible to strangers, except where these are intimately participant-observers. However, whoever may undertake the work of inculturation must have to take note of the essential qualities enlisted by Arrupe, which among other things include:

> . . . careful discernment to penetrate to the deepest meanings of the particular culture; and objectivity and interior humility which seek to transcend the grievances that persons may harbour because of previous mistreatment or injustice; persevering patience in order to avoid sterile polemics or "easy bargains with error"; . . .[73]

The supervisory role of the local ecclesiastical authorities is essential in inculturation. Without an openness and support from the authorities, all

---

[71]JOSEPH P. FITZPATRICK, <u>op. cit.</u>, p. 180-181.

[72]Cf.Vatican II, <u>Sacrosanctum Concilium</u>, nos 37-40.

[73]PEDRO ARRUPE, <u>op. cit.</u>, pp.261f.

efforts at inculturation would be in vain. As Chupungco points out, the Church leaders are not only to support the task of inculturation, but they are "to take the initiative, lay out the plan, lead and direct" it.[74]

On the basis of all these principles, inculturation would no more apply the method of evangelisation "which aimed at building christianity in a vacuum, having destroyed all that provided the preparatory roots in local cultures".[75] Instead, inculturation would be, in the very words of Azevedo,

> . . . a process of growth for the local christian community through the critical appraisal of its own culture. They would dig out the age-old "semina Verbi" as improved or perhaps as disfigured by their own cultural pilgrimage through generations. They would put aside meanings and values which were really felt to be irreconcilable with the christian message. In no way, however, would it be demanded of them that they renounce their cultural heritage and adopt foreign cultural patterns. Then, in the light of the christian message, they would eventually grasp the teleological orientation of their culture, its ultimate meaning.[76]

In these few lines an effort has been made to understand clearly what one is up to in talking of inculturation. This enquiry has equipped one with not only clear concepts, but also the reasons, dimensions, guides and principles for proceeding with our models in this work. After these observations one gets more convinced, and concludes with Chupungco, that "inculturation, properly done, is an ideal means of "Christianising" the entire culture, that is to say, of imbuing culture with the spirit of Christ and his Gospel".[77] However, inculturation is not an easy task.

In the subsequent section, the possibilities of inculturation within the rites of passage, especially among the Igbos, will be looked into.

---

[74]ANSCAR CHUPUNGCO, op. cit., p. 53.

[75]JOHN MARY WALIGGO, op. cit., p. 26.

[76]MARCELLO DE CARVALHO AZEVEDO, op. cit., p. 27.

[77]ANSCAR CHUPUNGCO, op. cit., p. 85.

CHAPTER 5

5   INCULTURATION OF THE RITES OF PASSAGE

5.1   **Choice of the Rites of Passage for Inculturation**

An individual normally passes through a natural cycle of birth, maturation, old age, and death. In whatever culture one looks at, life consists of successive motions from one stage to another, involving change from one status to another. The various phases in this passage from birth to death are generally crisis moments. In order to confront these moments with their corresponding crises, and ensure a successful transition from one to another, practically in every culture, people evolve a system of rites and ceremonies to punctuate and accompany these transitions, so that life's experience and tensions involved in them can be adequately dealt with. It is these rites that are referred to as the rites of Passage. It is the aspects of this phenomenon that has been chosen in this work to serve as sample for the Inculturation of the faith in the culture of the Igbos.

The choice of the rites of Passage is made after a thoughtful consideration of the fundamental facts about the Igbos, as well as from the motivations arising from the vivid facts laid bare by Mbiti when he writes,

> Africans like to celebrate life. They celebrate events in the life of the individual and the community. These include occasions like the birth of a child, the giving of names, circumcision and other initiation ceremonies, marriage, funerals, harvest festivals, praying for rain, and many others. Some of these rituals and ceremonies are done on a family basis, but others are observed by the whole community. They have a lot of religious meaning, and through their observation religious ideas are perpetuated and passed on to the next generations.[1]

The Community psychological mentality of the Igbos, which has been treated above, is another major factor that prompts the choice of the rites of passage. It is through the rites of passage that the individual is incorporated into his traditional community.

After seven years of intensive Apostolate and experience of a thickly

---

[1] J. S. MBITI, Introduction to African Religion, Heinemann, London, 1975, p. 19

populated section of Igboland, one has come to a conviction that the nerve centre of the Igbo culture is intricately intertwined with the rites and ceremonies connected with the transitional phases in life of the Igbo. About seventy-five per cent of the cultural problems confronting Christianity in Igboland is centred on the rites and ceremonies connected with the crises moments in life. During these moments of crises, the Igbo Christian finds himself drifting between the double roles of trying to be loyal to his traditional foundations, as well as standing for the Christian cause, whose demands he tries to meet up as long as, and only if the traditional community and its cultural obligations do not stand on his way. The very moment one meets with obstacles, it becomes quite clear that his convinced and fundamental roots are in the traditional system. This is the point which Arinze alludes to as he remarks:

> In moments of difficulty in life, whether it is death or sickness, in his life-cycle event, birth of a child, matrimony, burials and funerals of relatives, building or constructing of a modern house, in trade as well as in socio-political life, the Igbo have not completely left the practice of traditional religion.[2]

So, the transitional rites and ceremonies can be seen as the pressure moments of the Igbo culture. They are the awareness periods in the propagation and transmission of the culture. One strongly believes that unless an inroad is made into the culture through these nerve centres and stress moments, by gainfully employing them in the process of the inculturation of the faith, the double and parallel-roads existence will continue to characterise Igbo Christianity. One considers the awareness moments as very important for the Inculturation of the faith.

Through the transitional rites, which concern not only antenatal and postnatal infants, children, youths, adults, old people, but also even the dead, the cultural involvement of these levels of existence is demanded. Every individual passes through these various stages in any given culture, whether the stages are specially ritualised or not in the culture.

It is therefore the intricacy and the overriding value of the rites of Passage for the Igbos that prompt our choice. They are considered the necessary wave-lengths in the transmission of Igbo culture. By their means, an entrance is gained into the heart of Igbo Culture. If the Christian Faith must have a meaning for the people, it must have to penetrate this heart of Culture as a fertile seed, in order to germinate and flourish in the transformation of the traditional modal structure of the Igbos. Shorter reminds us here that the theology of the Multicultural Church is "the recognition that faith must become culture, if it is to be fully received and

---

[2]FRANCIS CARD. ARINZE, "L'incarnazione del Vangelo nelle culture", in <u>Studi Cattolica</u>, no. 290/91, 1985, p. 245

lived".[3]

There may be other alternative ways of bringing the faith into a culture, for instance, as has hitherto been done in Igboland. Such methods, however, have always left the faith on the periphery, since it remains external to the culture of the people. If inculturation is the rooting of the Christian message within the cultural values of a people, in order that the faith regenerate and bring forth fruits among the Igbos, one thinks of no other deeper and surer way than to go through the fundamental traditional values, which for the Igbos, are the transitional rites and seek to transform and perfect them. Such an inroad may even ensure the exposure of these platforms of culture to a continuous enculturative impact, which, as Herskovits observed, "is not terminated at the close of infancy. As an individual continues through childhood and adolescence to achieve adult status, he is continuously exposed to this process of learning, which can be said to end only with his death".[4]

One may preempt the characteristics of rites of passage, and see the Christian Faith in Igboland passing through a structural transition. In this sense, one discovers that the faith has already passed through the separation phase, when there was nothing whatsoever to do with Igbo Culture, and which stage has led to the present transition moment, which is marked by the present discussion for inculturation. It is hoped that with Inculturation the Christian Faith would incarnate among the Igbos.

5.2 **The Rites of Passage**

It was the Greek philosopher, Heraclitus, who observed and propounded that all is involved in change. Scarcely is there any being that is exempt from this constant change and motion. This philosophical observation was anthropologically orientated by Van Gennep, who sees everybody as individuals and as groups being involved in a transition. He observed,

> For groups, as well as for individuals, life itself means to separate and to be reunited, to change form and condition, to die and to be reborn. It is to act and to cease, to wait and rest, and then to begin acting again, but in a different way. And there are always new thresholds to cross: the threshold of summer and winter, of a season or a year, of a month or a night; the threshold of birth, adolescence, maturity, and old age; the threshold of death and that of the afterlife - for those who

---

[3]AYLWARD SHORTER, Toward A Theology of Inculturation, Orbis Books, Maryknoll, New York, 1988, p. xi

[4]M. J. HERSKOVITS, Man and His Works, New York, 1952, p. 40

believe in it.[5]

Gennep sees life as involving a series of passages from one age to another and movement from one occupation to another. He sees regeneration as a law of life and of the universe. In human beings, this fact becomes very pronounced. One observes a successive transition from the existential stages of birth to childhood, puberty, marriage, pregnancy, fatherhood, old age, death and ultimate funeral. In fact, the universe itself is governed by a periodicity which has repercussions on human life, with stages and transitions, movements forward and periods of relative inactivity. Even from the natural point of view, one observes a successive change in time from second to minute, from minute to hour, from hour to day, from day to week, from week to month, from month to season, from season to year, and so on. So, from these facts of change Gennep concludes,

> Transitions from group to group and from one social situation to the next are looked on as implicit in the very fact of existence, so that a man's life comes to be made up of a succession of stages with similar ends and beginnings: birth, social puberty, marriage, fatherhood, advancement to a higher class, occupational specialization, and death. For every one of these events there are ceremonies whose essential purpose is to enable the individual to pass from one defined position to another which is equally well defined.[6]

In all spheres, be it on the human or on the cosmic level, the change occasions a period of anxiety and uncertainty as well as danger both for the subject of the change and for all those around. As a result, these changes are marked and accompanied by ceremonies and rituals, whose purpose is to ensure that the transitions are successfully made, and to cushion the disturbances involved. Van Gennep calls these ceremonies the Rites of Passage. They aim at mitigating any attendant evil and disturbing effects.

But Rites of passage are "rites which accompany every change of place, state, social position and age". So they are not only one dimensional. There are also rites of passage, which are of a sociological and temporal nature. In this sense there are calendrical rites, whose aim is to ensure success and prosperity in the future, or to protect against danger and failure which could harm crops or animals. Rites of purely social nature exist such as the rites to mark the accession of power by a king. Gennep enumerates in his book various examples of such rites[7], whose details purpose and

---

[5]ARNOLD VAN GENNEP, The Rites of Passage, The university of Chicago Press, 1960, pp. 189-190

[6]Ibid., p. 3

[7]Ibid., pp. 18-25

space do not permit us here to treat. Generally, there are rites to mark the passage from scarcity to plenty - the first fruit festival, change from one state to another, movements between statuses, entry into new status, entrance into a political office or membership of an exclusive club or secret society. In each of these passages there are always accompanying rites. They all share one common characteristic. Their types determine their structural dimension. They can be simple especially when they are profane or civil rites. However, when an interplay of the sacred and the profane is involved, they can be very complex and intricate.

The purpose of this work constrains the restricted use of the term 'rites of passage' to mean the life-crises rites for the ritualization of stages in the life of an individual. Our treatment of the rites of passage is limited to the level which Lloyd Warner describes as

> . . . the movement of a man through his life time, from a fixed placental placement within his mother's womb to his death and ultimate fixed point of his tombstone and final containment in his grave as a dead organism - punctuated by a number of critical moments of transition which all societies ritualize and publicly mark with suitable observances to impress the significance of the individual and the group on the living members of the community. These are the important times of birth, puberty, marriage, and death.[8]

Our interest lies then in the ceremonies organised around the individual from the cradle to the grave. Rites of passage in our restricted sense concern the ceremonies through which an individual passes on all the most important occasions of his life. In cultures of semi-civilised peoples, such changes in life, as observed by Van Gennep,

> are enveloped in ceremonies, since to the semicivilized mind no act is entirely free of the sacred. In such societies every change in a person's life involves actions and reactions between sacred and profane - actions and reactions to be regulated and guarded so that society as a whole will suffer no discomfort or injury.[9]

It is the interaction between the profane and the sacred in some certain cultures that makes it more imperative to establish rituals in these moments of crises for the individual. And everyone is bound to follow the traditional rituals on account of their obligatory nature. It is only where a transformation has taken place, such as a revaluation consequent on a

---

[8] W. LLOYD WARNER, The Living and the Dead, New Haven; Yale University Press, 1959, p. 303

[9] A. VAN GENNEP, op. cit., p. 3

dialogical approach from a new religion in the place, as when an inculturation of the faith has taken place, that new rituals can replace the old traditional system. It has to be recalled that "the whole corpus of ideas evoked in ritual is the traditional knowledge of a society".[10] This accounts for the difficulties encountered, when one who has a religion different from that practised in his cultural ambient, tries to hold aloof from the obligatory established procedures and rituals of the society. Speaking of the obligatory nature of the rites, Mircea Eliade points out that,

> These "transition rites" are obligatory for all the youth of the tribe. To gain the right to be admitted among adults, the adolescent has to pass through a series of initiatory ordeals: it is by virtue of these rites, and of the revelations that they entail, that he will be recognized as a responsible member of the society.[11]

This work is geared towards surveying the possibilities for inculturation of the faith in the Igbo Rites of Passage. That is why it is essential to look at the structure of the Rites of Passage.

5.2.1 Structure and Characteristics of Rites of Passage

In any rite of passage, three basic structures are involved. Ordinarily any passage involves a point of departure - the terminus a quo, a movement, and a point of arrival - the terminus ad quem. So also in any rite of passage there are three stages - the previous status, the actual passing, and the new acquired status. Van Gennep calls these stages: separation, transition and incorporation. He prefers to call the rites accompanying these stages the preliminal, liminal, and postliminal rites. The threefold structure connotes the idea of previous separation - at times referred to as death, then the crossing of a threshold - transition, and an eventual reunion with a new situation - compared to a resurrection. The first stage of Separation consists of 'symbolic behaviour signifying the detachment of the individual or group either from an earlier fixed point in the social structure or a set of cultural conditions'.[12] During this period, one is isolated from the group. This is followed by a period of merger, which sees the individual undergoing a public ritual that accords him a new status. This

---

[10] J. S. LA FONTAINE, Initiation, Manchester University Press, Great Britain, 1986, p. 15

[11] MIRCEA ELIADE, Rites and Symbols of Initiation, Harper & Row Publishers, New York, 1958, p. x

[12] VICTOR TURNER, The Forest of Symbols, Cornell University Press, London, p. 94

stage signals a crossing of the threshold - a uniting oneself with a new world such as in marriage. Then finally one is integrated into the society as a changed and new person.

Although the three stages characterise rites of passage, yet they are not always equally important or elaborate in every rite. For instance, while rites of separation are prominent in funeral ceremonies, transitional rites play a prominent role in the ceremonies during pregnancy, betrothal and initiation; and rites of incorporation may be prominent in marriages.

The obligatory nature of the rites in the society has already been hinted above. It is noteworthy that, especially in semi-civilised society, societal groups and sections are carefully isolated, and a passage from one to another must be made through formalities and ceremonies. As Van Gennep points out in a symbolic manner,

> An individual or group that does not have an immediate right, by birth or through specially acquired attributes, to enter a particular house and to become established in one of its sections is in a state of isolation. . . . such a person is weak, because he is outside a given group or society. . . [13]

By this, all who do not participate in the rites remain outside the traditional system, and are therefore regarded as strangers. Such people are not accepted in the community and therefore have no place nor active voice in the goings-on in the society. Some consider such people who need to be brought into the system as polluting and from the remark concerning such polluting transitional individuals, the obligation and necessity of the rites shine clear. Turner writes:

> . . . one would expect to find that transitional beings are particularly polluting, since they are neither one thing nor another; or may be both; or neither here nor there; or may even be nowhere (in terms of any recognized cultural topography), and are at the very least "betwixt and between" all the recognized fixed points in space-time of structural classification.[14]

In other words, one who has not undergone or is about to undergo the rites are taken for no-status citizens having nothing, no property, rank, kinship position, nothing to demarcate them structurally from their fellows. They are indefinite, and neutral, having no identity, and therefore, are more often than not segregated, from the realm of culturally defined and ordered states and statuses. "They have physical but no social reality, hence they have to be hidden, since it is a paradox, a scandal, to see what ought not to be

---

[13]A. VAN GENNEP, op. cit., p. 26

[14]V. TURNER, op. cit., p. 97

146

there".[15]

One has to consider this point in order to understand the reasons for the pressure towards inculturation of the faith in this direction. Under this circumstance, how can the Christian stay aloof from the traditional system? Inculturation in this direction will open up an avenue and the possibility for the Christian to be in the helm of affairs in the traditional system.

Another feature noteworthy in the rites of passage is the fact that in the transitional rites, especially at the liminal stage of the initiation rite, the relationship between the instructors and neophytes is that of complete authority and complete submission. It is no doubt, then, that after the transitional experience one tends to hold on tenaciously to the traditions of the land. One would see the liminal stage in any of the rites as strategic. It is the elders who are the instructors of the neophytes, and as Turner further points out,

. . . it must be understood that the authority of the elders over the neophyte is not based on legal sanctions; it is in a sense the personification of the self evident authority of tradition. The authority of elders is absolute, because it represents the absolute, the axiomatic values of society in which are expressed 'the common good' and the common interest.[16]

Especially after the rite of initiation, the allegiance of the initiated to the traditional system and way of life is tremendous. From the impressions left in the minds of the initiated, the authority of the elders stand absolute and ought not to be debated upon. The effect of such impressions are permanent as Turner still elucidates:

The arcane knowledge or 'gnosis' obtained in the liminal period is felt to change the inmost nature of the neophyte, impressing him, as a seal impresses wax, with the characteristics of his new state. It is not a mere acquisition of knowledge, but a change in being. His apparent passivity is revealed as an absorption of powers which will become active after his social status has been redefined in the aggregational rites.[17]

The great importance attached to the liminal period results from its salient moment of reflection on the society, for,

During the liminal period, neophytes are alternately forced and encouraged to think about their society, their cosmos, and the powers that generate and sustain them. . . . In it, those ideas,

[15]Ibid.

[16]Ibid., pp. 99-100

[17]Ibid., p. 102

sentiments, and facts that had been hitherto for the neophytes bound up in configurations and accepted unthinkingly are, as it were, resolved into their constituents. These constituents are isolated and made into objects of reflection for the neophytes by such processes as componential exaggeration and dissociation by varying concomitant.[18]

5.2.2 **Role and Importance of Rituals**

Man consciously or unconsciously performs series of actions and behaviours sometimes accompanied by words, and may even at face value seem irrational, yet are replete with symbolic meanings. Man shakes hands, manifests signs of greetings, gives a kiss or an embrace. Our daily life is replete with such actions. Sometimes their intrinsic connection to the spiritual realities may be perceived, or they may be hidden to an outsider. Such actions can be private or public like the state ceremonial of laying wreath to the unknown soldier, or the match-past parade, or even the going on ward-round by a nurse in the hospital. All these fall into the same category which we refer to as rituals. A ritual is defined as a stereo-typed sequence of activities involving gestures, words, and objects, performed in a sequestered place, and designed to influence preternatural entities or forces on behalf of the actors goals and interests.[19] Rituals are staged events that follow a standard protocol whenever they are performed. They are social actions that require a group participation, through which transitions are structured, and which provide markers for bringing an individual into a new status. Rites owe their social nature from the fact that it is done by a society. It is within the life of a cultural community that rites develop and are assigned their meaning. It is really the tradition of the cultural community that give the rites their form and meaning. Therefore, the tradition of a people is looked upon as the legitimate binding force of the ritual.

Although rituals are social actions, yet each ritual is characteristically bound up with the sacred, since the crucial moments that are dealt with by rituals are sacred moments. Rite is typically a human action, bound up with word as human expression, which is of its nature profoundly religious. As Louis Bouyer clarifies

A Rite is precisely an action in which man feels himself active in a divine action: what man does is a divine action; it is an action which God performs through him, in him, in such a way

---

[18]Ibid., p. 105

[19]VICTOR TURNER, "Symbols in African Ritual", in JANETH L. DOLGIN et al., eds., Symbolic Anthropology, Columbia University Press, New York, 1977, p. 183

that he performs it in God by means of God.[20] (Free Translation from the italian version)

Liam Walsh thinks of rites as

> instances of that irrepressible human instinct to imitate and dramatise things or events or persons that are important for human life, to remember and to recreate them symbolically at certain times and in certain places.[21]

The major importance of rituals lies in the fact that they affect such critical moments in life as exemplified in the transitional stages of an individual by a controlling effect so that life's experience and tension in them can be adequately dealt with and brought under control. As La Fontaine puts it,

> Events and developments of the life-cycle constantly involve changes in conditions which do not occur without disturbing the life of society and the individual, and it is the function of rites of passage to reduce their harmful effects.[22]

It is this function that offers the reasons for the rites of passage.

Another value of rituals consists in their solidarity reinforcement of the community. This finds expression in the assertion made by Emil Durkheim, who saw rituals even though as religious actions, yet recognised that they are the 'means of reviving and strengthening the basic moral precepts on which social life is founded and endowing them with a compelling authority which appeared to derive from outside each participant'.[23] This value in rituals portrays some psychological effect, which compels people to participate in the rituals, especially in cultures characterised by community solidarity and common belonging. Walsh recognises this fact, hence he affirms:

> Rites and stories hold communities together and point them towards their future. As a group of people becomes self conscious and protective about its identity, its stories and rites become official.[24]

---

[20]LOUIS BOUYER, Il Rito e L'uomo, Morcelliana, 1964, p. 76

[21]LIAM G. WALSH, The Sacraments of Initiation, Geoffrey Chapman, London, p. 2

[22]J. S. LA FONTAINE, op. cit., p. 27

[23]Cf. J. S. LA FONTAINE, op. cit., pp. 23-24

[24]L. WALSH, op. cit., p. 3

Hence rites tend to ensure the stability and homogeneity of a cultural group. This leads one to the possible dynamism of rituals. It has already been established that rites owe their structural origin to the tradition of the land. The guardians and custodians of the tradition claim authority in stipulating the rites. The possibility of effecting a change in rituals depends on such authorities. As Walsh clearly points out,

> If those who control rites and their story lack the will or the imagination to see that life is never an exact repetition of the past but a continuity in change, they will cut the rites off from real life and thus destroy their value.[25]

La Fontaine describes the thinking of such custodians of traditions as conservative, in that they conceive of rituals as

> the property of the ancestors, the founders of all social life. It must be handed on, not tested, altered, improved, or even discarded. Since it supports experience and validates the seniority of elders, it is not surprising if they throw the weight of their secular powers behind it.[26]

Where rituals are conceived in this immobile and conservative way, they become so fossilised along with their cultural community. The forces of change are, however, so strong that rituals more often than not, get involved along with the change in culture, which has already been considered as dynamic. The reasons for ritual involvement in change is quite obvious.

> New generations with new life-experiences have to be told in a new way how the rite can have a bearing on their lives. Otherwise they will not find in the rite a way of dealing with the crucial moments of their life and a way of making appropriate choices about them. When rites and the words that go with them are not affecting choices about the serious issues of life they gradually lose their status, first for individuals, and eventually for a whole people. They drift towards being fable and folklore, while life begins to look elsewhere for way of dealing with its crucial moments and expressing its goals.[27]

As a result of this, new chances are offered for the introduction of new stories and new rites. 'Since societies are processes responsive to change,

---

[25]Ibid., p. 4

[26]J. S. LA FONTAINE, op. cit., p. 189

[27]L. WALSH, op. cit., p. 4

not fixed structures, new rituals are devised or borrowed'.[28] This is exactly the case in such cultures where a new religious affiliation threatens and disorientates the traditional religious beliefs. In such a situation, one finds great chances for Inculturation. Here lies directly our interest in talking of rituals in this work.

5.2.3 **The Individual Rites of Passage**

The limits of our interest in the study of the Rites of Passage is within the life-cycle stages of human existence. It is essential to look at the structure of each stage in the life-span of the individual.

First and foremost, an individual is conceived and born a child in the human family. One grows to be a teenager, an adolescent, and an adult respectively. At first one remains single, but may perhaps later on get married. With advancement in age one gets old, and ultimately dies, and is accorded a funeral rite which launches one into the next life. Directly corresponding to and accompanying these stages are the transitional rites of birth, puberty, marriage, old age and funeral. Although a more detailed study of only two of these life-cycle rites is envisaged in this work, yet it is worthwhile to take a look at the structure of each of the stages in general.

As has been hinted above, it is always difficult if not impossible in all cultures for an individual to enter any of these stages or statuses in life, or pass from one to another without participating in some sort of ceremony that serves to set the status apart from the others. It has also been observed that the rites perform the function of announcing to the society at large the nature and justification of the change in the status of an individual, as well as guide the individual on how better to readjust oneself in the new status. This, as has been explained, is a sort of shock absorber both for the individual and for the society.

In all the rites, the three fundamental structure and characteristics - separation, transition and incorporation are noticeable. The classical work of Van Gennep furnishes a valuable insight into the essential structure of these rites. As such, the work would serve as a major source of information in getting an insight into the general survey of the rites in each stage.

5.2.3.1 **The Birth Rites**

Life is generally considered as a gift of God in every culture. The arrival of a child, therefore, signals a sort of interaction between the divine and the human worlds. As such, this entrance and the eventual reception of the gift of life is always ritualised. In practically all societies, the stages

---

[28]V. TURNER, "Symbols in African Ritual", p.184

of Pregnancy and birth of a child is thickly punctuated with rites, since these stages mark the real entrance of a new human being into the human community. Such rites are highly regarded since they celebrate the veritable instances of the interpenetration of the sacred into the profane. Birth is a transition from the world preceding life to actual existence. Van Gennep includes the following aspects as constituting the childhood rites:- the cutting of the umbilical cord, first sprinkling with water and bath, loss of the remainder of the umbilical cord, naming ceremony, first hair cut, first meal of the family, first teeth, first walk, first outing, circumcision, and first dressing according to the child's sex.[29] Most societies have birth rites for individual and social reasons. Primarily, such rites serve the function of facilitating delivery and protecting both mother and child from the evil forces that may surround the events of birth. The rites, according to Van Gennep,

> are intended not only to neutralise an impurity or to attract sorcery to themselves but to serve as actual bridges, chains, or links - in short, to facilitate the changing of condition without social disruption or an abrupt cessation of individual and collective life.[30]

Another strong reason for the rites at this stage is of a social nature. It has been said that rites help to boost the communitarian solidarity of a cultural group. "Not only is the new born child considered 'sacred', but it is believed that he can be born only after he has obtained the favour of all those present."[31] As a result, the new life must be accorded a social recognition, be given a social identity, and become a member of the society. These two major reasons may be expressed through various rituals, as enumerated above.

Following the general structure of rites of passage, the three aspects of separation, transition, and incorporation are observable in the various rites of this stage. As Gennep describes it,

> Often the first rites performed separate the pregnant woman from society, from her family group, and sometimes even from her sex. They are followed by rites pertaining to pregnancy itself, which is a transitional period. Finally comes the rites of childbirth intended to integrate the woman into the groups to which she previously belonged . . . [32]

Much importance is attached to some of the rites of this stage on account

---

[29]ARNOLD VAN GENNEP, op. cit., p. 62.

[30]Ibid., p. 48.

[31]Ibid., p. 50.

[32]Ibid., p. 41.

of their significance. For instance, the naming rites signify the individuation of the child and its incorporation into the society. The purification rite serves an integrational function for the mother. It marks the social and physical return of the woman from childbirth and her incorporation into the normal societal groups and roles. This, in the Church circles, is equated with the 'Churching' ceremony. The circumcision, which is the cutting off of the foreskin of the sexual organs, is an act of social importance. It is a rite of separation from asexual world or from the world preceding human society and the rites of incorporation into the society of the sexes, and into the nuclear or extended family, clan or tribe.[33] In some societies, especially in the Muslim circles, circumcision is more a test of virility and a marker of young adult status than a point of entry into participation in the community,[34] while in the Jewish society, it is a mark of membership in a single community of the faithful. In some societies, where circumcision is performed for fertility purposes, the rites are celebrated at a later part of life, and serves as a prelude to marriage during the initiation stage.

One outstanding feature of these rites is the fact that they demand a societal celebration, involving not only the families of the child but the entire village community. This should be borne in mind when one speaks of Inculturation in this regard, since it serves to firmly place the new individual in the traditional context of his society.

5.2.3.2   **The Initiation Rites**

When one speaks of Initiation rites, three distinct aspects come to mind. The first aspect, which serves our purpose in the study of the life-cycle transitional rites, deals with the rituals whose function is to effect the transition from childhood or adolescence to adulthood, and which are obligatory for all members of a particular society. It is to this aspect that such terminologies as puberty rites, tribal initiations, or initiation into an age-group are applied. It is important to make a distinction between physical puberty and social puberty. One can grow to physical maturity without being yet recognised by his society as mature. While physical puberty can be early or late depending on the natural and genetical factors of an individual, social puberty is dependent on the social celebration and recognition through the rite of initiation.

The two other aspects that come into the concept of initiation concern the reception rituals into secret societies or groups or confraternity, as well as the rituals requisite for obtaining a higher religious status. These two forms are not of obligatory nature to all members of a society.

---

[33]A. VAN GENNEP, Ibid., p.52.

[34]The Encyclopedia of religion, 1987 ed., s.v. "Rites of Passage: Muslim Rites", by Dale F. Eickelman.

Whichever aspect one looks at, the same structure and essential features are common to all of them. They all share the tripartite form which is fundamental in all rites of passage.

Initiation to adulthood is an important rite of a mandatory nature, in the transformation of an individual into the fully social adult. As Mircea Eliade clearly observes,

> These rites are obligatory for all the youth of the tribe. To gain the right to be admitted among adults, the adolescence has to pass through a series of initiatory ordeals: it is by virtue of these rites, and of the revelation that they entail, that he will be recognised as a responsible member of the society. Initiation introduces the candidate into the human community and into the world of spiritual and cultural values.[35]

Hence, all uninitiated persons are contemptuously disregarded in the society. Through Initiation a social identity, 'a sense of social-emotional anchorage for the growing individual is established.[36] It is the initiation rites that establish a distinction between childhood and adult status, which is not dependent on physiological development but on social recognition through the community rituals.

Both males and females undergo initiation rites, though each according to its own platform. Male initiations, being more developed, widespread, and of a collective nature, are given very prominent and public attention, while that of females are more of individual ceremonies. The female initiation rite consists of the revelation of the sacrality of women and is intended to ritually prepare the young girl to assume her specific mode of being, which for Eliade means "to become a creatress, and at the same time is taught her responsibilities in society and in cosmos, responsibilities which among primitives, are always religious in nature".[37] There is in the female rite a solemn exhibition of the girl to the entire community - a ceremonial announcement that the girl is mature for her female roles as a woman.

Mircea Eliade gives an insight into the structure of the initiation rites. There is, first and foremost, the general preparation of the sacred Ground where the novices will be isolated during the ritual period. Then the novices are separated from their maternal comforting protection, which they have hitherto enjoyed, and ultimately isolated in the bush, where they are to be instructed into the religious and mythical traditions of the tribe. Then the novices will undergo some types of ordeals, which along with the secret ceremonies, which are interpreted to imply a ritual death that eventually leads to a sort of resurrection to a new life.

---

[35] MIRCEA ELIADE, Rites and Symbols of Initiation, p. x.

[36] Cf.J. S. LA FONTAINE, op. cit., p. 106.

[37] M. ELIADE, op. cit., p. 42.

154

Characterising initiation rituals are the role played by such features as secrecy, oaths, and tests or ordeals. Secrecy may not necessarily serve as an important feature in all initiations. Only in rituals of initiation into secret society or secret groups are they of paramount importance. One observes that such secret societies are characterised by their concern for secret knowledge, which may be accompanied by covert or subversive and even nefarious activities. In such cases secrecy plays a fundamental role. But ordinarily speaking, with reference to initiation for acquiring adult status, even though some of the rituals may be secretly performed and the knowledge transmitted to the individual is jealously held as exclusive only to the initiated, secrecy does not necessarily enter into the essential features of the initiation rituals.

Oath-taking is one of the aspects of the rites of initiation. The oaths may not necessarily be solemn and of equal importance in all forms of initiation ceremonies. They can even be only simple acts and mechanisms which compel the initiate to recognise the new state and obligations. They signify a commitment, since oaths generally serve the purpose of committing the individual "binding him or her to other members, and its breaking usually involves powerful sanctions; these may be misfortune or even death, whether at the hands of the group itself, or through some supernatural agency".[38] However, oaths are not necessarily parts of ordinary initiation rituals. In the rituals of initiation into secret societies, they are very important and are solemnly considered since the individual must be bound to preserve the secrecy of the group.[39]

Test and ordeals accompany the initiation rites. They are physical exercises of very terrifying nature, and are meant to test the ability of the initiate to endure hardships and manifest bravery in the face of life's difficulties.[40] They are, therefore, considered as physical signs of maturity. Such tests and ordeals can take the form of accepting scars on the body, being thoroughly whipped, tattooing, fasting etc. and in some areas, circumcision is a part of the ordeals. Even though these are physical exercises, they assume some spiritual dimension, as Mircea Eliade explains,

> . . . the various physical ordeals also have a spiritual meaning. The neophyte is at once prepared for the responsibilities of adult life and progressively awakened to the life of the spirit. For the ordeals and restrictions are accompanied by instruction through myths, dances, pantomimes. The physical ordeals

---

[38]LA FONTAINE, op. cit., p. 16.

[39]". . . initiates have died rather than reveal what they have promised to keep secret, . . ." -LA FONTAINE, op. cit., p. 40.

[40]"Courage and fortitude are developed by these tests, and they often alter the individual's physical appearance, lifting the natural creature to cultured human." - ROBERT F. MURPHY, Cultural and Social Anthropology, Prentice-Hall, inc., Englewood Cliffs, New Jersey, 1986, p. 188.

have a spiritual goal - to introduce the youth into the tribal culture, to make him "open" to spiritual values.[41]

One would consider the ordeals in their physically indifferent forms very healthy and commendable. They are oriented towards the cultivation of manly qualities such as courage, endurance, perseverance and obedience.

The tribal community utilises the moment of initiation as a formal traditional education of the initiates. Through this platform the traditional mysteries, history and mythical foundations of the community as well as personal secrets of human life are unveiled to the neophytes.[42] Evaluating the educative aspect of initiation rite, Eliade remarks:

> Learning how things came into existence, the novice at the same time learns that he is the creation of Another, the result of such-and-such a primordial event, the consequence of a series of mythological occurrences, in short, of a sacred history. This discovery that man is part and parcel of a sacred history which can be communicated only to initiates constitutes the point of departure for a long-continued flowering of religious forms.[43]

From the structure of the initiation rites, it is obvious that religious values come into play. Although initiation has more of cultural importance in the sense that it is through this that one begins to participate in the culture into which one is born, yet it involves the religious life of the individual. The individual through initiation gains an awareness and access to the spiritual values and religious life of the community. It opens one's way to the tribal mythological and cultural traditions.

It is important to note that initiation rite is a traditional ceremony that involves the whole tribe. While a new generation is introduced and integrated into the community, it is also by implication a re-actualization and regeneration of the entire community. From solidarity point of view, each successive initiation ceremony reinforces the community since it introduces new members into the community of adults, and through the rites the entire community is regenerated and reinforced. It is this factor that makes initiation rituals in some societies, as Eliade testifies, the most important of religious festivals. Attempts at inculturation in this direction is bound to yield maximum dividend.

---

[41]M. ELIADE, op. cit., p. 16.

[42]"Instruction is also given in ethical and social obligations in law and in kinship rules, and in technology to fit neophytes for the duties of future office." - V. TURNER, The Forest of Symbols, p. 103.

[43]M. ELIADE, op. cit., pp. 19-20.

5.2.3.3 **The Marriage Rites**

Once an individual has been formally introduced and exposed into the public awareness of the cultural society through the initiation rites, the individual is henceforth recognised as a mature member of the community. The next obvious expectation for the individual as well as the most eloquent sign of his maturity is the entrance into the marriage status. Marriage is the means adopted by the human society for regulating the relation between sexes. The rites of marriage constitute one of the major transitional rites of an individual on his earthly pilgrimage. Van Gennep sees Marriage even as the

> . . . most important of the transitions from one social category to another, because for at least one of the spouses it involves a change of family, clan, village, or tribe, and sometimes the newly married couple even establish residence in a new house.[44]

The transitional character of marriage clearly appears, as he further describes,

> To marry is to pass from the group of children or adolescents into the adult group, from a given clan to another, from one family to another, and often from one village to another. An individual's separation from these groups weakens them but strengthens those he joins.[45]

Since marriage marks a crossing from the stage of adolescence to assume a marital status, in nearly every culture, no matter how complex it is, such a transition is accompanied by a ceremonial ritual. The rituals have always the fundamental features of rites of passage. There are the separation aspects characterised in various cultures by the betrothal period. During this period, the two individuals wishing to marry each other, single themselves out from their normal and ordinary accustomed friendship circles, and spend their time on each other in an intimate and interested type of way. The betrothal stage forms a period prior to marriage that permits the parties to associate intimately and fairly constantly, ensuring that they are suited for each other. In fact, it is a trial period for them.

> It provides time prior to the definite commitment and the assumption of responsibilities to fuse interests and identities and for each to accommodate to the other in a movement

---

[44]V. VAN GENNEP, op. cit., p. 116.

[45]Ibid., p. 124.

away from the romantic attraction to a more conjugal relationship.[46]

This stage is followed by a real transitional ritual, which commits the couple to each other. Then, come the elaborate rites of individual union, according to the cultural stipulations of the society in question. The rites are always specific and very symbolic. The incorporational aspects, which normally forms the stage and the background of the actual liminal transitional ritual, is often commensalistic in nature. Aggregation and feasting together are always veritable expressions and concomitant of important events in social life. It is, however, the transitional ritual of individual union which marks the end of all marital negotiations, and the most significant of all the ritual aspects.

The rites which celebrate marriage vary greatly in duration and complexity in various cultures. While in some societies these rituals are so fragmentary that they are hardly considered existent, in other societies, they are so elaborate, diverse and complex that they can even last for weeks or months. It is interesting to note that while marriage ceremonies may be seen as social events, they always have both religious and economic implications and involvements. These dimensions even dictate at times, the pace of the entire social aspects. For instance, there are always in every marriage economic transactions such as the fixing of the bride price and the dowry. In every marriage, objects are transmitted from friends of one partner to those of the other. More important, however, especially for our discussion is the religious dimension of marriages. A religious ritual always accompanies the symbolic and actual transitional act of marriage. The religious ritual celebrates and ratifies the very symbolic union of the two young people. The symbolic union may even assume a simply social nature as joining hands, intertwining the fingers, kissing, embracing, pressing their heads against each other, giving or exchanging belts, bracelets, or rings or clothes, binding one to the other with a cord, offering the other something to eat or drink, eating together, seating on the same seat, drinking from the same liquid or container etc.[47] There are, however, symbolic acts that suggest a religious character. In this light should be seen such acts as eating together, pouring of rice or wheat on the head of the bride, imparting of paternal blessings and prayers for the couple - these acts have for their motive - the desire to promote the fertility of the union or ensure abundance of food for the household.

There are rites which allay the fears of inherent danger attendant upon entrance into the marital state. These rites are always regarded as very important for the marriage, and are at times subsumed and expressed through the prayers and paternal blessings on the couple. It ought to be noted that, being one of the life-cycle transitions, the idea of marrying

[46]THEODORE LIDZ, op. cit., p. 425.

[47]Cf. VAN GENNEP, op. cit., p. 132.

generates a sort of crises in the individual, which demands a ritual adjustment for the restoration of equilibrium in the social order. Hence, they are protective rituals. Marriage rituals are intended to insure the fertility of the union and obviate the dangers which accompany sexual intercourse. They serve as appeals to the higher powers and are, therefore, sacrificial rites and prayers. Pointing out the reasons for the religious rituals in marriage, William Crooke writes, "Marriage, . . . contemplates that the parties are under the influence of taboo, and the rites are intended to obviate its dangers, and in particular, those which may prevent the union from being fertile".[48] To supply the religious rituals in marriage pertains to the priestly functions in the community.

Another last point to be noted is the fact that marriage ceremony is an entire communitarian celebration, since so many are involved in a single marriage. It is not just something that concerns the two young people. It touches not only the two families in question - nuclear as well as extended, and also at times, it is an affair of entire village or town. It would be unwise to demarcate or duplicate such celebrations due to their historic and unique nature.

5.2.3.4   **The Funeral Rites**

One of the most stark realities of life that confronts one with so many unanswered questions is the reality of death. The ultimate questions that surround the experience of death leaves one speechless. If the humans are very meticulous in welcoming the gift of life at its initial stages with the birth rituals, they are even all the more careful and elaborate at the ultimate moment of the separation from the world of the living. Hence, in all cultures there are funeral rites. In practically every culture, death marks a physical separation of the individual from other living human beings. This is so radical that such separations are celebrated with funeral rites and ceremonies, which are intended to emphasise this fact of separation from the living society. Generally speaking, the major functions of death rituals are to ensure a permanent separation of the dead person's ghost or spirit from the survivors and an attempt to re-establish a solidarity not only among the survivors, but also the funeral rites, are intended to clear a person from any obstacles on the way and ensure a solidarity of the dead person with the world of the dead and dead ancestors.

Following the classification of Van Gennep, even though Funeral rites would at the first thought give the impression of consisting more of the separation aspects and rituals, the other aspects are equally and even conspicuously identifiable. There are the transitional or liminal as well as the incorporational aspects. It is to be observed that where funeral rites

---

[48]WILLIAM CROOKE, The Natives of Northern India: Native Races of the British Empire, A Constable, London, 1907, p. 206.

serve the purpose of integrating the deceased into the world of the dead, the rites are very elaborate and assume great importance.

The very event of death characterises the separation aspects. The moment of death registers automatically the physical reality of separation of the dead person from the living humans. The most prominent rite of this stage is the mourning of the dead, whose duration depends on the closeness of the relationship between the mourners and the dead person.[49] Other rites of separation, according to Van Gennep includes: the various procedures by which the corpse is transported outside; burning the tools, the house, the jewels, the deceased's possessions; putting to death the deceased's wives, slaves, or favourite animals; washing, anointing, and rites of purification in general; and taboos of all sorts. The physical aspects of the separation rites are: the grave, coffin, cemetery, closing of the coffin or the tomb. It includes also the collective rites of expelling souls from the house, the village, and the tribe's territory.[50]

The transitional aspect is very prominently characterised by the more or less extended stay of the corpse or the coffin in the deceased's room (as during a wake) in the vestibule of his house or in the assembly of his one time companions in the Church or workplace - during which some last respect and tribute is paid to the deceased. Gennep reveals that the transition stage can stretch into days, weeks, months and years, when they are then celebrated as commemorations.[51] What, in some cultures, is referred to as second funeral or burial is nothing other than the same extended transitional aspect being celebrated. Lafitau is, therefore, right in observing that,

> Among most savage nations, the dead bodies are only in safekeeping in the sepulchre where they have initially been placed. After a certain time, new obsequies are given them, and what is due them is completed by further funeral duties.[52]

The incorporation aspect is generally the shared meal during or after funeral and at commemoration ceremonies. The meal takes place sometimes when the period of mourning is lifted, or as in the case of a double-staged funeral, when it takes place usually at the end of the first stage. It is then thought that the deceased partakes of this meal in

[49]"During mourning, social life is suspended for all those affected by it, and the length of the period increases with the closeness of social ties to the deceased (e.g., for widows, relatives), and with a higher social standing of the dead person." - Cf. VAN GENNEP, op. cit., p. 148.

[50]Cf. VAN GENNEP, op. cit., p. 164

[51]Ibid., p. 148.

[52]LAFITAU, Moeurs des sauvages ameriquains, II, 444, quoted in VAN GENNEP, op. cit., p. 148.

company of all the relatives who gather to participate in the meal. The purpose of this communion is to reunite all the surviving members of the group to remain in solidarity with one another, and sometimes also with the dead person. It may also be seen as a symbol of the last commensalistic union with the deceased. The rites which lift all the regulations and prohibitions of mourning such as the special dress, carrying of shaved hair, indoor restriction etc. should be considered rites of reintegration into the life of the society.

The actual shape and elaborations accorded to funeral rites in any culture is dictated by the belief of the people regarding death and the after-life, as well as the facts of the sex, age and social status of the deceased person, and the circumstances surrounding his death.[53] So, some dangerous dead are not entitled to a funeral rite. Such dead are "condemned to a pitiable existence, since they are never able to enter the world of the dead or to become incorporated in the society established there.[54] They include those bereft of family, the suicides, those dead on a journey, those struck by lightning, those dead through the violation of a taboo etc.[55]

Generally speaking, most cultures have a belief in the life after death. While some hold on to a rebirth or reincarnation, others such as in Hinduism and Buddhism have a strong belief in liberation (Moksha) after death for the deceased. This is not the same thing as the resurrection of the dead along with retribution, which christians believe. These beliefs condition people's attitudes in funeral rites, and dictate the specifications and dimensions of the rites. In Hinduism, for instance, the funeral, referred to as Samskara, prepares a person for existence after death. The Indians had an earlier custom of cremation of the dead, which later came to be seen as a ritual sacrifice through which the deceased person is born again into the company of his ancestors. Hence the funeral for them is a rite of passage from the earthly existence to the world of the fathers.[56] Worthy of note, however, is the peculiar fact that in Hindu funeral, 'they do not refer at all to the common Indian beliefs of rebirth (Samsara) and liberation (Moksha). These Hindu rituals are founded on a different world view that celebrates life and fertility, shrinks from pollution and death, and when death comes, ritually transports the dead to the world of the fathers'.[57] Even in traditions where

---

[53]In some cultures, for example in Africa, people who die in accidents, or as a result of some diseases are normally thrown away and not given a funeral in the real sense of it.

[54]VAN GENNEP, op. cit., p. 160

[55]Ibid., p. 161.

[56]The Encyclopedia of Religion, 1987 ed., s.v. "Rites of Passage: Hindu Rites", by PATRICK OLIVELLE.

[57]Ibid.

mummification obtains, its purpose is precisely to make rebirth, the life beyond the grave, possible. Funeral may even have the utility of disposing of eternal enemies of the survivors.

The age of the deceased has an influence in the rites, since dead children are normally given a hushed burial as distinct from the elaborate burial of a titled adult, which can stretch into days, weeks, and even months in some cultures.

Therefore all people see funeral as a ritual intended to pave a way for a better experience in the after-life.

We have taken a bird's eye view of the various stages and rites that punctuate the life-cycle of an individual. This observation is discernible in all cultures. The specific difference to these general observations in individual cultures may arise out of the specific world view of such people. For instance, among the Igbos, besides these four main stages in the life span of an individual, there is the revered stage of elders in the community. Worthy of special note for this work is the status of the traditional headship, which only the most aged person in the whole community becomes. The peculiarities that characterise the transitional rites among the Igbos would now form the object of our attention.

5.3 **The Peculiarity of the Igbo Transitional Rites**

One has taken a lot of pains to go through the fundamentals of the Igbo cultural system at the earlier stages of this work. The intention of the enquiry is to enable an outsider to take note of the specific difference in the cultural life of the Igbos. Surely many of such differences go to register the Igbos as people with a very rich cultural heritage. It is such peculiarities that characterise and identify the Igbo rites of transition. So, in common with every other people, the Igbos share the same fundamentals of the rites of transition. Over and above other cultures, the Igbo transitional rites have their specific peculiarities which one can categorise into religious, social, and political dimensions.

First and foremost, the Igbo transitional rites are deeply penetrated and intertwined by the deep religious sense of the Igbos. It has already been noted that religion is the centre of the life, activity and psychology of the Igbos. An expatriate once documented of the Igbos, that

> they are, in the strict and natural sense of the word, a truly and a deeply religious people, of whom it can be said, as it has been said of the Hindus, that 'they eat religiously, drink religiously, bathe religiously, dress religiously, and sin religiously. In a few words, the religion of these natives as I have all along endeavoured to point out, is their existence, and their existence

is their religion.[58]

In making such a remark about the Igbos, Major Leonard only acknowledges and alludes to the fact which Mbiti, speaking globally of the African peoples, would re-echo as the implications from the people's world view. According to Mbiti,

> It is religion, more than anything else, which colours their understanding of the universe and their empirical participation in that universe, making life a profoundly religious phenomenon. To be is to be religious in a religious universe.[59]

The religious implications in the transitional rites, therefore, arise from this all-comprehending religious vision of the universe by the Igbos. In strategic transitional moments of life, the Igbos, overwhelmed by this religious sense, resort to what Mbiti prefers to call Instant Religion.[60] In such moments, the Igbos are constrained to turn to the traditional religion as a "genuine means of finding an outlet for their feelings of joy or tension generated by the particular crisis or important event".[61] It is on account of this fact that religious implications are talked about in the transitional rites of the Igbos. The transitional rites have a deep religious implication. For instance, the physical and social ceremonies associated with pregnancies, birth, and childhood are, over and above the social implications, regarded with deep religious feelings. They simply see these rites from the perspective, as Mbiti puts it, "that another religious being has been born into a profoundly religious community and religious world".[62]

This religious implication of the rites of passage for the Igbos has to be borne in mind in discussing inculturation in Igboland. Unless this religious perspective is utililised and the seeming vacuum in the Christian celebration of the transitional moments are filled up, the facts of what S. N.

---

[58]A. G. LEONARD, The Lower Niger and Its Tribes, Frank Cass, London, 1968, p. 429.

[59]JOHN MBITI, African Religion and Philosophy, p. 262.

[60]"Instant Religion is that which shows itself mainly in moments of crisis like sickness, desperation, emergency, death and tragedy; and comes to the surface also at key moments of life like birth, wedding, death . . . ". - J. MBITI, ibid., p. 275.

[61]Ibid.

[62]Ibid., p. 120.

Ezeanya would call - the Endurance of Conviction[63] - observable today among the Igbo Christians will continue to obtain. Chris Ejizu notes some of these facts, which, inspite of the overwhelming influence of christianity on the traditional system, for which reason the traditional religion has been reduced to a phenomenon for only a quantitatively minute percentage of Igbos made up of the illiterate and aged ones, has continued to survive and makes its influence felt even in our modern society among the literates. He testifies that

> . . . different forms of ambivalence . . . still prevail in the lives of many members of the Christian Churches, even if such practices are carried out secretly today . . . . The world view of most Igbo professing christians remain that which is inherited from the traditional religion. Certain traditional beliefs . . . still persist in the minds of many professing christians today. These show up in any serious life crisis in the lives of such christians. They waste no time in seeking the traditional aids to solve such problems. Diviners and protective charm-makers still number among their clients a good percentage of Igbo baptised christians.[64]

Hence, from this fact of continuity inspite of discontinuity, he concludes,

> Igbo traditional religion persists as a force of considerable consequence in contemporary society, even if it had undergone a number of modifications.[65]

This conclusion confirms Major Leonard's assertion that "Igbo social system is so entirely woven in with their religion that, even if they wanted to, they could not get away from it".[66] This religious dimension, therefore, dovetails with the social and political implications.

From the social aspects, the peculiarity of the Igbo transitional rites is observable from the strict, unalloyed fidelity of the Igbos to the traditional social system with its laws and customs - the Omenani - which has an intimate relationship not only with the traditional religion, but also with the ancestral allegiance. The transitional rites are deeply concieved as dictates of this traditional law. Every Igbo is always cautious not to go against, or

---

[63]Cf. CHRISTOPHER I. EJIZU, "Continuity and Discontinuity in African Traditional Religion: The Case of the Igbo of Nigeria", in Cahiers des Religions Africaines, Vol. 18, n. 36, p. 212.

[64]Ibid.

[65]Ibid., p. 213.

[66]A.G. LEONARD, op. cit., p. 429.

do anything contrary to these traditional dictates.[67] This explains why such practices as the transitional rites are taken seriously and regarded as obligatory. The societal force behind the transitional rites of the Igbos arises from this link with the ancestors, who, through the 'Omenani' dictate such rites to be performed. There is, therefore, a direct link between the transitional rites and the ancestors. For instance, the Igbos believe that a new born child is always a coming back in existence of one of the dead ancestors. There is, therefore, a belief in reincarnation. The simple aspects of semblances between a new born child and any of the dead ancestors is enough for the traditional Igbo to conclude and confirm the fact of reincarnation.

Also, through the initiation rites the traditional statutes originated by the ancestors are further transmitted and perpetuated, and thus, the traditional standard set by the ancestors are maintained. The marriage rites insure a steady flow in the ancestral lineage by guaranteeing the flow in offspring. This is a physical prolongation and quantitative expansion of the lineage.[68]

As one gets old, one becomes a veritable mouthpiece, through which the ancestors, who, according to the Igbos, continue to influence the affairs of the living in the lineage, speak to the Igbo community. This is the reason why the authority in the traditional system rests in the hand of the oldest man in the community. He is, as it were, the nearest link with the ancestor and even, physically speaking, he is nearest to the land of the ancestors. When one finally dies, one is received into the company of the ancestors, provided one is accorded a good and befitting burial and funeral rites.

Hence all the Igbo transitional rites have a strong base in the ancestral belief, and thus obtain their importance and value from such relationship. Their valency for inculturation, therefore, can be associated to the positive valency of the Igbo solidarity with the ancestors. Schineller makes a reference to this positive valency as he remarks:

> A strong sense of solidarity exists in Nigeria between the living
> and the dead. Parents and grandparents who led good lives
> and died well are honored and remembered, and their presence
> is felt in the family, in the lives of those who remain behind.
> They protect the living and mediate to them the power and love
> of God. Is not this precisely at the heart of Catholic belief in

---

[67]"The Igbos believe that their lives are profoundly influenced by their ancestors and this belief has far-reaching sociological consequences. Any departure from the custom for example, is likely to incur displeasure and vengeance of the ancestors". - E. K. MEEK, Law and Authority in a Nigerian Tribe, Oxford University Press, London, 1937, p. 61.

[68]In answer to a catechismal question: What is the meaning of everlasting life? - an old neophyte replied: It means that anybody who is begotten should also beget another, and this continues without end.

the communion of saints and in the veneration of saints?[69]

The ancestors are evoked as the source of the traditional authority. Consequently, since it represents the absolute axiomatic values of the society in which the common good and common interest handed over by the ancestors, the traditional authority dispensed by the elders is absolute in the traditional community; hence the political implications of the transitional rites among the Igbos.

The Igbos have been presented above as a people with a deep sense of solidarity and possessing a communitarian psychology. This means in effect that the transitional moments and their celebrations cannot but be seen as the entire community's big moment and celebration. This fact will be dwelt upon in the subsequent section.

Still dealing with the social level, one observes another peculiarity of the Igbo transitional rites from the role and the social value of the rites in the establishment of the social status of the individual. One cannot be regarded as a free-born of the land if one does not go through the birth, initiation, and marriage rites as dictated by the tradition of the land. It is the fact of going through these traditional rites that constitutes and establishes one as an authentic member of the Igbo community. It is interesting to note that, while, for instance, the birth rites celebrate the gift of life - which is the greatest gift that man can get, as symbolised even in the Igbo nomenclature: 'Nduka-aku' (life is greater than wealth), and 'Ndubuisi' (life is the greatest), it is at the same time an indirect celebration of the parenthood of the new-born. One needs only to consider the fact that for the Igbos, a woman who has no child is taken as someone useless in the community, or as one who is not in the good book of the ancestors, or may have attracted their hatred and hostility. That is why a woman feels fulfilled not only by the birth of a child, but only when she begets a male child.[70] A man who has no male child sees himself and is regarded in the community as useless.[71] Consequently, in the birth rituals, one celebrates and appreciates this gift of life, and at the same time the parents are publicly recognised, acclaimed and boosted, more especially if it is a case of the first pregnancy, where these celebrations have also social and economic importance attached.

Finally, one of the distinctive aspects of the Igbo transitional rites is

---

[69]PETER SCHINELLER, A Handbook on Inculturation, Paulist Press, New York, Mahwah, 1990, p. 89.

[70]"A woman who cannot or has not given birth is a social misfit. If she has never conceived she is openly ridiculed and told that she is not a woman." - E. I. METUH, Comparative Studies of African Traditional Religions, p. 200.

[71]This explains also why the Igbos take special pride in having many children in the family. It is an eloquent testimony of God's special blessings, more especially if the children are of both sexes.

the factor of their traditional eschatological importance. The Igbos see the various transitional rites as consequently dictating and leading someone to the ultimate realisation of the purpose of life. The involvement of the transition rites in the Igbo concept of salvation is clearly manifested by Osuji, who observed that

> The concept of salvation for the Igbo includes union with one's 'Umunna' community; living upright life; dying in a very good age; and having children through whom the lineage, the torch of life for one's group is not extinguished; being accorded full burial rites after death . . .[72]

One is in union with his 'Umunna' community only when one has participated in the traditional demands of his community, which concretely means undergoing the traditional rites of transition.

Briefly, it has been seen that while the Igbos have the same fundamental characteristics with other cultures, the specific difference in Igbo culture with reference to the rites of passage lie in the religious, psychological, social and political factors, which qualify their way of life, belief and world view. One must then, take note of these important dimensions, and channel one's efforts in supplying the alternatives that will satisfy the fundamental cravings of the Igbos through Inculturation. As can be seen above, the values involved are very precious for the Igbos. The value of life is involved. The status symbol of the Igbo and his philosophy is involved. The link with ancestors is also another deep-rooted distinctive value for the Igbos. Since not every dead can be an ancestor, it is a pointer to the fact that the Igbo, in speaking of salvation, then, has boldly in mind the eschatological reunion with God, in company of their ancestors, who are their traditional saints. Such a reunion is only possible after a truly ritualised and organised life.

5.4 Communitarian / Solidarity Factors of the Igbo Rites of Passage

The communitarian psychological factor has been listed above as one of the distinctive elements that ought to be highlighted in discussing the transitional rites of the Igbos. It was purposely mentioned only in passing in the preceding section because it is intended to be given a wider treatment on account of its importance among the Igbos.[73] As a logical consequence

---

[72]C. C. OSUJI, The Concept of Salvation in Igbo Traditional Religion, Doctoral Dissertation at Pontifical Urban University, Rome, 1977, p. 68.

[73]E. Ilogu writes: "Emphasis is placed on the commune rather than the individual,. . . . Yet the individual's responsibility to the commune is clear and never shirked because social expectation as well as shared values are

of the "'I' because of 'we'" concept of the Igbos, it can even be concluded that the ontological base of the solidarity of the Igbos, which provides and assures the Igbo of a solid base of security is the community.[74] It is the community that authenticates the identity of the individual, and this factor generates a strong sense of co-responsibility and a sort of compulsory interest in one for the others among the Igbos. If the individual derives his identity from the community, it simply implies that "the degree to which the individual is rated on the socio-psychological integrational scale in the community derives its credence from the degree to which he responds to the modelling influence of the psychological community".[75] The overall effect of such a relationship is a concrete existential togetherness, which expresses itself in a strong awareness of communal sorrow on account of the adversity of one, and a corresponding joy in the event of an individual success.

Reflecting on the already discussed concept of the rites of passage in general, as the various ways and expressions of a traditional community through which it meets up with, counterbalances, and insures the transitional moments for the individual and the community,[76] one sees the rites of passage as a product of each traditional community.[77] Every product bears the imprint of its maker. And the imprint becomes a perspective through which the identity of a product and its authenticity is guaranteed. Therefore, where a traditional community is characterised by such a deep sense of

---

commonly observed and the social ethos of the village is jealously guarded and upheld both by religion as well as by the accepted practice and prohibitions of the community". - Cf.EDMUND ILOGU, Christianity and Igbo Culture, NOK Publishers, Ltd. New York, 1974, p. 22.

[74]"The Igbo community denotes first and foremost . . . ontological quality of human relations. It is ontological in so far as all members of the community are believed to descend from a common ancestor. . . . This link which binds all members of the same family by propagation is broadened to include all the members of the community or clan who are believed to be descendants of the same ancestor. Everyone considers himself as member of a definite community and as a part of the whole." - J. P. C. NZOMIWU, The Moral Concept of Justice among the Igbos, A Doctoral Thesis in Moral Theology, Academia Alfonsiana, Rome, 1977, p. 38.

[75]CLETUS EZE ALEKE, op. cit., p. 235.

[76]Confer the very beginning of this chapter in section 5.1. above.

[77]In fact, A. A. Schneiders refers to them as 'the cultural residue of communal living, of the sharing of common experiences, hardships, attitudes, values, and interests'. According to him, "through these media the community gradually assumes a psychological character, and one begins to speak of community attitudes, desires, hopes and feelings". Cf. A. A. SCHNEIDERS, Personality Development and Adjustment in Adolescence, Milwaukee, Bruce Publishing Co., 1960, p. 417.

communitarian philosophy and solidarity as one truly finds among the Igbos, the transitional rites cannot but be seen as necessarily demanding a traditional communitarian character as an essential requisite. Even though the traditional rites may be celebrated here and now for a concrete individual person, yet prominence is always given to the communitarian aspect of the rite. Allusion is made to this fact as Schneiders, discussing the personality of the adolescent, argues:

> If therefore . . . personality can be partly defined in terms of the relations that exist between the individual organism and the persons and events that come within the range of his experience, the conclusion is inescapable that the community in all of its aspects will figure prominently in the development of personality.[78]

Hence, the Igbo rites of passage flow from the community and in each transitional rite a strong sense of communitarian solidarity can be identified. Such a communitarian attention follows the Igbo person not only at the developmental stages of life, but in fact punctuates all the transitional moments of the Igbo even to the ultimate point of burial and lying in the grave, as the Igbo funeral rites clearly testify.

With such a sense of the community in Igboland, one observes the daily experiences being made as new children are born, grow into what is considered as traditional maturity, get married, grow into old age, and eventually die. One notes also the strong sense of solidarity which is manifested in and by one and all in the community as they actively participate in the moments of joy or sorrow of every member of the community, irrespective of the degree of personal relationship between them. Illustrating the development of this sense of solidarity in the Igbo individual, Cletus Aleke writes,

> He witnesses grief, death or misfortune . . . of a relative. It requires of him to sacrifice his time and provide personal support and affection as is demanded of him and of others in the community. He is not only called upon to participate in the sorrows of others but also to share in their joys, and above all to offer service to the whole community.[79]

In such ways and also through the obligating communitarian influence one is imbued with a strong sense of solidarity and traditional corporate feeling for one another.

Surely this traditional corporate feeling of the Igbos is diametrically opposed to the unfortunate individualistic style of living evidenced in some

---

[78]Ibid., p. 407.

[79]C. E. ALEKE, op. cit., p. 241.

parts of Europe, where the singleness of living fossilises into the erection of imaginary as well as concrete walls of shame against human beings. In such contexts one would easily pick a quarrel with his neighbours simply, for example, for being greeted by the other on the way. Instances abound of cases where people live next door to one another for years without knowing or saying a word to each other. In order to evaluate better the positiveness of the Igbo solidarity, it may be interesting to make a personal comparison between this Igbo style of living and the individualistic type which Mbiti enumerated as the possible dangers of urbanisation.[80]

It is, in fact, in order to recognise, appreciate and try to preserve this positive value of the Igbos that one notes this factor as important in Inculturation within the Igbo rites of passage.

Taking a cursory glance at the Igbo transitional rites, one can see the simple relationship that exist between the rites and this communitarian factor, as well as the concrete expressions of solidarity in the transitional rites.

Through birth and the rites surrounding birth, one is introduced into the Igbo community. In the celebration of these rites the physical presence of a sort of representation of the traditional community is demanded. By undergoing the traditional initiation rites, membership in this community is consolidated, ratified and publicly recognised. Igbo Marriage is not an affair between only two individuals, as is the case in some western countries. It is something that concerns not only the families of the individuals involved, but also the entire kindred and village, and even at times, it touches the entire community. Through the traditional marriage a permanence and a quantitative expansion of the membership to the community is ensured.[81] Growing to old age among the Igbos is a transitional passage that introduces one into a position of authority among the Igbos. Being the oldest in the community authorises one to possess the 'Offor' - the status symbol of authority of the traditional community. This, in effect, means that

---

[80]Mbiti writes: ". . . amidst the many people who live in the cities, the individual discovers that he is alone. When he falls sick, perhaps only one or two other people know about it and come to see him; when he is hungry he finds that begging food from his neighbour is either shameful or unrewarding or both; when he gets bad news from his relatives in the countryside, he cries alone even if hundreds of other people rub shoulders with him in the factory or bus. The masses around the individual are both blind and deaf to him, they are indifferent and do not care about him as a person. Almost at every turn of his life the individual in the city and under modern change discovers constantly that he is alone or even lonely in the midst of large masses of people". (Cf., J. MBITI, African Religions and Philosophy, p. 225.)

[81]It is interesting to remark that Igbo Priests and religious people, who, by virtue of their vocation and vows cannot marry, are always looked upon and considered as people who do not wish a perpetuation of the community.

one becomes the immediate spokesman of the community before the ancestors and also the living representative of the ancestors in the Igbo community. As a result of a good-lived life, death, and through funeral rites one is introduced into the extended company of the ancestors in the land of the dead.

In all these rites, which are moments of joys and sorrows, the Igbos stand in solidarity behind the member - actively participating, contributing whatever is demanded of them - be it time, affection, money, gifts and services. There is also the aspect of commensalism, which is anthropologically considered as an eloquent expression of solidarity and togetherness. Indeed, this togetherness is manifestly expressed in funeral rites and ceremonies, where practically every member of the community is expected -nay- compelled to be physically present, interrupt his daily work, provide food and drink for the wake-keeping (depending on the degree of relationship), participate in the physical mourning of the dead (if one is a woman),[82] and take part in the actual burial of the dead, which is demonstrated by throwing or leaving some earth on the grave of the dead. Such a solidarity in funerals has two motivations. One is to unitedly launch one into a reunion with the ancestors[83], and the other is to distract the attention of the bereaved ones from brooding over the loss.

From the importance of the community to the Igbos, any alienation from this traditional community is tantamount to robbing one of the "traditional solidarity which supplied for him land, customs, ethics, rites of passage, customary law, religious participation . . . ".[84]

It is an observable fact that today not only the christian missionary ventures but also other factors such as urbanisation, with their traditional cultural destructive tendencies, are becoming obstacles to the communitarian solidarity of the Igbos. However, one needs only to note the overall drift of people from the cities back to the rural areas of the parts of Igboland on weekends, month-ends, or on traditional feastdays and other such strategic moments in the life of the Igbo village community as the performance of the transitional rites, in order to be convinced that it is not the intention of the Igbos for such values to die out. The regular return to the villages is for the purpose of maintaining this sense of solidarity with their kit and kin in the villages. During such returns, irrespective of one's religious affiliation, everyone is expected to actively join the village community in demonstrating their sense of solidarity. In fact, such a solidarity response to the call of the traditional community takes precedence before any other personal or group programmes. In one's concrete experience as a one-time parish priest in Igboland, all parish programmes had always suffered serious set-backs on such traditional occasions. Therefore, one is inclined to think with Ejizu that

---

[82]Every woman is generally expected to bemoan the dead by crying loud and shedding tears at the arrival at the place of death.

[83]Cf. G. T. BASDEN, Among the Ibos of Nigeria, p. 117.

[84]Cf. J. S. MBITI, African Religion and Philosophy, p. 219.

even though some factors are seriously militating against some of the Igbo cultural values, yet it would be erroneous to think that on account of that, the Igbo cultural values are dying out. Even if some aspects are dormant, others such as this sense of solidarity prove themselves very much alive, and provide reasons for Ejizu's conclusions of 'Continuity and Discontinuity' among the Igbos.[85]

The Inculturation of the Igbo Rites of Passage, therefore, is expected to utilise the Igbo communitarian solidarity as a booster for the Christian Faith.

5.5   The Prospects of Inculturating the Igbo Rites of Passage

From the foregoing insight into the valency and importance which are attached to the rites of transition in general, but with special reference to these rites among the Igbos, one sees Inculturation work in this direction as not only important and desirable, but also as very strategic. In his opening address to a very recent discussion / Seminar on Inculturation, the Bishop of one of the most fertile areas proposed for this Inculturation in Igboland, Bishop M. U. Eneja, referring to the prospects of Inculturation, remarked:

> This time is most opportune. On the one hand, Nigerians wish Christ and his Church to fully come to them. Circumstances are suitable. The soil is well prepared. The Christians, the clergy, religious have grown in numbers. The laity is dynamic. Church societies are multiplying and spreading, bringing healthy effects on the population.[86]

One would see this remark as an urgent invitation to the all-important work of inculturation. It has been manifested above that the transitional rites form a very essential and sensitive transmitting wave-length for the Igbos. As such, this call becomes, first and foremost, a call for the creation of this contact point for the Igbos. From the remark above, one could have the impression that such a work may seem easy to embark upon. However, a close look at the prerequisites for inculturation in this direction reveals it as an uphill task, fraught with a lot of problems and obstacles. It is not going to be easy for the Church, nor for Igbo Christians, and also for the Igbo

---

[85]". . . it has not been completely bludgeoned out of existence. It continues to persist as a living system in the life of its faithful remnant located mainly in the rural parts of Igboland, while evolving in different ways in the other existing systems in present-day Igbo society". - Cf. C. EJIZU, op. cit., p. 214

[86]UGONNA IGBOAJA & OBIORA IKE, eds., Inculturation: Where do we Stand?, Lay Apostolate Publications, Enugu, 1990, p. 6.

culture. It ought to be borne in mind that the transitional rites of the Igbos have flourished as their traditional way of life for centuries even before the advent of civilisation. Since the advent of Christianity, these traditional ways of life have existed on parallel basis to the christian rites, without involving any process of transculturation. To talk now of the inculturation of the christian faith within this traditional system can be equated to a reconstruction of the foundation of an already existing edifice. This is definitely going to be a herculian task, for it is always easier to erect a brand new edifice on a new foundation, than to reconstruct an old existing house. After a hundred years of evangelisation, inculturation work on the foundations of Igbo Culture would mean digging deep into this foundation to undo what has been poorly or badly done at the beginning of evangelisation. Surely both systems have already fossilised, and therefore, may prove difficult opening up to each other for a transculturational process which is implied in inculturation.

Secondly, achieving inculturation within the Igbo transitional rites, demands a thorough knowledge, not only of the cultural concepts and valencies involved in the transitional rites, but also of the christian theological foundations and principles.[87] An enquiry into the situation of things reveals that only a very negligible number of the Igbo clergy are acquainted with a knowledge of all that is involved in the Igbo traditional rites. Real studies and interested research into this area had been hampered on account of the negative and disinterested attitude of the Church, and, therefore, of Christians, to the traditional elements of the culture in question. A study of Theology alone is simply not enough for such a work. In order to make the christian principle the source of animation in the traditional system, which is the purpose of inculturation, an authoritative and authentic knowledge of the traditional system and its implications is called for. As such, a thorough research in this direction is essential.

At this point in time, it is even disheartening to note that there seems to be a lack of unanimity and a sense of cultural awareness on the part of the ecclesiastical personnel. While some would see any research in this direction as taking a leap in the right direction, others would see it as being anachronistic. Inculturation work, it must be said, necessarily demands a concerted and unilateral treatment. Otherwise while one tries to construct, the other dismantles.

Even from the part of the laity, there is a glaring lack of authentic knowledge of the culture and the traditional system since they have been dissuaded right from the start from having anything to do with them. As a result, even though they are aware of being alienated from their very cultural foundation, yet some look askance at any moves in the direction of Inculturation. Records of the past reveal resentments from the side of the

---

[87]"The complexity of the matter demands the interdisciplinary collaboration of cultural anthropologists, sociologists, and linguistic experts."(ANSCAR J. CHUPUNGCO, Liturgies of the Future: the Process and Methods of Inculturation, Paulist Press, New York, 1989, p. 45.)

laity over any efforts even to indigenise. Such efforts have always been criticised as 'watering down the faith'. It is exactly on account of this fact that one must even have recourse not to the Christians but to the traditional members as authentic depository sources of information about the traditional system in the event of inculturation exercise in Igbo culture. Both the clergy, laity and everybody should be interested, prepared, and open to learn the fundamentals of the culture in order to carry out inculturation. It is strange to observe that only of a very recent past is the study of the Igbo traditional culture and religion included on the curriculum of studies in some of our Seminaries and Institutes of higher Learning. The recommendations of Dr. Iwe in this regard ought to be given attention. He advocates that:

> . . . there will be need for a deliberate inculcation of cultural consciousness in our people. This is a measure that will inspire them to examine and appreciate the nature, import and purpose of culture. Such an inspiration would awaken in them the desire to recapture and assert the fundamental values and institutions of their culture.[88]

One cannot really constructively criticise what one does not know. There ought also to be a readiness for this.

The complex nature of the Igbo transitional rites even tend to complicate issues in an eventual inculturation exercise. It calls for a special attention in order to establish the essential elements and be able to sieve them out from superstitions.

There is also no gainsaying that any attempt into inculturation in the Igbo transitional rites may necessarily demand a christian readjustment or have a liturgical implication. As A. Chupungco remarks,

> Adaptation to the culture and traditions of peoples is above all a liturgical matter regulated by liturgical principles, criteria, and methods. Surely adaptation requires that there be a dialogue between liturgy and culture.[89]

And besides,

> To be faithful to sound tradition and to foster legitimate progress at the same time is an art requiring expertise in the science of liturgy, the virtue of flexibility, and often a great faith in the wisdom of the church.[90]

---

[88]N. S. S. IWE, <u>Christianity, Culture and Colonialism in Africa</u>, Department of Religious Studies, College of Education, Port Harcourt, 1985, p. 189.

[89]A. J. CHUPUNGCO, <u>Liturgies of the Future</u>, p. 11.

[90]<u>Ibid.</u>, p. 1.

From the Magna Charta of the Vatican II regarding the Liturgy, allowing of flexibility and legitimate progress, while maintaining a faithfulness to sound tradition[91], one is glad that the way is quite open for Inculturation. However, considering the stand of certain local ecclesiastical Authorities in their unreadiness to admit of any liturgical readjustments other than 'what obtains in Rome', one remains very doubtful of any hopes of progress. Such attitudes of carbon-copy allegiance have at times been influenced and orchestrated by economic factors at the detriment of other existential pastoral needs of the local church. It is no wonder, then, that on account of such motivations, some very dynamic and laudable initiatives of some people have been nipped in the bud and deprived of seeing the light of day. This accounts for the apparent standstill and dormancy which have become a rule of life, and which plague many local churches. It is perhaps necessary, therefore, to remind us of the fact that "flexibility, which allows the liturgy to respond to the pastoral and cultural needs of every local church, is one of the prominent and, it is hoped, permanent gains of Vatican II".[92] And where there is a reluctance to adapt, it means a rejection of legitimate progress.[93]

Granted that the present consciousness and readiness observable in some areas in Igboland in the pursuit of Inculturation is constantly maintained, and that all rally round to boost this consciousness with a concerted effort, it is our humble expectation that this would make our dreams for inculturation in Igboland come through. The success of inculturation lies in the fact of beginning to experiment, for it is said, that a child who is afraid to stand or fall, and on account of this does not practice, will never walk at all. As Shorter puts it,

> Inculturation is not a purely intellectual problem. It concerns culture or the way of life of people. The only way in which inculturation can possibly be realized is through experimentation. If experimentation is prohibited, inculturation is delayed. Church leaders may be afraid of mistakes being made, or of losing control, but these are risks that have to be taken. Without the possibility of making mistakes and of learning by mistakes, nothing can be achieved.[94]

It is our firm belief that inculturation can be carried out in the field of Igbo transitional rites. Inculturation is expected to delve deep into the essential but key elements and values in the rites, seek a way of making the christian

---

[91]Cf. VATICAN II, Sacrosanctum Concilium, nn. 37 -40.

[92]Ibid., p. 8.

[93]Cf. Ibid., p. 11.

[94]A. SHORTER, Toward a Theology of Inculturation, p. 252.

faith to animate these values, elevate and beautify them. By so doing the traditional system is upheld and boosted in such a way that the values can be said to be catholic as they are traditionally authentic.

For instance, inculturation ought to look into ways of integrating the Igbo traditional birth rites and ceremonies with the christian rite of Infant Baptism, as we intend to propose in this work.

Even with its intricate connection to the masquerade cult in Igboland, inculturation of the initiation rites is yet possible. One recommends firstly, that a dialogue with the Masquerade society be initiated, with the aim of discussing the pressure points. Fortunately enough, today, only very few of the old veterans, who still practice the traditional religion, constitute the supreme authority in this matter, although they can be adamantly conservative, and may even allow no discussion of the issue. It is generally supposed that, on account of the changing circumstances, through dialogue, and counting also on the possibility of Igbo christians finding their way into the traditional decision-making body, it is possible to see Christianity emerging as the end-point of a passage from the Igbo traditional history. If "in the great historical civilisations in which the mysteries proliferated, we no longer find the situation characteristic of primitive culture", as Mircea Eliade observed, but rather an occasion of initiation of youths, which eventually makes initiation to become a sort of collective regeneration and spiritual renewal of a community, then, it is a pointer that initiation rites can generally undergo a transformation and change from its pristine form to a different spiritual end-point. Hence the revealing of the great mysteries of the traditional community, characteristic of initiation rites, ought not to be seen as something of a fixed and static nature, but as something that can be transformed and even be replaced by other mysteries of higher religious values. Therefore, revealing of the mysteries is a dynamic potential not necessarily tied to the very specific primitive circumstances. In his book on Initiations Mircea Eliade gives several examples of how the traditional patterns of initiation show a capacity of being indefinitely utilised, reanimated, and enriched with new values. He observes:

> It is as if initiation and its patterns were indissolubly linked with the very structure of spiritual life; as if initiation were an indispensable process in every attempt at total regeneration, in every effort to transcend man's natural condition and attain to a sanctified mode of being.[95]

Seen from this perspectives, the archaic patterns becomes potentials that can be taken over and utilised for various spiritual ends and charged with new religious orientation and content, yet preserving their cultural traditional structure. In this regard, the primitive Christianity provides ample examples of the possible utility of initiation rites of cultures. Here, the present form of the rite of christian initiation for adults comes to mind. One sees ample

---

[95]MIRCEA ELIADE, Rites and Symbols of Initiation, p. 114

opportunities for the Igbo rites of initiation to be integrated and enriched with the christian rite of confirmation. This definitely should exclude everything that has to do with superstitious and false worship. In such an exercise, it is possible to evolve a new spiritual orientation that is not alienated from the traditional system. One agrees with Eliade in his conclusion that,

> . . . . the initiation elements in primitive christianity simply demonstrate once again that initiation is an inseparable element in any revaluation of the religious life. It is impossible to attain to a higher mode of being, it is impossible to participate in a new irruption of sanctity in the world or history, except by dying to profane, unenlightened existence and being reborn to a new, regenerated life.[96]

It ought to be remembered that initiation rite is the official Igbo tribal recognition of the manly qualification and fitness of an individual. This tribal recognition can be integrated with the christian character formation, which is specially celebrated in the confirmation rites. The ample record of the certain initiatory themes which christianity took over and re-evaluated from other cultures provide a precedence in this matter.[97] However, a thorough study of the implications is essential.

Even when one observes a general tendency to suppress and desacralise Igbo initiation rites, it ultimately ends up in the reduction of these values to the level of unconscious or subconscious existence in man. These, eventually, exert their influence in man, even if only on the imaginative plane, and from time to time, they rear their heads in a camouflaged way. This goes to confirm the remark of Eliade, who writes:

> It is true that in the case of modern man, since there is no longer any religious experience fully and consciously assumed, initiation no longer performs an ontological function; it no longer includes a radical change in the initiand's mode of being, or his salvation . . . . Nevertheless, they continue to function, and that is why I said, that the process of initiation seems to be coexistence with any and every human condition.[98]

There is a big chance for Inculturation, then, within the Igbo initiation rites.

With reference to the Igbo traditional marriage, so many thoughts and suggestions have been made for a possible creation of an integrated ritual from both the christian and the traditional systems of marriage. It is however unfortunate and regrettable that the appropriate ecclesiastical quarters have not yet given a go-ahead order in this direction. It exists as

---

[96]Ibid., p. 118.

[97]Cf., Ibid., p. 121.

[98]Ibid., p. 128.

a lofty ideal only in the air or on the pages of the manuscripts. The merging is advocated as a type of inculturation in order to avoid the parallelism as hitherto observed in Igboland, where the same marriage is ritualised first of all on the traditional platform, and later on, especially after the marriage has been consummated, only to be again ritualised on the christian platform. There is no need for such a duplication, when it is possible to merge the celebrations, without entering into syncretism. The traditional context needs only to be furnished with a christian character, thereby merging the two structures into a unified central celebration, in such a way that it can be said to be truly traditional as it is christian. It ought, however, to be noted that after the performance of the traditional ceremony, the couples are legitimately considered as married. Is it not anachronistic to perform the christian marriage of already married people? The same can be said of the other Igbo traditional rites of transition. They offer to christianity in Igboland a very ample opportunity to be boosted and traditionally recognised as a way of life that serves the interest of the people, and therefore, greatly valued. This means much for the strong rooting of the faith. This is, however, not an easy task. As has been reflected above, it demands much study, enquiry, considerations and authentic knowledge of both christian faith and the traditional rites in question. Only experts can venture to delve into such a task. But it is a task rich in its expectations. Iwe's prerequisites furnishes us with a conclusion to this section. A successful inculturation would demand, as he outlined, among other things:

> . . .cultural leaders of intellectual stature and moral and mental maturity, men of creative originality, citizen of historical understanding and prudence, a sober and mature sense of religion and christian sense, sensibility and wisdom, cultural protagonists and propagandists, thorough civic education and maturity, mass culture-consciousness and appreciation, local community leaders of practical wisdom in a progressive cultural mood . . .[99]

Given all the possibilities examined above, inculturation within the Igbo rites of passage is a task that gives much hope and joy to look forward to and to actually undertake. Through inculturation in the framework of the transitional rites, the Igbo christian would be influenced from the childhood period, and insured through the stormy periods of growth and maturation. No doubt, such a christian and cultural foundation, good and authentic as it is, cannot but flower into a successful and ripe old age and an eventual enjoyment of a rich funeral, which indeed becomes a launching the dead into the company of the ancestors, seen from the traditional perspective, as it is also even in a more eminent way, an enjoyment of the company of the officially recognised saints in God's house.

---

[99]N. S. S. IWE, op. cit., p. 190.

CHAPTER 6

6   **PROPOSED MODELS FOR INCULTURATION**

In the discussion of the foregoing section on the prospects of inculturating the Igbo rites of Passage, the difficulties involved in ushering in Inculturation among the Igbos was vividly clarified. It may, therefore, seem somewhat deceptive to talk so easily of proposing a model for Inculturation. The proposition of a model in paper does not necessarily mean the actual practice in concrete reality. The workability of a proposed model depends on the fulfilment of the possible factors and conditions mentioned, and the removal of the various obstacles on the way. Only then could one consider Inculturation as possible. Any model should be seen as one out of several perspectives and possibilities. Hence the model being proposed should not be seen as a blue-print. One intends here simply to show that inculturating the Faith in the Igbo traditional birth rites and the traditional Headship is possible, and promises a very rich dividend for the faith.

One has chosen to use the Birth rites and the traditional Headship as bases for Inculturation. At first glance, reasons for choosing them are evident. The Birth stage is the beginning of life, while the old-age is the final stage of a matured life. The inception of life is accorded its overriding importance in the life of any individual on account of the value attached to life. All care and measures are taken in every culture at this period to welcome, protect and preserve life. Life is the greatest treasure of any individual irrespective of the culture in which one lives. It is even more so for the Igbos, with their special value and conception of life. On account of this importance, a lot of rituals are concentrated at this stage of life. The traditional rites pose problems for the faith and call for action. It is no wonder that the double allegiance of the Igbo Christian is more noticeable and rampant at the early rites of childhood. If one succeeds with Inculturation at this early stage of life, it would wield much influence and even control the future life.

At some stages of this work, special study was made of the enculturative process of the human being. It was discovered that the impressions created at the initial stages of life have an enduring influence in the later stages, and that any psychological crisis at the initial childhood period remains throughout life. For this reason the Birth rites have been chosen for inculturation.

Some other specific and basic factors bearing on the value of life and this stage of life for the Igbos, also influence the choice. Those factors are the already mentioned values which include the fulfilment of the parental personality through childbirth, and the Igbo concept of life and everything connected with it. The overriding reason and the main reference point in this model chapter is the conviction that through the inculturation of the christian faith within the Igbo Birth rites and the traditional leadership contexts, a firm fertile root and strategy for the flowering of a convinced faith for christians is ensured, with the obvious result of dismantling the hitherto baptised-but-not-converted attitude and solving the problem of the parallel allegiance to the christian faith and to the traditional system. It is evident that, given the fact of cosmic totality of the Igbo Culture, i.e. the total harmony and unity of faith and culture of the traditional system, inculturation of the faith will serve the function of paving a two way traffic process of penetration and integration, so that the christian faith becomes the soul of Igbo Culture in these rites. It is expected, as Franciscus Seda clarifies, that it is faith that preserves culture, even though faith should be developed into the culture of a people. According to him,

> Faith should be developed into culture. Otherwise it is not fully
> discerned, fully thought and fully lived. Culture is needed to
> preserve faith. On the other hand culture is developed around
> a faith. Culture can only survive by the faith it possesses. Faith
> is the soul of culture. Culture without faith is culture without
> spirit, without life.[1]

The effect is envisaged to be a transference of the convinced allegiance and devotion of the Igbos from the objects of traditional religion to the object of christian religion - a sure guarantee of the flowering of the christian faith. The faith will be buoyantly enriched by the traditional context - a veritable tapping of the traditional system, without syncretism or watering down of the christian faith. These two factors must be borne in mind as one proposes a model. It should realise the end of all evangelisation work as summed up by Pope Paul VI in Evangelii Nuntiandi:

> It is . . . a matter of reaching and overturning, by force of the
> Gospel Message, the criteria of judgement, the ruling values,
> the points of interest, the lines of thinking, the sources of
> inspiration, and the pattern of living among human beings that
> are contrary to God's message and Salvation plan.[2]

---

[1]FRANCISCUS X. SEDA, "The Task of the Catholic University in the Dialogue between Faith and Culture in a Plural Multireligious Society", in ARIJ A. ROEST CROLLIUS, ed., Inculturation, Working Papers of Living Faith and Cultures, XI, Gregorian University Press, Rome, 1989, p.101.

[2]POPE PAUL VI, Evangelii Nuntiandi, no. 19.

6.1   Inculturation Within the Igbo Birth Rites

When one speaks of the Igbo Birth rites in general, so many rituals that characterise this stage of life are involved. Constituting the Igbo Birth rites, as has already been hinted, are such rituals as pregnancy rites, birth rites proper and after birth rites.

The type and mode of pregnancy rites, following the research carried out, are so varied among the different sections of Igboland. They range from 'Ije Nkpe' (consultation with fortune-tellers to know the mind of the deity and expectations of the pregnancy), to the placatory and protective sacrificial rituals such as: 'Igba aja Umunna' (kindred sacrifice), 'Aja Mkpowaibe' or 'Ize ife Ajani', as one finds in places like Enugu-Agidi; 'Ikpa agbara Ime' in some parts of Enugu-Ezike. There are other indifferent rites as 'Itu-Eze' or 'Ikufo Eze' (perforating the teeth) - reckoned as a more beautifying feature, 'Ineta Eze' (viewing the teeth), and 'Irunye Aku' restrictive rituals found in Ezeagu areas. In Ahoada areas it is at this time that the circumcision of women take place. There are still other medicinal rituals as taking of herbs and concoction to ensure a fast and safe delivery. Most of these rituals are meant to solicit the favour of the deity for the gift of child and also have a reassuring value for the pregnant woman[3]. They have, therefore, psychological and social effects.

At the birth of child there begins a recovery period for the mother referred to as 'Omugwo'- a period of intensive care of both mother and child. Characterising this stage are such rituals as 'Iga mmanya Omugwo' (provision of paturitional wine), 'Isa ala' (washing of the breast - preparation for breast-feeding), the 'Otubo' (Umbilical cord) ritual, 'Isi Ji Uda' (cooking yam of delivery), 'Iwacha Uno' (Purification), and 'Nchegbe nne na nwa' (giving drink to mother and child).

As after-birth rituals are the traditionally important rites of circumcision ('Ibe Ugwu'), the Naming ceremony - 'Igu Afa', 'Ikuputa nwa (Outing), and traditional Outing ceremony or what, in Christian circles, is referred to as Churching ceremony - 'Ije ahia nwa'.

All these rituals are situated at the inception, which is a strategic period in the life of an individual. A grip of this strategic period means a grip at the traditional foundation of the ontological potentials of the young infant, even before the formal enculturative process sets in. It is at this inception period that the Igbos believe the new child is firmly rooted, insured and anchored at the traditional ancestral foundations of the society. Ignoring this stage and interfering in the later period of the child, is tantamount to working with the shoots of a firmly rooted tree, which defies every attempt at re-channelling its source of growth, as long as the root remains intact in its foundation. On the contrary, an involvement of the faith with culture even at this early stage through inculturation is possible through the conscientization and conscious responsibility of its community. As Walsh admits, "a child is vulnerable to and, therefore, receives every act or

---

[3]Cf., F. A. ARINZE, Sacrifice in Ibo Religion, p. 39.

carelessness that enfolds it, beginning from the womb of its mother".[4]

In as much as no stage should be ignored in ensuring a firm rooting of the child, one seriously advocates that major attention should be focused especially on the rites after the birth of the child on account of their traditional importance and significance among the Igbos.

6.1.1 Integration of the Christian Faith with Igbo Birth Rites

It is axiomatically stated in Mathematics that parallel lines can never meet. Inculturation is being discussed simply because it is glaringly clear that Faith is not incompatible with the culture of peoples. Culture that stays on parallel lines, and at times, even in opposition to the Faith does not engage in any type of dialogue with the Faith.

Our exposition of the Igbo Culture has revealed that Igbo culture is not incompatible with the christian faith. We have explored the beautiful potentials of the Igbo, which should glorify and make the christian faith in Igboland to flourish. Seeing the faith and Igbo culture as incompatible could lead to a vehement opposition to Igbo culture. A Jesuit missionary, commenting on the compatibility of some Igbo cultural values, remarks:

> . . . for example some aspects of the strongly knit family structures, much of the drumming and dancing, many art forms, many rituals and prayers connected with the major life events of birth, marriage and death quite compatible with christianity and indeed quite beautiful, were abandoned, with resultant feelings of loss, diffidence and homelessness among the converts.[5]

From their very nature, faith is something that comes from God, while culture is learnt and acquired by man. If faith should develop in a culture in order to be 'fully discerned, fully thought and fully lived'[6], then, faith must tow the line of inculturation, which is a two-way kind of process - not only of penetration and integration, but of readiness to give and to receive, which is a true mark of dialogue. It is only though such a process that faith can serve as the soul of culture, in order that culture survives. Surely not every type of evangelisation can penetrate culture. The type of evangelisation evidenced in Igboland that existed with assumptions of incompatibility with the culture cannot but remain on the periphery and outside of culture. Only

---

[4]LIAM G. WALSH, Sacraments of Initiation, Geoffrey Chapman, p. 103.

[5]J. B. SCHUYLER, "Conceptions of Christianity in the context of Tropical Africa: Nigerian reactions to its advent", essay in Christianity in Tropical Africa, ed. C. C. Baeta, London / Oxford, 1968, p. 210.

[6]Cf., FRANCISCUS X. SEDA, op. cit., p. 101.

an 'inculturated evangelisation which seeks to arouse and develop the christian faith should . . . reach the heart of culture'. Describing the effect of such a faith integrated with culture, Marcello Azevedo further writes:

> Through a process of inculturated evangelisation which is respectful and critical, dialogic and dialectical, the gospel message may succeed in becoming a new source of inspiration stemming from the very core of the presuppositions of culture. Thus a culture emerges which is at the same time new in its perspectives and faithful to both its original and deep human cultural teleology and the liberating and transforming action of the Spirit.[7]

Discussing the relationship of the christian faith with non-christian religions, the Fathers of Vatican II declared the good things and positive potentials in such cultures as 'preparatio evangelii'. In the same light, and especially in his thesis on anonymous christians, Karl Rahner regards such potentials as supernatural or grace-filled elements, which an evangeliser needs only to stimulate and utilise in bringing the anonymous christian to an explicit consciousness of the latent Christ in his own religious system, since there is no other revelation outside of Christ. Commenting on those grace-filled elements, Shorter maintains,

> It follows that the 'grace-filled' elements which Karl Rahner discerns in non-Christian religions are not simply ignored in the evangelisation process. They are important components of the new cultural form adopted by the christian faith after evangelisation, and they may also offer insight to the Universal Church in the exchange which takes place between the particular churches.[8]

What is recommended, then, is a dialogical communion between faith and culture. When that happens the faith cannot but renew, correct, purify, complete and restore the culture in dialogue, which means performing the function of yeast in culture.

With reference to our subject of discussion, the christian faith is expected to enter into dialogue with the Igbo Birth rites. Such a synthesis will first and foremost, reveal the false rituals, dispose of all superstitious elements and replace them with authentic religious attitudes, while holding fast to the non-superstitious elements in the culture. Let us see how such

---

[7]MARCELLO AZEVEDO, "The Challenges put to the Christian Faith by Modern Contemporary Culture", in ARIJ A. ROEST CROLLIUS, ed., Inculturation, Working Papers on Living Faith and Cultures, XI, Gregorian University Press, Rome, 1989, p. 66.

[8]A. SHORTER, Towards a Theology of Inculturation, p. 97

a dialogue and integration can look like in the various aspects of the Birth rites. The possibility of this integration depends on which rituals are compatible with the christian Faith.

6.1.1.1   The Christian Faith and the Pregnancy Rites

Psychologically and humanly speaking, it is clear that the pregnancy period, being a moment of joy for the woman and her family, is a phase of uncertainty, anxiety and insecurity. This is on account of the fear of the unknown and all the more because of the value of life involved. This applies generally in all cultures. Anthropologists have this to say:

> Pregnancy is the foreshadowing of birth. It is, therefore, in itself a crisis condition, or a preliminary phase of the critical event of giving birth. Most peoples seize upon the gestation period as calling for a cultural relief of their anxieties. Chief among these anxieties are that (1) the child will not develop ideally, (2) the fetus will miscarry, and (3) the birth will be difficult. Pregnancy tabus and injunctions are supposed to bring freedom from these fears.[9]

In a very particular way, the degree of the anxiety and insecurity heightens for the Igbo woman, as a result of the strong value of life and child-birth of the Igbos, as well as the societal implications involved[10]. It has already been pointed out that for the Igbos, the birth of a child means for the mother the fulfilment of her womanhood and her full acceptance and the consolidation of her position in her marital home. Such reasons can lead someone into psychological and physical tensions in this stage. These are the major reasons why the pregnancy rituals are performed. They are meant to ensure a hitch-free birth, health of the new life and its mother, and provide a psychological relaxation for the pregnant woman.

With the deep religious sense of the Igbo, regulations and religious rituals are demanded in such precarious and therefore, dangerous period. Any type of haphazard ritual would not give the Igbo the psychological satisfaction needed. The ritual should be one that registers in the nerve centre of the source of anxiety and insecurity. The ritual ought to reassure

---

[9]EDWARD ADAMSON HOEBEL & EVERETT L. FROST, Cultural and Social Anthropology, McGraw-Hill Book Company, New York, 1976, p. 155.

[10]"To realize the urgency, spontaneity and earnestness of such sacrifices for children it will help to bear in mind that for the Ibos, marriage without children has completely lost its meaning. The Ibo woman could well say with Rachel: 'Thou must need give me children, or it will be my death.'(Gen. 30:1) - Cf., F. A. ARINZE, Sacrifice in Igbo Religion, p. 40.

a firm and strong contact with the giver of life and restore a feeling of security. Unfortunately those consulted by most villagers in such moments are diviners and fortune-tellers. These exploit the situation and supply the needed satisfaction.

However, the christian faith makes it clear that all life belong to God, and it is He that determines everything. This is expressly clear in St. John's Gospel: "Through him all things came to be, not one thing had its beginning but through him. All that came to be had life in him . . ."[11] This theological fact is the reason for our firm belief in God. It means that all have God as their source of existence and owe him honour and absolute dependence for everything. The Psalmist reinforces this fact:

> All creatures depend on you
> to feed them throughout the year;
> you provide the food they eat,
> with generous hand you satisfy their hunger.
>
> You turn your face away, they suffer,
> You stop their breath, they die
> and revert to dust.
> You give breath, fresh life begins,
> You keep renewing the world.[12]

On account of this, it becomes imperative for all creatures to look up to God for everything and in all situations of life. "Our help comes from the Lord who made heaven and earth".[13] Every assurance and security which we need as creatures in all our daily difficulties should be sought for and got from this Almighty God. Through the Psalmist God tells us:

> I rescue all who cling to me,
> I protect whoever knows my name
> I answer everyone who invokes me,
> I am with them when they are in trouble;
> I bring them safety and honour,
> I give them LIFE, long and full,
> and show them how I can save.[14]

When, therefore, diviners and fortune-tellers, who are consulted for rituals in pregnancy, claim to manipulate or re-channel the course of events of life through any other power or means outside of God, they either deceive

---

[11]Jn. 1: 3 - 4

[12]Psalm 104: 27 - 30

[13]Psalm 121: 2

[14]Psalm 91 : 14 - 16

themselves and those who approach them for a foreknowledge of the reality, or they are challenging God.

In the Igbo case, however, these diviners exploit the situation and, by any means whatsoever, try to restore this sense of security and psychological relaxation. Christians continue to wonder about the success of these diviners. The answer is clear. Any ritual which pays attention to the individuals and the factors involved, and shows interest in these individuals, would definitely capture the devotion and the allegiance of the Igbo. An observation of the christian ritual shows for instance the blessing of a pregnant woman, done in a very haphazard, disinterested and impersonal manner, that leaves the pregnant woman in doubt of its authenticity. That is why she goes home and consults a diviner who, even though he uses useless means, yet convincingly restores confidence in the woman. Why must there be always these parallel rituals for the same person? Experience reveals that where the Igbo is assured of a personal and interested ritual treatment, there would be no room to contain those who frequent such places. The various charismatic centres and healing homes in Nigeria such as Elele in Port Harcourt, where more personal and interested touch of patients are experienced, is an eloquent testimony of this fact.

In integrating the faith, therefore, in such a cultural structure, one thinks of a possibility of supplying a christian ritual for the pregnancy period. It has to be somewhat different from what it has hitherto been. It needs not be a stereo-typed general type of ritual, but should be so elastic in order to give adequate attention and a real human touch to the psychological situation of the pregnant woman. Such a ritual could even be preceded by a sort of dialogue with the pregnant woman, the findings of which could be incorporated and utilised in the ritual, hence, room should be made for spontaneous prayer in the ritual. It would not be out of place to include in such a ritual a sort of physical contact with the woman by way of a symbolic blessing and sprinkling of her womb with holy water.

The Igbos would be in favour of offering sacrifice for the pregnancy. It is important afterwards or even to situate the ritual within the Holy mass requested by and celebrated for the pregnancy. There is nothing as convincing to the Igbo as a ritual that is interestedly performed with a tinge of personal touch. It becomes glaringly clear that the woman has been personally and spiritually cartered for in her need. Such a ritual cannot but convey a psychological message which will have a soothing effect on the woman. It should leave her convinced of a divine protection both for herself and for her child in the womb.

However impressive the ritual may be, it should not be thought that the ritual would replace the medical and clinical attention for the pregnant woman. One would even insist that purely medically recommended traditional concoctions, made from roots and herbs, which have been found helpful for allaying pains during pregnancy could be recommended. Care should be taken to see that no superstitious means are involved in the production of such concoctions. It is indeed the mind of the Church that,

Whatever goodness is found in the minds and hearts of men, or in the particular customs and cultures of peoples, far from being lost is purified, raised to a higher level and reaches its perfection, for the glory of God, the confusion of the demons and the happiness of men.[15]

Therefore, with reference to such rituals as 'Ikufo Eze' and 'Igbawa Obu' - which are purely aimed at beautifying the woman, in order to influence the beauty of the offspring -, and 'Ineta Eze' which are performed in Ezeagu areas, and female circumcision performed around Ahoada areas at this period, since they are not necessarily hooked on to any idol worship, they could be recognised if they are not accompanied by such worships. This would be a cultural recognition that has no repercussion for the christian faith.

But the other sacrificial rituals such as: 'Ize ife Ajani', 'Igba Aja Umunna', 'Aja Nkpowaibe', 'Ikpa agbara Ime' of Enugu-Ezike areas, 'Ije Nkpe' and 'Isa Ishu' of Ezeagu region, and wearing of protective charms as well as consultative rituals of the fortune-tellers and diviners - on account of the false worship and superstitions involved are recommended for purging. It is the aim of all evangelisation to purge culture:

It purges of evil associations those elements of truth and grace which are found among peoples, and which are, as it were, a secret presence of God; and it restores them to Christ their source who overthrows the rule of the devil and limits the manifold malice of evil.[16]

In order to supply for and satisfy the spiritual yearnings of the family, who in the normal traditional rituals offer for sacrifices such living animals as cocks, egg, white cloth and kola-nuts - all being meaningful symbols for Igbos, one recommends that allowance be made so that these items be still offered along in offertory procession as offerings by the family for the Mass celebrated for their intention. Instead of these being sacrificially offered on idols with the blood smeared on the womb of the pregnant woman as is usual, it now becomes a wholehearted gift for the same motive, to be used for and on the needy and poor members of the community. As a substitute, bread and wine, consecrated into the body and blood of Christ would be offered as most acceptable offering to God.

An open, personal and concrete but interested christian dialogue with the Igbo pregnancy rituals would surely come out with a satisfactory and salutary effect for both the faith and the Igbo culture.

---

[15]VATICAN II, Lumen Gentium, no. 17; (Cf., Ad Gentes, no. 9)

[16]VATICAN II, Ad Gentes, no. 9

6.1.1.2   The Christian Faith and the Igbo Birth Rites

"The arrival of a child in the family is one of the greatest blessings of life. African peoples greet this event with joy and satisfaction".[17] This observation of Mbiti is given its most eloquent expression among the Igbos. In some parts of the Imo State like Okwuato as well as other parts of Igboland, the announcement of the arrival of a child in the community is greeted by the whole village and hamlet with spontaneous and hilarious expressions of joy and jubilation, singing and dancing of traditional songs such as: "Onye ihe oma di mma, bia gburu anyi aka, Ala anyi di mma eeh!" (meaning: Let anyone who cherishes goodness come to embrace or shake our hands, for our goddess 'Ala' is indeed good!).

Generally this new gift of life and its beginning are greeted with deeply religious and traditionally celebrated symbolic rituals within a cultural framework. The motive for these traditional rituals range from purely social to religious, cultural and hygienic reasons. Let us have a view of some of them.

6.1.1.2.1   The Paturitional Period: 'Omugwo' Rites

The first immediate phase is the actual birth of child and the recuperative moment for the mother and child known as the 'Omugwo' period. This stage is characterised by the special care taken of the mother and child by way of nutritional entertainment and their secluded life. It is within this period that such rituals as 'isi ji uda' (rite of eating yam foo foo of the delivery), 'emume otubo' (umbilical cord ritual), 'Isa ala' (preparatory rite for breast-feeding), 'iga mmanya omugwo' (rite of parturitional wine), 'nchegbe nne na nwa '(rite of commensalism for mother and child) are performed. Most of these are simply plain and symbolic expressions which do not necessarily involve false worship. Their motives are either hygienic, social or anthropological. As long as no other external religious motives are brought into these rituals, they are not inimical to the christian faith. This period ends with the traditional purification rites - 'ikpo ntu nwa' or 'nsi-ulu-enyi', which should bring the seclusion period of the mother to an end. She can henceforth be about her normal household affairs. The termination of her seclusion is celebrated by the inner circle of the extended family, who are invited and sumptuously entertained. It is also referred to as 'ikuputa nwa'- introducing the child to the extended family - a sort of prelude to the formal social birth of the child before the whole community.[18] An inculturation strategy could be a possible visit of the family by a Church

---

[17]JOHN MBITI, Introduction to African Religion, p. 82.

[18]Cf., TONY UBESIE, Odinala ndi Igbo, p. 77.

representative as a gesture of goodwill wishes. It would be best if the priest visits the family, registering if only his physical presence, or even giving both mother and child his first blessing after childbirth. In this way, his presence begins to be felt even at this stage in the extended family level.

6.1.1.2.2   Igbo Naming Ceremony: Traditional yet Christian?

"When a child is named, he is both individualised and incorporated into society".[19] Of Africans in particular, Mbiti writes,

> The name is considered in African societies to be very much part of the personality of the person. Therefore, it is taken seriously, and chosen with care and consideration. Often names of people have a meaning, and it is this meaning which must be given due consideration.[20]

The naming ceremony can be considered as the first major ritual of great traditional importance. Commenting on the Igbo traditional naming ceremony, Obiukwu refers to it as 'the turning point in the history of the Igbo child'. According to him, ". . . it has a double dimension; social and religious. With it a child is incorporated and received officially into 'umunna' (extended family) community".[21] It is exactly strategic importance which the traditional naming ceremony has for the Igbos that makes it imperative that serious thoughts be given to ways of integrating this rite with the christian faith.

A view of the description of the ceremony, which Obiukwu furnishes us with, may help to give us more insight into the details for consideration. According to him, the ceremony takes place in 'Obi' ancestral compound - normally before the ancestral shrine of the extended family. The chief actor is the Okpara / Onyishi - the traditional head of the extended family, assisted by the other heads of the nuclear family. The ceremony is witnessed by an invited cross-section of the community. The chief actor performs the rite thus:

> Having washed his hands, he takes up white chalk and draws some lines on the ground . . . . takes one of the kola-nuts, . . . gives thanks to Chukwu (God), to Ala, to the ancestors and all the good spirits of the community, prays for himself, . . . the whole members of the family, for all present and finally for the child about to be received into the umunna. . . . breaks the

---

[19]ARNOLD VAN GENNEP, op. cit., p. 62.

[20]J. MBITI, Introduction to African Religion, p. 87.

[21]S. OBIUKWU, op. cit., p. 36.

> kola-nuts throws some on the altar, and some pieces on the ground. He eats parts of this nut, breaks and shares the rest of the nuts to all present.
> The child is . . . handed over to Okpara, who . . . lays it with its back flat on the ground. He consults the parent for the choice of name for the child, then, picks it up, addresses it, recounts for it the accepted norms of conduct in the community.[22]

Among other things that follow are the symbolic handing over of working tools with admonitions and other symbolic actions. He finally concludes by a formal calling of the chosen name. The child is thus publicly and fully received and incorporated into the extended family. The ceremony culminates by thanksgiving offering to 'ala', ancestors and guardian spirits, and the ceremony is brought to a conclusion by feasting. In the other cultural areas of Igboland slight variations may exist, but the main structure remains the same. This represent a sample for us of a naming ceremony of the Igbo child.

We gather even from this description as points to look into: the value of the naming ceremony and the significance of the Igbo names; the community-centred factor expressed in the extended family context; the ancestral implication; the role of the nuclear head of the lineage - the Okpara - of the family in the rite and the festive mood of the rite.

With reference to the significance of the naming ceremony and even the relevance of the given names, it should be noted that

> Names are not merely considered as tags by means of which individuals may be distinguished, but are intimately associated with various events in the life of the individual as well as those of the family and the larger social group.[23]

This is very much true of the Igbos. Also, as has already been remarked, for the Igbos, and in fact for all Africans,

> an indigenous name . . . personifies the individual, tells some story about the parents and / or the family of the bearer; and in a more general sense, points to the values of the society into which the individual is born.[24]

---

[22]Ibid., pp. 36 -38.

[23]H. WIESCHHOFF, "The Social Significance of Names Among the Ibo of Nigeria", American Anthropologist, vol. 43, 1941, p. 212.

[24]EBO UBAHAKWE, "Culture Content of Igbo Personal Names", in F. C. OGBALU & E. N. EMENANJO, eds., Igbo Language and Culture, vol. 2, University Press Ltd., Ibadan, 1982, p. 27.

Igbo names are pregnant with significant and descriptive meanings. Apart from shedding light on the occasion or circumstances of birth of the individual such as the psychological, seasonal, temporal and congenital circumstances, they tend to give clues through which a family history could be reconstructed. They thereby supply for the disadvantages and shortcomings of illiteracy. "From the list of names in a family, it should be possible to reconstruct or glean something about the history, the aspirations, fears, hopes and vicissitudes of the family . . .".[25] Also the beliefs, mentality and historical circumstances are reflected in most Igbo names. Hence, Anozia is right in concluding that "Igbo names present us with the most authentic and most ancient records of their beliefs and ways of life that comes down to us".[26] The scale of values reflected in the Igbo names in their descending order of importance runs thus: God, deities, and spiritual beings; virtuous qualities; kinship; natural phenomena; social entities; calendar; titles; non-virtuous qualities; natural physical objects; parts of the body; material assets; occupation. A great majority of Igbo names manifest the peoples' awareness of their complete dependence on the spiritual beings, namely: the Supreme God, the deities and ancestral spirits, and their religious sentiments. The spirituality attached to such names is very provocative:

> They express among other things, confidence, faith, gratitude, hope, fear, humility, joy, reverence and repentance. These are sentiments spontaneously coming from the hearts of the parents and relatives who give the names to their children.[27]

If these values play very important roles in our faith as christians, one wonders what could be more christian as such Igbo names. In the official ecclesiastical documents it is clearly stated that the conferences of bishops may allow catechumens to keep the name they already have, or take a traditional christian name, or one that is familiar in their culture, provided this can admit a christian interpretation.[28] What theological reasons could, then, be given as grounds for not recognising and using the Igbo names? Could the traditional contexts of the giving of Igbo names not be strategically inculturated? Ezeanya evaluates the positive effects that should accrue from such an exercise:

> By making use of the Igbo names at the christening and

---

[25] Ibid., p. 28.

[26] P. I. ANOZIA, op. cit., p. 89.

[27] S. N. EZEANYA, A Handbook of Igbo Christian Names, C. M. S. Press, Port Harcourt, 1967, p. 10.

[28] Ordo Initiationis Christianae Adultorum, Vatican City, 1972, General Introduction, IV, no.88, p. 38.

naming ceremony, christians will be preserving a splendid heritage. They will be paying deserved tribute to the memory of the deeply religious Igbo ancestors.[29]

Another important point that ought to be considered is the traditional communitarian aspect. This is a feature already fully discussed in line with Igbo solidarity. The naming ceremony is a ritual where the communitarian factor is demonstrated. It is expected that all the members of the extended family and the traditional community be physically present for this ceremony. Even the fact that such names as 'Igwebuike' (multitude is strength), 'Ibebuike' (one's neighbour is his strength), 'Ubammaduka' (the greater the crowd the better) are purposely given to individuals, goes to emphasise the importance of unity and solidarity for the Igbos. The reason for such names is simply to "inculcate in them the indispensable value of solidarity and the vital necessity of building up an authentic intimate bond among them".[30] It has been expressed that it has not been easy for Igbo christians to identify with their fellow brothers and sisters on account of the dichotomy created between them and their relations in the traditional community in the past. It is during these ritual ceremonies which are moments of joy as well as in moments of sorrow that this communitarian factor is expected to be manifested. What a beautiful and strategic impression it would create if, within this communitarian aggregation for the naming ceremony, the presence of the christian community or even some christian participation is registered. One wonders why there should not be a recognition of the traditional naming ceremony, reflecting and integrating it in the christian baptismal rites. It offers an opportunity to tap the potentials of the communitarian factor through the recognition of the traditional context, and using this ceremony to construct a traditionally oriented preliminary rites of infant baptism.

The traditional naming ceremony in Gabon offers an example of a practice worthy of emulation in the construction of a traditionally oriented rite of infant Baptism among the Igbos. In Gabon the rite of naming coexists with a rite analogous to baptism, so that the baptism is regarded as a lustration, a purging and purifying rite, a final rite of separation from previous world. Arnold van Gennep quotes and describes a vivid picture of such a co-existence thus:

> A basin of water is provided and the headman of the village or family sprinkles water upon it, giving it a name and invoking a blessing that he may have health, grow up to manhood or womanhood, have numerous progeny, possess riches.[31]

---

[29]Ibid.

[30]M. MOZIAH, op. cit., p. 241.

[31]SIR DANIEL WILSON, West Africa, quoted by A. VAN GENNEP, op. cit., p. 63.

To think of such an example points immediately to a restructuring of the rite of Infant baptism. This would aim at accommodating the traditional context which furnishes the communitarian psychological factor. It must be observed that hitherto this community-centredness and solidarity with the traditional community have always been missing in our Infant baptisms. This is a vivid fact, which was openly revealed in the deliberation for a new Era of Evangelisation in Nigeria, during which it was remarked that,

> The naming ceremony gathers together kith and kin, a cultural group. The child is acknowledged and received into the kinship, with thanksgiving to God. Our baptism ceremony at the moment does not generate anything like the emotions of the naming ceremony. Besides, we lose a privileged moment for evangelising.[32]

When one, therefore, advocates for this community-centred ritual, one is re-echoing and actualising some authors, who suggest that "the Igbo naming ceremony which is a community-centred event should be examined critically as a possible basis for constructing a baptismal rite that would be authentically Igbo".[33]

The naming ceremony for the Igbo is one of the most important means of expressing and influencing solidarity. In it, the child is formally recognised and accepted into the community, where all members, through active physical presence, eating and drinking together[34], show their solidarity to the new child and renew the same among themselves.[35] It, therefore, follows that an active presence of Christianity in this ceremony would mean a gesture of solidarity not only with the child, but also with his community - both christian and traditional. This is, in effect, a movement towards the inculturation of the faith within the system.

A direct recognition of the traditional naming ceremony would definitely come up with some religious implications as to the relationship with ancestors and attitudes towards them, the value of the Igbo traditional shrines and altars, with their accompanying cultural and ancestral symbols. There is also to be the problem of religious attitude to such places, by way of traditional offerings and libations.

---

[32]JAMES C. OKOYE, "A New Era of Evangelisation", in New Era of Evangelisation, p. 10.

[33]J. P. C. NZOMIWU, "The African Church and Indigenisation Question: An Igbo Experience", in AFER, VOL. 28, NO. 5, oCT. 1986, P. 330.

[34]It should be noted that togetherness in eating and drinking - Commensalism - is a positive and powerful anthropological factor and determinant of solidarity.

[35]Cf., M. MOZIA, op. cit., p. 213 - 214.

The question of the value, relationship and attitude of the Igbo to ancestors has been exhaustively treated in the earlier chapters of this work.[36] It is seen that there is a very real, strong and living contact between the Igbos and their ancestors. The fact that they are regarded as the traditionally canonised saints leaves much room for dialogue and discussion. Much consideration should go into a correlation of the Igbo ancestral attitude with the christian teaching on the communion of the saints. One notes the similarity existing between the Igbo traditional understanding of the ancestral spirit and the christian understanding of patron saints. One must, however, recognise that this idea for the Igbos is more concrete and vividly expressed in their day-to-day life. Perhaps the theological clues for solution to this may be sought in Karl Rahner's concept of the 'Anonymous christians', being referred to the dead, who never had the opportunity of hearing about Christ in their life-time, and who lived so decent and in a God-fearing manner. The solution of this question would be a very strategic step in the process of Inculturation.

With reference, then, to the naming ceremony, it ought to be remembered that the ancestors are cooperators with God in the gift of fertility manifested in an unbroken procession of posterity in the ancestral lineage. Hence, ancestors occupy a very important place in naming ceremonies. For the Igbos, the ancestors become officially the child's patron spirit - guiding and protecting the child from possible contingencies which might result, much more as a child's parents do. It should not surprise to note that in the ritual, response to this spiritual relationship is made through libations or other offerings to the ancestor. Arinze points out that:

> In the case of sacrifices to the ancestors and the kinder spirits . . . . there seems to be no doubt that the Iboman feels a union with them when eating the sacrificial meal. He gives a part of the kola-nut to the spirit and chews the rest. He gives a part of the fowl, fou-fou and wine to the spirit or ancestor and divides the rest with his neighbours.[37]

Full active involvement of christians in such sacrifices has always been problematic, because christians do not meddle with anything offered to idols or what is involved in false worship. If the chief actor in such ceremonies must necessarily perform the offerings and pour libations, he must make use

---

[36]Refer to Chapters 3 & 4.

[37]FRANCIS A. ARINZE, op. cit., p. 103. "In Sacrifices to them the Igbos invariably start with the kola-nut, for the kola-nut symbolises friendship. It is the traditional sign of welcome and when split and partaken of with others it constitutes a pact of loyalty and oneness" - E. G. PARRINDER, African Traditional Religion, p. 88.

of his own share of the common items. [38]

Another aspect that may create some christian discomfort may be the fact that this ceremony is performed normally before the ancestral shrine of the family. This is normally situated in one central corner of the house. It is there - **'onunna'**: 'mouth of fathers' that the ancestral symbols and ritual staffs and spears of authority are housed[39]. The fact that these symbols have been physically handed down from the olden times by the various forefathers in an unbroken chain of succession, down to our times creates some aura of awe, reverence and respect for the ancestors whose symbols these things are. These symbols are legacies of the past and physical linking objects with the dead members. To the oldest as the physically nearest member of the community to the ancestors is assigned the special care of these traditional treasures and symbols of traditional authority. The respect, reverence and highest position accorded to the eldest, accrue from this factor. Therefore, ordinarily, under most circumstances, people "feel comfortable in the precincts of the ancestral shrine, for one is being observed and cared for by family forces whom he is caused to respect through annual reminders of their vast powers over him".[40]

The admonitions of St. Gregory to Bishop Augustine of Canterbury among the Anglo-Saxon furnishes us with food for thought in respect to the shrines. It was recommended that,

> . . . the temples of the idols in that country should on no account be destroyed. He is to destroy the idols, but the temples themselves are to be aspersed with holy water, altars set up, and relics enclosed in them. For if these temples are well built, they are to be purified from devil-worship and dedicated to the service of true God. In this way, we hope that the people, seeing that its temples are not destroyed, may abandon idolatry and resort to these places as before, and may come to know and adore the true God.[41]

---

[38]The sacrifice may take the form of libations, and small quantities of food, or the killing of an animal, pouring out the blood on the altar or on the ground, and cooking the rest for participants. Therefore, it is the blood which is given to the spirits, and sometimes fat and intestines because blood is the life. Whatsoever is offered to the ancestral spirits are commonly placed at their shrines and have a communion significance. - (Cf., E. G. PARRINDER, African Traditional Religion, pp. 87 - 88).

[39]AUSTIN J. SHELTON, The Igbo - Igala Borderland, State University of New York Press, Albany, 1971, p. 63.

[40]AUSTIN J. SHELTON, The Igbo - Igala Borderland, p. 64.

[41]THE VENERABLE BEDE, A History of the English Church and People, transl. by L. SHERLEY-PRICE, 1955 (Penguin ed.), Harmondsworth, Middx. 1, 30.

Besides, when one considers the extreme importance and cultural value of these traditional symbols of authority for the Igbo, one reckons that they are absolutely irreplaceable as legacies of the past. One does not even need to replace them. The very moment christianity enters into dialogue with the traditional system, purification of these symbols by christianity is possible and imperative, so that they could be highly treasured without the attitude of worship. The right attitude to be given to these items of the past should be like those observed in the places of special honour and respect, where principal personalities must go to pay tribute and honour to the past heroes, and lay wreaths of remembrance. The question of invoking the ancestors in those places is in order, since it is possible to be even spiritually in contact with the dead members of our family. All said and done, this x-ray of the naming ceremony has revealed the possibilities whereby christianity can pave a way into the traditional system in such a fully traditionally charged instance of cultural expression. When the faith enters the heart of the Igbo community, its integration, in the words of Uzukwu

. . . becomes a sort of planting the seed which will sprout on African soil, becoming the leaven in the mass . . . . This is like becoming flesh within a receiving community to allow his message rock and be rocked by the very roots of the tradition of the receiving community.[42]

The naming ceremony offers an opportunity for spreading out the rite of infant baptism for the Igbos, which in turn makes room for accommodation and recognition of the traditional system. It situates the faith at the same time, in a privileged position to influence the system and the individuals involved in the process of inculturation. One observes even that the present-day mode of infant Baptism, whereby the rites are performed all at a go, leaves little or no lasting impact on the individual nor his traditional community. A ritual that is spread out to integrate the traditional rituals, and which, thereby, progresses gradually and establishes a stronger contact with the community of the new child, cannot but have a long lasting impact and influence, besides, making the christian faith take root and feel at home in the culture of the Igbos.

6.1.1.2.3 Rite of Circumcision - an Incorporation into both the Cultural and the Christian Communities?

Circumcision is a cultural and tribal feature, which, with other practices

---

[42]ELOCHUKWU E. UZUKWU, ed., Religion and African Culture, Spiritan Publications, Enugu, 1988, p. 164.

that have to do with the mutilating or splitting or perforation of the body for various reasons, fall into the same category. Generally, such practices as pulling out a tooth, cutting off or perforating the ear lobe, tattooing, scarifying or cutting the hair - all these have the natural motive of modifying the personality of the individual. Over and above these, circumcision rite tends to have a more cultural significance. The motive is to thereby separate one from the mass of humanity and assign to someone an identity which automatically and permanently incorporates him into a defined group. In the case of female circumcision, the excision of the erogenic centre, the objective is to remove the appendage by which the female resembles the male, and hence it is a rite of sexual differentiation on the same level with the assigning of dress, instrument or tools proper to each sex in the various cultures. It is, therefore, a mark that identifies one among his native community as a distinguishing mark so to speak.

Invariably, circumcision is performed either within the first eight days of birth or postponed to a later period, when it is integrated within the rite of tribal initiation into adulthood. It is this connection, that corroborates the idea of tribal incorporation. It is believed that the blood shed during circumcision binds one to the land - the mother earth of the particular cultural area, as well as to the past generations. Mbiti explains:

> This circumcision blood is like making a covenant, or a solemn agreement, between the individual and his people. Until the individual has gone through the operation, he is still an outsider.[43]

No doubt, circumcision in some culture is given some sexual significance: a sort of shedding off of the state of inactivity and the unveiling of the state of sexual activity. It is to the existence of such significance in cultures that Schmidt points to as he writes:

> It seems more and more evident among the semi-civilised peoples that circumcision was supposed according to their simple and incorrect ideas, to facilitate the reproductive act, and it is usually performed during mysterious puberty feasts when manhood is reached.[44]

However, this significance seems to be today untenable, on account of the resulting hygienic and sexual disadvantages, for which reason present-day physicians dissuade circumcision, especially for females.

In direct reference to this work, the research carried out among the various cultural areas of Igboland show that circumcision is a common

---

[43]J. MBITI, Introduction to African Religion, p. 93.

[44]PETER WILHELM SCHMIDT, in L'origine dé l'idée de Dieu, chapter IV, trans. J. J. PIETES, ANTHROPOS (Vienna, 1908), pp. 602 -603.

practice of the Igbos. This is generally performed on the eighth day after birth, even though around the Ndoni areas, that of the female is performed during pregnancy. In some areas like Enugu-Ezike, it is limited only to males. The Igbos adduce three reasons for circumcision: aesthetic motive, tribal identification, incorporation and a symbolic integration into the world of sexual activity. Traces of similarity between the Igbos and the Jewish race have been noticed in various aspects.[45] The question of circumcision is one of these. From this observable similarity, the cultural significance of circumcision of the Igbos as an integrative community becomes more plausible.

With reference to the christian faith, however, it must be acknowledged that membership to the community of the faithful does not depend on the belonging to a specific race as obtains in the Jewish community. Through membership of christian community by Baptism "there are no more distinction between Jew and Greek, slave and free, male and female, but all of you are one in Christ Jesus" (Gal. 3 : 28; Rom. 10 :12; 1 Cor. 12 : 13). "In that Image there is no room for distinction between Greek and Jew, between **circumcised and uncircumcised** . . . (Col. 3 : 11). From this point of view, the baptismal rite is distinct from the traditional circumcision rite. As Walsh points out,

> Baptism is not a rite of tribal or cultural initiation. It is a rite
> of freely chosen entry into a community in which the only basis
> of belonging is the choice of God, and in which there is no
> longer Jew or Greek, slave or free, male or female.[46]

It is, however, the intention of indirectly establishing the difference that motivates the desire of integrating both rites. It is such a union which should make the christian membership to shine out and act as a perfection. While the traditional rite identifies the individual as a concrete member of a human tribal community, the reception in the pre-baptismal ritual is the acceptance of the individual into the membership of God's people. It is possible to reconstruct an integrated ritual that can accommodate both rites, so that the pre-baptismal reception becomes a recognition of the tribal origins and the authenticity of the child in his traditional community. The transition of the child to membership of a wider horizon of God's people would become transparently manifested[47]. The transitional symbolism of this gesture could leave a lot of impact and influence on the tribal community of

---

[45]Confer Chapter 1.

[46]L. G. WALSH, op. cit., p. 71.

[47]Would this not agree with the transitional sentiments which St. Augustine tried to identify in the newly baptised, expressed thus: "Today is the octave of your birth; today is perfected in you the seal of faith which was given among our fathers of old on the eight day after physical circumcision". - ST.AUGUSTINE, Sermons, 8.

the child. Such an influence would be registered in the parents and relations of the child, who are the immediate community of this child and are expected to play an important role in the eventual upbringing and christian nurture of the child, whether they are christians or non-christians. Walsh points out that the rite of infant Baptism

> . . . draws the community and the parents of the child into the rite in a way that expresses their acceptance of responsibility for the christian nurture of the child, without which the Baptism cannot normally be celebrated.[48]

A reconstruction of an integrated ritual for the tribal circumcision rite and the pre-baptismal rite of reception into the christian community can be seen as an opportunity for making an in-road into the cultural centre of the Igbo child. This should be seen as strategic for the imprinting of the demands of christian way of life in the minds of the tribal community of the child.

Since both the naming ceremony and the circumcision rite are more or less celebrated at the same time among the Igbos, both could form a strong base for the construction of an initiatory celebration of the pre-baptismal aspects of the rite of infant Baptism, which one here recommends to be spread out a bit, and gradually celebrated in stages. Through this method, a traditionally symbolic expression of the rite of infant Baptism would be manifested within the significant and strategic moments of the socially sensitive and traditional gestures of the Igbos over a new child. Hence, one reinforces the call for a structural reconstruction of the rite of Infant Baptism.

6.1.2 Can the Churching Ceremony and the Igbo Traditional Outing Ceremony co-exist?

'Ipu - Ahia' - Outing into the market of both mother and child after birth is another important traditional rite among the Igbos.[49] After about two to three months after delivery, when the mother is quite refreshed and is back to her normal physical fitness, this ceremony takes place. Fully dressed in her best attire, and amidst relations and friends and neighbours, both mother and child make their first official outing outside the home. The venue for this outing is the traditional public square, the public forum, which is normally the biggest market place in the area. Here the mother and child pay homage to the traditional shrine, situated always in a strategic section of the market square.   It is here that the sentiments of gratitude and thanksgiving, as well as offerings and prayers are expressed to the deity of

---

[48]Ibid., p. 70.

[49]Cf., VICTOR C UCHENDU, The Igbo of Southeast Nigeria, p. 60.

the land. Then follows the joyous and jubilant procession round the entire market, during which both mother and child are heartily congratulated and ushered with gifts in various forms. When this is over, the whole entourage settles down in the family stand in the market, where the rest of the day would be spent in a joyous and exuberant atmosphere of festivity, which is punctuated by eating, drinking and merry-making.

This ceremony has an important significance for the traditional community. It is an equivalent ceremony which, in the christian circle, is celebrated as the Churching ceremony. Owing to the hitherto lack of dialogue between the christian faith and the Igbo culture, both ceremonies are celebrated parallel, at times one after the other. Generally speaking, the outing ceremony marks the termination of the seclusion period of inactivity for the woman. The outing of mother and child is for the purpose of officially manifesting and publicising the new birth as well as the eventual public acclamation and reception of mother and child. This is necessary for their full integration once more into the social and public life of the community.

Seen in its entirety, the ceremony has religious, social and economic motives. It marks the first formal and public act of Thanksgiving and homage to the deity of the land for the gift of the new child. The precedence of this aspect before any other goes to show its religious importance for the people. Homage and thanksgiving through prayer and gift offerings are made to the deity, who is regarded as responsible for the gift of life. The social aspect lies in the reintegration of the mother and the new child within the active society. This is manifested by the jubilant reception and the free for all festival of the community. The economic motive is self evident. One should imagine that the arrival of the new child has occasioned a lot of financial spending and expenditure for the family. The presentation of gifts to mother and child in this ceremony serves as an indirect reimbursement for such incurred expenditures of the family. This is also a manifestation of the Igbo sense of solidarity. Seen in the light of this work, the outing ceremony, which, as it were, culminates the birth rites deserves attention. Regarding the religious aspects, the purpose of the outing ceremony coincides with the purpose of the Christian Churching ceremony. It is essential that the woman pays tribute to God, makes a thanksgiving for the gift of the child and for her safe delivery. It is, however, the object of such tribute and worship in both systems that raises the points of disagreement. It is this aspect that presents a problem for an integrated and unified celebration.

As long as the traditional shrines in these strategic public places have false-gods as their object of worship, paying homage to them remains inimical to the christian faith. For, "You must worship the Lord your God and serve him alone (Dt. 6 : 13; Mt. 4 : 10). Besides, it has already been demonstrated that God is the author of all life. Such homage and thanksgiving should be addressed to him and him alone. For the Igbo traditional public places to qualify for such religious attitude, they should be subjected to conversion and purification similar to the ones referred to in the admonitions of St Gregory (already quoted above)[50]. It is only after such a purification exercise that one could accord the public places purely traditional and social status, where honour and tribute to the dead ancestors can be paid without any religious bias. Even if the objects and symbols transmitted from the ancient past are preserved in such places, they should not be for the purpose of religious attitude. They should be seen as museum objects. But this is difficult for the Igbo, who has a very real and concrete relationship with his ancestors, hence through these objects the Igbos call up a lively and sentimental relationship with the past generations. Latria is a theological term that limits expressions of religious worship only to God alone. Ordinary visit in honour and memory of the past generations after such places must have been purified and blessed should not attract any objections, since such places in even the christianised countries of Europe are equally very highly regarded and guarded. Wreaths are even laid in such public places, which is an expression of some spiritual sentiments. One foresees, however, the possibility in future of even celebrating the Eucharist in purified locations of these strategic traditional public places, especially when the christian faith must have penetrated into the heart of Igbo culture.

As an alternative, therefore, one proposes a single and unified celebration of the outing ceremony for the christian woman, which should begin with a Church service - either a liturgy of the Word or in a very eminent way, the celebration of the Eucharist, which is the veritable Thanksgiving to God. In order to accord this ceremony its culminating character as the final ritual celebration of the birth rites, one goes even further to propose that the actual and remaining culminating ritual of the infant Baptism be performed in this ceremony. This should serve as a completion of the full incorporation of the child within the christian community, which may have already begun in the suggested pre-baptismal celebrations, as well as the full integration of the mother in both the traditional and christian communities. This ought to supply for the religious motives of the outing ceremony. After this, the purely social and economic aspects should follow. The jubilant procession of the mother and child escorted by their train to the market square, which remains a meeting ground for all - christians and non-christians - should be encouraged. As a gesture of traditional value, the mother and child could pay a visit as a courtesy call and a mark of respect to the stand of the traditional elders in the market square. In line of this recommendation, a unified rite could be developed.

6.1.3 Igbo Birth Rites and the Christian Baptism

Igbo birth rites are the fundamental traditional rites which introduce and insert the Igbo child into the culture of his community. The rite of

---

[50]Cf., section 6.1.1.2.2 above.

Christian Baptism, on the other hand, is the fundamental requisite for membership into the christian community. It is the first and most important step in the christian's journey through life. Both realities have as subject an individual human being at the initial stages of his journey through life. While the traditional rites aim at rooting the individual within the cultural foundations, the Baptismal rite aim at channelling the new life in the secured foundation of faith. This observation leads one to pose questions about Culture and Faith, which are the points of reference of the Igbo birth rites and the christian Baptism respectively. Already at the introductory section of this chapter, it has been established that faith and culture are not opposed to each other, but are compatible, and therefore, need each other. The symbiotic relationship that exists between them has been demonstrated. It is, therefore, necessary to view the structure of both rites to explore the possibilities of an integrated co-existence, not in the hitherto parallelism that has characterised the existence of both realities among the Igbos. The search is rather for points of convergence, which would enable both rites to dovetail and influence each other so that a unified coexistence could be realised for the greater good of the individual.

Examining the structure of both rites does not necessarily mean a comparison, for as long as they belong to different levels, there is no question of comparison. While culture is man-made, the faith is God-given. One intends, therefore, simply to show the points of similarity and areas of agreement. Chupungco recommends that

> Before entering into the area of inculturation it is necessary to make a preliminary comparative study between the christian liturgical forms and the corresponding cultural elements. The object of such a study is to discover the points of convergence on which interaction between the liturgy and culture can operate.[51]

Both rites are being discussed because of the importance they have in the life of the people in question. One has gone a long way to express the value of the traditional birth rites for the Igbos, for whom also the rite of Baptism ritualises the beginning of life in Christ. Baptism ritualises the symbolic passage from birth to life and inserts the christian as an inseparable member of the mystical Body of Christ. It is the christian Baptism that gives an individual his original christian existence and identity, inaugurating his membership of the Church. What the Igbo birth rites set out on the cultural level to achieve - recognition, integration and consolidation within the traditional community, the christian Baptism in an eminent way on the spiritual level achieves. Both are for the Igbos indispensable.

Looking at the structure of both rites, so many points of agreement are revealed. The structure of Infant Baptism or even Baptism in general

---

[51]A. J. CHUPUNGCO, Liturgies of the Future, p. 27.

reveals a rite that can be divided into three phases: the pre-baptismal, the baptismal and the post-baptismal aspects. The central and most essential core is the bathing in water, with the invocation of the names of the Trinity. Preceding this central core are the secondary rites that accompany and symbolise the transition of the individual from one way of life to another. These are the rites and gestures of welcome and introduction of the new individual into the membership of the christian community. In the adult rite of Baptism these secondary rites are conspicuously separated and variously distributed, such that the transitional character are fully manifested, a transition from a way of life dominated by sin and the devil to another - the christian way of life. These secondary rites in their theological significance are meant to mark the gradual introduction of a person to the new way of life and his gradual transition into the community of this way of life. With the gradual transition as a preparation, the central core of the rites - the pouring of water, becomes a real acceptance of the climax of the christian way of life and a real entry into the new life. The post-baptismal aspects are the ceremonies which symbolise and express the new life of the baptised. The baptized is anointed with chrism and associated with the christian symbols of light and innocence of life.

While a lot of similarities are observable between the Igbo birth rites and the pre-baptismal rites, the baptismal and the post-baptismal rites find their possible similarities in the traditional initiation rites, which, however, lie outside the scope of this work. Hence, we are interested with the secondary rites of the pre-baptismal stage. The similarities border on the subject of both rites. Both deal with the beginning of life of a new child. In both cases, the community of the child are the same. The attention of the parents of the child and his community are called for. Invariably the community of the child remains the same in both rites. It should be remembered that the christian community is drawn from the members of the traditional community. Invariably the sponsors in the baptismal rite are presumed to be also present in the goings-on in the traditional ambient, since sponsors are always chosen from the friendship circles of the family. During such big traditional ceremonies in the family the presence of such friends are not lacking.

The dissimilarity would be the fact that in the baptism of the child in the church, his traditional community in the sense of the symbolic cultural representation by the elders, are normally lacking. In both rites naming ceremony are involved. The rite of identification of the candidate is present in the two rites. There is formal reception into the community in both systems. While circumcision rite identifies and welcomes the individual in the cultural circle, the signing of the cross on the forehead identifies and welcomes the candidate in the pre-baptismal rites. The need for sense of solidarity is felt in the two rites. While the solidarity of the Igbos is outstandingly demanded and manifested during the birth rites, which are occasions of joy, Walsh speaks of the solidarity expected also in baptism. He explains,

The response of the individual to the grace of Baptism is

always cultivated and carried within this response of the community. The cultivating and carrying takes the form of a comprehensive solidarity with the human situation of the person to be baptised . . . . A christian community that would, for example, disregard the fact that one of its catechumens was hungry or suffering some other human degradation, on the grounds that Baptism was only concerned with the good of souls, would hardly have much success in encouraging an appropriate response on the person to the saving love of God.[52]

Transitional character is manifested in both rites. The birth rites set the ball rolling for all the other rites of passage. It is the same in the case of Baptism. Roguet leaves no one in doubt as to the transitional character of the sacraments in general. He explains:

. . . sacraments are not only halts, milestones, or even landmarks placed all along a human life, to give it a certain christian colouring. The sacraments are in themselves the christian life, the sacraments are in themselves a movement, a voyage and . . . an adventure.[53]

Appeal for protection and sponsorship is made to the good dead heroes of the community in the both rites, except that while in the christian baptism the appeal is made to confirmed and proclaimed past heroes, in the traditional birth rites such heroes are looked for in the dead ancestors. God is, however, requested for blessings in the two.

One striking remark to note is that the rite of infant Baptism as is presently practised among the Igbos, with its here-and-now one staged celebration fails to impress on the family of the child. Enough opportunity is not given even to influence and to interact with the family and the community of the child, who are expected to play an important role in the christian upbringing of the child. A child coming from non-christian families, that gets so baptised is surely not going to be suspended in the air or deprived of contact with his traditional community. He must grow in the midst of this traditional community. That is why one feels that the lack of contact or of more opportunity to influence this traditional community is a grave matter. More closer contact is bound to influence the upbringing of the child. It is in this light that one would see the advantages of a baptismal rite that is gradually phased and celebrated. The phases could be integrated with the traditional birth rites, for more exposition and contact with the traditional community of the child. Even from pedagogical point of view this is an important factor in the conscientisation of the natural environment

---

[52]L. G. WALSH, op. cit., p. 102.

[53]A. M. ROGUET, Christ Acts through the Sacraments, The Liturgical Press, Collegeville, Minnesota, 1960, pp. 35 - 36.

of the child to be baptised. This is even more the case especially in areas where the family and relations of the child as well as his community are predominantly non-christians. A protracted and gradual celebration of the rite favours such a conscientisation.

The above observed convergence in the two rites compels one to seek for allowances which would permit movement in the direction of co-existential integration of the two rites. Vatican II legislates on this point and furnishes a possibility of the use of such golden opportunities for inculturation. Vatican II approves that

> In mission Countries, in addition to what is furnished by the christian tradition, those elements of initiation rites may be admitted which are already in use among some people in so far as they can be adapted to the christian ritual in accordance with articles 37 - 40 of this Constitution.[54]

The alluded numbers 37 - 40 concern the conditions for taking up such elements. These guard against taking over anything that is bound up with superstitions and errors, and assign the function of specifying the area for changes to the competent territorial ecclesiastical authorities. No. 40 speaks of areas and places, where radical adaptation of the liturgy is demanded, and sets the conditions for such procedures. One reads:

> The competent territorial ecclesiastical authority must in this matter, carefully and prudently consider which elements from the traditions and cultures of individual peoples might appropriately be admitted into divine worship. Adaptations which are considered useful or necessary should then be submitted to the Holy See, by whose consent they may be introduced.[55]

This provision from the teaching of the Church in our time gives a green light for the Inculturation within the Igbo traditional rites. Clarifying on the nature of elements that qualify for the adaptations recommended by Vatican II, Chupungco specifies:

> They can be elements of daily observance connected with family and social life, or else traditional rites set apart by society to mark significant occasions. The important thing is that they should possess the quality of 'connaturalness' for signifying certain aspects of the sacramental reality . . . . they should be able to frame christian initiation in the context "of a

---

[54]VATICAN II, Sacrosanctum Concilium, no. 65.

[55]Ibid., no. 40.

people's distinctive traditions and culture".[56]

So, included are such elements as rites connected with marriage, birth, new year, sowing and harvesting, which, according to Chupungco, the Bishops of the mission lands claimed "All that is needed is to purify them of some stains of superstition before incorporating them into the sacred ritual of the Church".[57]

It is on the basis of these expositions that one recommends the incorporation of the Igbo basic traditional birth rites exposed above, namely - the naming ceremony, the circumcision rite and the outing ceremony into the rite of infant Baptism to be restructured. The incorporation of these rites into the Baptismal rite would envisage the spreading out of the baptismal rite into the phases analogous with the traditional rites. This would put an end to the one single celebration of the rite, and make way for a more influential contact and interaction between the christian faith and the traditional life of the child, even right from his traditional home. This means in effect a recognition of the child's traditional ceremonies as well as opens the way for dialogue with the christian faith. Ultimately, this will do away with the double celebration of the rites.

In concrete, one talks of the possibility of making the traditional naming ceremony and circumcision rites as parts of the pre-baptismal rites, which can then, be situated within the traditional ceremonies so that it becomes the recognition of and the building on this as a framework. This becomes as well an indirect recognition of not only the child, but also his history, that of his family, his traditional community, and his culture. It is from this christian oriented traditional background that the child for baptism is presented to Christ, who recognises the traditional authenticity of the child. When ultimately in the recommended outing ceremony the child is fully baptised, it becomes a christian with a recognised cultural background - a boosting of the co-existence of culture and the christian faith. This would even make the transitional aspect of the christian Baptism to shine out, since it becomes a movement from birth to a fullness of life in Christ, who is the epicentre of existence, without losing one's roots in his culture. Such attitude of respect and esteem for non-christian elements would prove to be fruitful means of inculturation. Baptism could, then, be seen as an entrance into a culturally oriented christian faith.

6.1.4 Is the Celebration of Christian Baptism within the Traditional Community Possible?

A glance at the title of this section may suggest an impression of

---

[56]A. J. CHUPUNGCO, Liturgies of the Future, p. 126.

[57]Ibid., p. 129. (Cf., Acta et Documenta, Series II, 5, p. 427).

radicalism. This is, however, far from the intention here. The proposals made in the foregoing sections recommend a spreading out of the rite of infant Baptism to two or more phases. The intention for this spread out is to create opportunity for the faith to come in contact with the environment of the child. It is foreseen that the various phases would demand different background as locus for the celebration. While it is foreseen that the core of the rite, i.e. the Baptism proper with water should be celebrated in the Church as recommended during the outing ceremony, the pre-baptismal rites integrated with the traditional birth rites is thought to take place outside of the Church. This agrees even with the liturgical structure of Baptism. This, the Liturgy explains, is necessary to bring out the transitional symbolism. Since the traditional rites being considered for integration with the Infant Baptism are normally celebrated in the traditional context, and the intention for the integration is exactly to influence this context, purify and uplift it, the question arises, then, as to the possibility of celebrating the pre-baptismal rites within the context of the traditional community, i.e. in the home or in the meeting ground of the traditional community. In the treatment of the single traditional birth rites, the traditional places of worship and shrines have been discussed and recommendations as to the requisites for the free use of such places by christians have also been made. This section presupposes these facts. The question projects and thinks of a future situation, whereby the integration of the faith and culture may have so worked out that the traditional strategic places are neutralised and purified in such a way that christians and non-christians can freely interact in these places without any religious inhibitions. Such a situation is already today envisaged, counting on the possibility of Inculturation in Igboland. Already in some towns, in an attempt to tap the social and psychological importance of the public grounds and the market squares for the Igbos as rendez-vous of the community[58], some christian communities have begun to site and situate Churches and meeting halls around these traditional rendez-vous[59]. This is intended to capture the attitude, attachment, and psychology of the Igbo people for such places, and use them as evangelisation strategy. Even if Churches are not sited in these places, except that they are rendered non-inimical for the use of everybody, the question is, if the pre-baptismal

---

[58]Such places are the 'ilo', which Basden saw as "the rendez-vous of great crowds of haggling buyers and sellers . . .". In such places according to him, "meeting for many purposes are held in these open-spaces: for the adjustment of differences between individuals, for the celebration of fixed feasts, offerings of common town sacrifices and on specially appointed occasions. Hundreds of people will assemble when an important question is under discussion, or a great function is in progress". - G. T. BASDEN, Among the Ibos of Nigeria, p. 49.

[59]In the newly created parish of Ugbaike in Enugu-Ezike, Nsukka Diocese in Nigeria, the new Parish Church under construction is exactly sited in the vicinity of the traditional market square.

celebrations and even the actual baptism could take place in these places. Employing the use of our much referred-to principle recommended for the Anglo-Saxons, and allowing exceptions to the normal regulations about sacred places, which, however, are mellowed down for mission lands, one proposes a celebration of the rites in such strategic places. In such places an important use could be made of the communitarian solidarity of the Igbos, their traditional festive psychology, and the traditional value of the places. Inculturating in such a potential would make an enormous impact among the Igbos. The desire of the Igbos for the inculturation in such strategic structures provokes the remark of Father Stan Anih in his diocesan article for the centenary celebration, where he expresses:

> I am inclined to say that Christianity in our century has converted many human faces but must in the second century face the difficult task of converting the social face - the symbolic values and communal conscience of our people.[60]

What would debar a priest from assembling the christian community and so impressively performing even the actual rite of Baptism, since the pre-baptismal rites as recommended above presumably may have been celebrated in the traditional homes, in such strategic places and in the presence of the traditional community, whom the celebration is meant to influence? This could be seen as an expression of a fruitful dialogue with the system. In areas, where the scarcity of priests is the case, is it possible for the Catechist or a lay Christian to perform the special rite of Infant Baptism in the absence of the priest, in such a context? In Igboland where the oldest in the community has a privileged status, which aspect would be fully discussed in the subsequent section, granted that this oldest in the traditional Community is a christian, is it possible that he, in the absence of the priest within this traditional context, be given the privilege and function of baptising infants in such extraordinary circumstances? It should be noted that such a person qualifies on both levels: as a christian, he can always baptise like any one else in extraordinary cases in the absence of the priest, provided one has the intention according to the mind of the Church; as the eldest in the traditional community it belongs to him to officiate in birth ceremonies. Should the Church not delegate such a privileged person in the traditional community to officiate at times, even for the purpose of making the christian faith be homely to the people? Provision for such exceptional cases seem to have been made in the Church teachings on the Sacred Liturgy, as one reads in the documents,

> Likewise a shorter rite is to be drawn up, especially for mission countries which catechists, and also the faithful in general, may

---

[60]STAN ANIH, "A Hundred Years of War between Christianity and Igbo Culture", A Paper for the Enugu Diocesan Centenary Celebration, 1985, p. 19.

use when there is danger of death and neither priest nor
deacon is available.[61]

This provision could be stretched to accommodate the point under
consideration. The post-baptismal aspects of the infant Baptism could be
left out and reserved for the priest to be completed at a later period. It
ought also to be noted as Chupungco assures, that,

> For welcoming children who have been baptised by the short
> rite and converts who have already been validly baptised SC
> 69 ordains that new corresponding rites be drawn up. Such
> rites should respectively show, that the supplementary
> ceremonies are not for validity but for the integrity of baptismal
> liturgy.[62]

It is with this in mind that one argues in the subsequent part of this work for
the installation of Christians as the traditional Head of the Igbo traditional
community. This would enable practising Christians to enter into the major
mainstream of the traditional administration. The effect of this would be that,
as insiders, they could influence and convert the structures and values, not
by destroying them, but by demonstrating how the traditional administration
could be discharged through the application of sterling christian principles
within the strategic traditional structures, not by use of charms and false
religious worships.

This proposal becomes more plausible when one observes that the
priest, as the ordinary minister for the sacraments, may not always be at
hand in each successive traditional event in the villages and at the same
time. The scarcity of priests and other official functionaries is a factor and
reality to reckon with in so many areas in Igboland, in spite of the ever
increasing number of candidates for the priesthood. Besides, today various
Igbo traditional communities reckon with a membership of swelling majority
of such old christians and fallen christians at the helm of affairs. From the
internal organisational arrangement in some local Churches in Igboland[63],
christians, having such strategic influence on the traditional community could
be delegated and assigned the function of officiating in the birth ceremonies
within their area in the cultural community. This would also demonstrate the
apostolic character of the lay people. Vatican II reminds us that:

> The laity . . . are given this special vocation to make the

---

[61]VATICAN II, Sacrosanctum Concilium, no. 68.

[62]A. J. CHUPUNGCO, Liturgies of the Future, p. 111.

[63]In Enugu Diocese, for instance, there are six major administrative
groupings according to sex and age: Catholic man, women, young men
(senior and junior), young women (senior and junior), in all levels : diocesan,
parish, town, village, kindred and family.

church present and fruitful in those places and circumstances where it is only through them that she can become the salt of the earth.[64]

On this basis, the Igbo laity can, therefore, be entrusted with even more apostolic functions like the one under discussion, as the document further enlightens:

> Besides this apostolate which belongs to absolutely every christian, the laity can be called in different ways to more immediate cooperation in the apostolate of the hierarchy, like those men and women who helped the apostle Paul in the Gospel, labouring much in the Lord (cf. Phil. 4: 1-3; Rom. 16: 3). They have, moreover, the capacity of being appointed by the hierarchy to some ecclesiastical office with a view to a spiritual end.[65]

It would be a wonderful and impact-creating experience, if, in a gathering of the traditional community, a church minister or someone delegated by him in line with the above recommendations, conducts a liturgy of the word, in an atmosphere of traditional festive celebration, which is always punctuated with singing and dancing.   Within this ambient the rite of baptism as recommended above, could be celebrated. This would be thought-provoking for the non-believing traditional community. The emotional impact it would create on them could have more positive results for the flourishing of christianity in Igboland.

Summary

In the above lines, we have tried to suggest some practical steps in the inculturation within the traditional birth rites of the Igbos. It is one thing to make a proposal, another, however, to put the proposal into practice. It is not an easy task. It demands an intensive dialogue, confrontation and interaction between the systems in question. This would streamline the areas of opposition, and seek to align the points of convergence between them. The survey of the structure of the Igbo birth rites reveal a lot of possibilities that should be utilised. It is irritating to see on the one hand that the Igbo birth rites and the christian Baptism offer so many areas of convergence that could be beneficially put into use for the merging of the hitherto parallelism existing between them, and on the other hand, to observe that no serious efforts have been shown from the side of the

---

[64]VATICAN II, Lumen Gentium, nos. 31 & 33.

[65]Ibid.

Church to inculturate in this direction. One is convinced all the more after this enquiry, that pursuing Inculturation in the lines suggested above, will not be all that too easy, but it promises a far-reaching positive result. It definitely would set the stage for a deeper dialogue between the two structures. It is only through dialogue that the ways for mutual enrichment, which is a stepping stone to the desired goal of inculturation, so that the faith would enter the nerve centre of culture to act as leaven and soul of culture, would be achieved. Surely the Igbo birth rites are the gateways into the cultural nerve centre of the Igbos. The propositions above aim at influencing this cultural centre. Errors may be found on the proposed way, but one is convinced that it is through a series of mistakes that one ultimately arrives at success.

6.2 Inculturation in the Rites of the Igbo Traditional
Headship: 'Onyishi' or 'Okpala' or 'Diokpa'

It may sound a bit strange and paradoxical that, while the contemporary society is worried about the increasing rise in the population of the aging people and are doing everything possible to combat the concomitant social problems, one writes in advocate for the leadership of the same category of people, who are reckoned as biologically and naturally weak and inactive. While the contemporary society sees the problem from the social point of view, it is the intention of this work to focus on the religious and cultural dimension of the problem in Igboland.

It is an indubitable fact that when one gets old, the physical organs tend to wear out, and the physical processes of the individual tend to run down. At old age, one's energy diminishes, resistance to illness decreases, and the body generally become slower and less flexible.[66] It is also to be admitted that in senility the brain no longer discharges its essential functions as organ of adaptation. As a result of this, the old person is viewed as in the stage of second childhood, during which one necessarily and almost completely depends on the care of another.[67]

Arising from the two factors, some prejudices are harboured against old people. Some see them as so physically degenerated that they have no personality worth talking about. Others would see them as people with already fossilised and fixed ideas, hence admitting of no possibility of change. There are still some who see the state of being old as an undergoing of a social death, which leaves one not merely a senior but as a second class citizen. No matter how true these prejudices may be, one should not lose sight of some psychological and anthropological factors. It must be admitted that, even though they may be less adaptable, older people are more experienced. Their short-term memory may be impaired, but their long-term memory is relatively enhanced. It is due to this fact of long memory and wider perspective that old people are by nature conservationists. With their wide range of experience and long range vision they are more qualified to serve as arbiters, since they stand more chance of making clearer judgements.

Anthropologically considered, the aged people are considered most secure in societies where they have high prestige. In slow changing cultures, the elderly are always held in high esteem and greatly respected. In such societies people look up to them to draw from their wealth of knowledge and great cultural experience.

In particular reference to the Igbos, just like the Samoans, old age

---

[66]Cf., G. R. LOWE, The Growth of Personality: From Infancy to Old Age, Pelican Books, Great Britain, 1985, p. 245.

[67]Cf., THEODORE LIDZ, The Person, p. 514.

is regarded as the best time of life. Contrary to the view that aging is a process of disengagement of the person from his society to a state of inability, for the Igbos, older people are well integrated into the life of the society. The old people feel themselves to be valuable participants and even cornerstone of the family and village affairs. It is no wonder, then that they are being discussed as highly functional in handling such a serious matter as community leadership in Igboland. Every cultural way of life is oriented in the direction of its people's world view. Judging from the value and importance given to the ancestors by the Igbos, one should not be surprised about the respect and honour shown to elders, most especially, to the oldest in all the levels of the traditional community. This is on account of the physical nearness of the oldest to the ancestors. Such a one is therefore, the nearest living representative of the community to the dead ancestors. He is the mid-point between the living and the dead. This accounts for the major reason why Igbos do not welcome the idea of old people's home, which is the order of the day in Europe.

When one speaks of leadership or headship in Igboland, it is essential today to make distinctions. With the growth of civilisation, the present condition witnesses two different leadership structures. There is the State-structured systematised governmental leadership, which takes responsibility for the whole land irrespective of tribal affiliation, in terms of developmental infrastructure, running of essential services, and provision of utilities and essential human needs for the people - such as roads, water, electricity, health programme, schools etc. There is, on the other hand, on the kindred, village and town levels, an equally very influential and powerful traditional administrative structure. This controls and influences the concrete day-to-day aspects of every member of the community. The influence of this traditional structure binds the community irrespective of where one resides. Hence people fear the traditional system more because of its binding authority, which is rooted in the tradition of the land and based on the authority of the ancestors.

When one, therefore, speaks about the traditional leader or head in this work, one has this traditional structure in mind. It is the eldest person in each level of the community that becomes the traditional head - the 'Onyishi' - 'Okpala' - 'Diokpa' - as he is variously referred to in the different sections of Igboland. In such a context, one experiences the leadership which La Fontaine speaks about in his writing thus:

> In some descent systems, authority flows along genealogical channels, linking men with their ancestors through their fathers; effective power rests in the hands of the 'fathers' until death.[68]

Hence, in the extended family, kindred, village and town levels, the oldest living male becomes the traditional leader. But he must be transparently honest and behave well. The post is incontestable. Whoever grows to be

---

[68] J. S. LA FONTAINE, op. cit., p. 32.

the oldest inherits the post, the corporate will, and the corporate property of the community. It is against this background that one can best understand, appreciate and truly evaluate the implications for inculturation within the Igbo traditional headship.

By talking about the inculturation within the traditional headship, one thinks of the inculturation of the rite of installation of such a traditional leader, as well as what concerns his daily role in the community, which has religious, social and political implications.

The special interest in the choice of the traditional leadership as a base for inculturation is on account of the already considered central role of the traditional leader in the various rituals, in the Birth rites for instance. The choice is also on account of the overriding influence such a post and its occupier wields in all questions in the life of the community. The authority reposed on the traditional head among the Igbos is so great, that one could even say that he is the pressure point and the driver of the cultural machinery of the Igbo traditional community.

The second obvious reason is based on the truth contained in the remark made by Nzomiwu, who, pointing to the attitude of the Igbos to the elderly as a veritable potential for inculturation of the fourth commandment, writes:

> If respect for the aged is understood as expressed in certain
> behaviourial patterns which a junior person ought to exhibit to
> those considered socially his or her elders, the message of the
> fourth commandment should come naturally to the Igbos.[69]

The subject has a very important reference to the demands of the fourth commandment. In paying allegiance to the ancestors, whose representative the oldest is, the Igbos are simply trying to be faithful to the demands of the fourth commandment.

Effecting inculturation within this powerful base of the Igbos would guarantee a rooting of the faith in the mainstream and powerhouse, which definitely would radiate into other aspects of the traditional life of the Igbos. Any vehicle will always move in the direction dictated by the man on the steering. It is therefore, an important strategy for the flowering of the faith.

6.2.1 Can a Christian Become the Igbo Traditional Head?

The christian religion has already celebrated the first centenary of its advent in Igboland. This means that the pioneers of early christianity in Igboland should be all getting very old by now. Also with the statistical predictions, it is simply obvious that in the year 2000, so many would be definitely falling into the old category and would be battling with the concrete

---

[69]J. P. C. NZOMIWU, op. cit., p. 329.

problems and situation of being old.

In Igboland, if it is the elders who become the traditional leaders and steer the helm of traditional affairs, it simply means that Igbo christians in great numbers would find themselves assuming this enviable class and status in the Igbo society. In fact, in so many Igbo communities, christians have already become the oldest in their traditional communities. Experiences of the past in the assumption of this traditional leadership in some areas have left so many questions for christianity to answer. Hitherto, in the event of a christian growing to become the oldest in his community, it has always meant a big loss for christianity. Since the post is incontestable, a christian who becomes the oldest, must necessarily take it up. He cannot refuse to become the oldest of his community. Unfortunately christianity in Igboland has been very slow in making provision for this for christians. Hence, Igbo christians are worse prepared for this post. Finding themselves in such a post, christians have always felt like they are caught up in a tight spot, with no other alternative than to decamp from the faith they have built up all these years. After a whole life-time of good christian living, one is confronted at the tail end of life, with this reality, which forces one to bow exit to christianity, and take up the demands of the traditional assignment dictated by one's age and the tradition of the land. One must cast the faith overboard simply because there has been no serious dialogue between christianity and this Igbo traditional structure. In taking up the traditional headship of his community, one must discharge not only the political and social roles, but also the religious aspects of the community. Unfortunately the religious demands run contrary to the christian faith. It is exactly religious reasons that compel one to quit christianity. Many a time it is demanded that, in order to enjoy the rights and privileges attached to this post, the oldest must discharge the religious roles of false worship of idols. It has been very difficult for many to resist the temptation of foregoing the attached privileges. That is why so many end up being fallen christians at this stage of their life. It is this factor that provokes a christian reaction which calls for inculturation. There is acute need of a dialogue with this system, in order to make it possible for christians to take up this post without any religious inhibitions. Unless this dialogue is engaged upon, the situation will become more hopeless for christianity in the future, when so many christians would be expected to assume the traditional leadership of their communities. Besides, this would even influence the younger generation, who would see no reason for remaining a christian, since they would ultimately fall away at the end. What is the use then?

The problem is: how can a christian take up this office and be able to discharge the expected roles without abandoning his faith at this crowning moment of christian living? This is an existential problem in the extended family, village and town levels in practically all parts of Igboland. The problem concerns not only one person in each of the levels, but as many people as there are extended families, villages and towns in the whole of Igboland. That is why it must be very seriously handled.

In response to the raised question, it is not only possible but indeed a fact that christians grow to become the traditional head of their community.

There are already cases of such taking up of the traditional headship by christians. Since there is no officially approved procedure in use by christians in reference to the problem, people have been using individual initiatives, trying to abhor anything that has to do with non-christian sacrifices. As such, emphasis is only laid on the festival aspect of the installation. An informant, himself a christian who has become the traditional head of his village in Imilike Ani in Nsukka area, describes his installation thus:

> I inquired from other christians who did such before me. I feasted them - (all the elders, Ndishi, Onuobu and Ogaa 'provosts' in the umunna). But I did not kill goat and hen. I went to the market and bought a chest of goat, a hand of it and a chest of hen (obu ewu, aka ya, and obu okuko) and gave them. They were very happy. They did not perform anything as sacrifice as I told them beforehand. They ate and thanked me and went home . . .[70]

Even from this account, so many points at stake remain unclear and unmentioned. It is the missing but salient issues in the problem that provokes the negative reaction given by another informant, who, when confronted with the question of the traditional headship of the community by christians, remarked:

> When a christian becomes an elder it is difficult because he cannot call on or even pay libation to the ancestors. When a christian becomes the oldest, the community would no longer know how to live; they would have neither customs, laws nor wisdom any longer. They would stray into disaster because nobody will accept the responsibility till he dies and within this period, everything will be static.[71]

From these two commentaries, two points remain clear. The first point is that christians do take up this traditional headship, and secondly there is absolute disregard by christians of the traditionally treasured ancestral practice involved. They do away with everything that has to do with the allegiance and ancestral symbols, which, however, form the bulwark of the traditional system, for which reason the eldest is respected. One would see this as a dodging of the problem and not as a solution. One would think that it belongs to the christian to demonstrate exactly what makes what wrong in the traditional practice, and to supply what is more authentic. In

---

[70]Research Information given by Mr. Gabriel Onah of Imilike Ani in Nsukka area of Igboland on June 30, 1989.

[71]Research Findings supplied by Mr. O. B. Ogbonna of the Department of Philosophy, U. N. N. , April 1989.

as much as a christian can become the traditional head without this practice, this would, however, create a cultural problem, which causes dissatisfaction among the non-christians. In order to set matters aright so that neither the christian faith nor the culture of the people suffer, a dialogue with this system is called for. The giving and receiving aspect of dialogue, which brings about inculturation, is essential.

6.2.2 Burning Issues in the Igbo Traditional Headship

In the foregoing clarifications, a lot has been hinted in the direction of the points at stake in the assumption of the office as the Igbo traditional head at any of the cultural levels by a christian. The traditional head has already been described above as the oldest living member of the community. It is not an appointed office, rather, one grows into this office. If the oldest refuses to take up his office, no living member of the community would dare to substitute him. Being the traditional head means becoming the paterfamilias of the lineage. It entails the performance of the religious, juridical as well as the political functions of the community. This spells out the three dimensional roles, which should be looked into. In effect, the eldest is the chief priest of the lineage, administers the office of justice as the traditional chief judge, and takes decisions or confirms and ratifies these among the council of elders.

As head, he is ipso facto the custodian and depository of the traditional symbols of the ancient and historic connection with the past of the community, among which are the much revered sacred symbols of the ancestors - 'arua' or 'ofo'- and the symbols of justice.[72] The authority and authenticity of these symbols derive from the fact of their historicity as the concrete expressions of the unbroken continuity of the lineage and of relationship with the dead ancestors. These have a value for the traditional Igbo community which can be compared to the value of the Ark of the Covenant or the Torah to the Jews of the old Testament. On the importance which the Igbos attach to the symbols, Meek wrote:

> The authority possessed by virtue of seniority by descent or by priesthood has a material embodiment among the Ibo. This institution is that of the **ofo**. It is a stick, sometimes roughly shaped to represent a human figure . . . . Each senior householder holds the family **ofo**, which he assumes at a

---

[72]"The **onyishi** always carries **oho**: it shows people that he is the eldest man. Anyone who holds it cannot tell lies to people. **Oho** is related to the old people, the **ndichie**." - ONYISHI UGWU ONO of Umune Ngwa, quoted by A. J. SHELTON, The Igbo-Igala Borderland, pp. 63 - 64.

special ceremony . . .[73]

As such they are regarded as sacrosanct by the Igbos. The traditional head is expected to take possession of these symbols. The main point of his installation rite is the formal acceptance of these symbols and taking responsibility over them. Gennep paints a picture of what such an installation can involve:

> There is a handing over and an acceptance of the sacra, which here are called 'regalia' and which includes drums, a sceptre, a crown, "relics of the ancestors" and a special seat. They are at one and the same time the symbol and the receptacle of royal magico-religious power.[74]

In the Nsukka area, the title of 'onyishi' is taken up thus:

> Any man whose turn comes up, when the onyishi dies, will become the new headman. On that day when he makes offering to the **arua** he will gather the other elders together and he will feast them. He will cook a goat and have palm wine, and he will tell the elders that he is the eldest man and is the one who must keep the **arua**, so the staff will be moved to his lineage house where he keeps his forefathers.[75]

As the head, the house of the oldest becomes the venue for the traditional meetings, since he is restricted to his house, but must chair all traditional meetings, by virtue of his being the representative of the living before the dead ancestors and vice versa. He is, in fact, regarded as the symbolic representative of the traditional values and is obliged to follow the traditional laws of the land - the 'Omenani'. It ought to be noted that the elders of societies were transmitters of tradition, the guardians of ancestral values and the providers of continuity.

In practical terms, one would see the burning issues involved in the Igbo traditional Headship as knotted and tap-rooted in the famous problem of the ancestral relationship of the Igbos. Much attention and space have been given to this subject in the earlier part of this work. The burning issues of the traditional headship pose serious questions that must be answered in the eventual inculturation within this strategic pressure point of Igbo culture. Whatever questions and answers are involved must also be seen in the light of the demands of the fourth commandment of God -

---

[73]CHARLES K. MEEK, "An Ethnological Report on the Peoples of the Nsukka Division, Onitsha Province", Lagos: Manuscript, 1931.

[74]A. VAN GENNEP, op. cit., p.110.

[75]Account given by ONYISHI ELEJE NWASOGWA of Amuukwa, Nsukka, quoted by A. J. SHELTON, op. cit., p. 185.

'Honour thy father and mother' - of which the Igbo ancestral veneration is a concrete and an eloquent expression. This problem ought to be seen in comparison to the observable practice in the burial grounds or cemeteries in European countries. How does one relate the traditional expressions of reverence to ancestors by the traditional head to the devotion shown to the dead ancestors in European cemeteries? The difference lies in the fact that while living animals are offered in sacrifice by the Igbos, very expensive marbles and flowers are employed in Europe. The attitude in both has much to do with material expressions.

Another dimension of the problem deals with the question of whether the Igbo christian should drop his religion because of the demands of becoming the oldest in his culture. It deals with the question of how the christian Igbo oldest can best demonstrate concretely his fidelity to the fourth commandment - a relationship to his forefathers, who are no more alive. What attitude should he adopt in demonstrating his reverence and honour to these good and honest forefathers[76], without giving them honour due only to God?

The problem touches also on the issue of the preservation of the Igbo historic and cultural symbols. Is there any relationship between the practice of preservation of the cultural symbols through the traditional head and the existence of european Museums - a record of the historical past of humanity.[77] These and many other allied questions are the points at stake. Many more of such questions would be dealt with in the following paragraphs, which treat the problem in a more detailed way. The issues are categorised into three divisions corresponding to the three major roles of the Igbo traditional head thus: the religious, social and political implications.

6.2.2.1   Religious Involvement and Its Implications

Among the Igbos there is the concept of cosmic totality, whereby everything is seen as interconnected with the spiritual reality. As such, everything has a spiritual relationship. It is obvious, therefore, that the headship factor, which is rooted in the ancestral relationship, having a religious implication in Igbo culture, must be also involved in this religious implication. As the Paterfamilias, it belongs to the oldest to offer sacrifices to ancestors. Arinze explains:

---

[76]No bad or dishonest person can be an Igbo ancestor.

[77]It is disheartening to note that some of these symbols in questions have found their way into the Museums in Europe. They were found as very unworthy to be kept by christians by the early missionaries, only to be decently transported to Europe to feed the Museums. The very owners of these symbols must now pay heavily just to have a look at these ancient symbols.

It is he who 'gives food' to the ancestors. It is he who offers the occasional kola and libations for the good of the whole family. It is he in a special way who sacrifices the fowls in the annual feast of Alom Mmuo in honour of the ancestors.[78]

It is expected of him to invoke and worship the ancestors daily, in the normal morning prayers - '**Igo Ofo**'- made with the ofo and before the ancestral shrine.[79] As a custodian of the traditional sacra, he is expected to have a shrine for the ancestral symbols.

Each compound has a forefather shrine (**onunna**: 'mouth (of) fathers') and every lineage has a larger ancestral shrine in which major lineage offerings to the forces of the ancestors are made. Each clan has an ancestral shrine house set apart; this is **ulo arua**, 'house (of) spears' - arua referring to ancestral force as it is symbolised by the ritual staffs and spears of authority.[80]

The traditional head is even more religiously implicated by the installation ceremony, which is punctuated by religious rituals surrounding his official acceptance of responsibility as the oldest.

The concrete technically religious implications can be framed under the following questions. When a christian is involved, what form of religious ceremony should the installation take? What must a christian do with regard to the traditional sacra, being the essential symbols of his office? Should he accept these symbols and the responsibility over them? As the things that make him an ancestral representative would be lacking if he does not accept the traditional symbols, what could substitute these symbols, which should have the traditional historic value, authenticity, and trustworthiness for all the people, like the Ofo? If he should, on the other hand, accept the symbols, how should he regard them and what should be his attitude to them? In order to have a specific difference that ought to characterise his tenure of office, what could he adopt as his personal symbol as a christian, since, while he inherits the symbols of his predecessors, he is expected to have

---

[78]F. A. ARINZE, op. cit., p. 78.

[79] " . . . the man washes his hands, . . .makes signs on the ground with chalk . . . places down his Ofo. he breaks the kola nut, chews and spits a part of it on the Ofo, and generally throws a little to the invisible spirits outside, ... Greeting and salutations are made in this invariable order: to Chukwu, the spirits, and the ancestors. Then he makes petitions for himself, his family, his kindred, and his property. Now follows curses against his enemies: may Chineke (God) repay them!" - (F. A. ARINZE, op. cit., p. 25.)

[80]A. J. SHELTON, op. cit., pp. 63 - 64.

his own specific symbol?[81] In a nutshell, one of our informants summarises these points at stake thus:

> When a christian becomes an Onyishi, many things are at stake. . . . the (Igwuyi Nna) installation ceremony, no christian will accept the Arua and Nna, even to hold Ofo is a taboo for them so that the things that make an Onyishi a proper ancestral representative on earth is lacking. . . . The shrine of Nna, that symbol of unity will also be missing in his obi . . . [82]

What to do with the symbols remain a crucial question in the problem. If christians refuse to have anything to do with the symbols, the problem develops a cultural implication, as the same informant further analyses:

> Another important problem is what to do with the 'Arua', 'Ofo' and 'Nna', . . . how, where, and who keeps these items, since it is only the eldest man in a lineage who has the right to keep them. The truth is that all these antiquated items will be lost before long and that is together with the sanctity, sacredness, and reverence attached to them. This is very important, for even if they are devilish items, they are part of our history, our identity and the mirror with which we can see our past; to lose them is to miss our identity, . . . [83]

Before one attempts to propose answers to these problems, let us take a look into the other implications.

6.2.2.2   The Social Implications

Apart from the religious implications, becoming the traditional eldest necessarily implies some social difficulties for the christian. This post has been described as a very enviable status among the Igbos, because one thereby becomes the highest and the first person in the community. While some of the social implications do not necessarily spell danger to the

---

[81]There are normally the shifting **arua** staffs which are transfered from one haeadman to the next and the non-shifting ones. This non-shifting ones, according to Shelton, "is a completely iron staff which remains with the onyishi; when a new onyishi assumes control over the arua he must have a smith make his personal **okaka** as his insignia of office" - (A. J. SHELTON, op. cit., pp. 104 - 105).

[82]SILAS C. MAMA, "Making of Onyeishi in Ubollo" Research Findings, University of Nigeria, Nsukka, March 1989, pp. 7 - 8.

[83]Ibid., p. 9.

christian faith, there are, however, some aspects that may be regarded as entanglements that could ultimately lead to religious implications. In majority of cases, when it is foreseen that a christian would be the next head, some uncompromising non-christians in the council of elders, would come up with a legislation that attaches the privileges of the office with the conditions of full responsibility over the traditional symbols. Hence, to enjoy the fringe benefits of the office, one must take up the religious functions involved. These benefits are in the nature of the yields and revenue accruing from the landed property and the cash crops of the community, which the oldest, by virtue of his position, dispenses and controls. He is also entitled to a share of special parts of meat in major feasts in the entire community. It is from these benefits that the oldest person maintains himself. When and where such a legislation is in force, therefore, it has always constituted a very big temptation for christians. Most of the christians who, at this point of their life abandoned their christian faith, have invariably been lured by these social benefits of the office. This is, however, not always the case. Some have stood their ground and heroically foregone the benefits. Under such cases, the landed and cash crops always remained fallow and untouched as long as the christian incumbent was in power. In some extreme cases the death of the incumbent might even be hastened or he would be done away with through devilish means.[84]

Another area that is inimical to the christian faith is the movement of houses. In some areas, when one becomes the oldest, he must transfer his dwelling to the ancestral home of the lineage. These homes are often situated within the precincts of the traditional sacred places, sacred because of their historical value as the abode where the forefathers had lived. These precincts are at times not spiritually healthy for christians on account of the nefarious traditional religious activities that take place there. As Ezeanya describes, such places are

> . . . set aside solely as a dwelling place for a particular deity and / or a place where it may be consulted with the concomitant rituals or simply as a place set aside for the performance of certain religious functions, like making offerings to ancestors.[85]

The traditional Igbo prefers such sacred places because he "feels

---

[84]"If his behavior becomes too consistently erratic the gathered elders can quite easily depose him and replace him with an elder from among them who satisfies the needs of seniority and at the same time is somewhat more amenable to their suggestions and to what they define as 'good thinking'." - A. J. SHELTON, The Igbo-Igala Borderland, p. 188.

[85]S. EZEANYA, "'The Sacred Place' in the Traditional Religion of the Igbo People of the Eastern Group of Provinces of Nigeria", West African Religion, 6 (August) 1966, p. 1.

comfortable in the precincts of the ancestral shrine, for he is being observed and cared for by family forces . . ."[86] Since the house of the traditional head becomes the meeting venue for important matters, the environs of the ancestral abode is made to express the physical relationship with the dead ancestors.

However, the question is, if the ancestral home of this nature would be conducive for the faith of a christian who becomes the traditional head? Dialogue for inculturation should argue for readjustments such as the possibility of erecting separate homes distinct from these spiritually uncomfortable precincts. Such readjustments should ensure that while the christian culturally feels at home, he should have a very conducive atmosphere for his christian faith.

As to his entitlements in the community, the christian traditional head would be exposed to accepting parts of items already sacrificed to idols. Of course, as a christian, he should note that he is looked up to by everybody for giving examples of active faith. Hence, he should be prepared to forgo anything that is inimical to his faith. However, we are interested here in noting the fact that all these factors are implications for a christian. Since it is important not to shy away from this office as a free-born of the land, solutions must be sought for these implications through dialogue in inculturation.

6.2.2.3   Political Implications

The role of the traditional leader in the administration of justice in the land, which is exercised as the chairman of the Council of Elders is another problem area for the christian Igbo leader. Lowe once remarked thus:

> In so far as adulthood is a period of responsibility, authority, and influence, adults are usually expected to be in charge of things. They are no longer trainees but graduates, and are expected to train those younger and less experienced than themselves. They are executives and policy-makers and whether they uphold the status quo or try to change it, they represent, more than any other age group, the way things are in society.[87]

In this remark, one finds reasons why christians should be encouraged to take up the traditional headship. The Igbos, like the Chinese, have this type

---

[86]A. J. SHELTON, op. cit., p. 64. "The shrine areas or the environs associated with familiar spirits are . . . places where one can relax and feel relatively comfortable" - Ibid., p. 80.

[87]G. R. LOWE, op. cit., p. 224.

of political administration, where the elders and titled people decide and make policies for the traditional community. This has been highlighted in the Igbo political structure. It belongs to the eldest of the community to chairman this highest decision and policy-making body. On grounds of faith, the presence of christians have been conspicuously lacking in various councils of elders. Whatever is decided in this council, which the traditional head confirms and ratifies binds on everybody in the community. When a christian accedes to this post, it is seen as an honour for Christianity as well as an opportunity to apply christian principles to the cultural traditions. However, there are implications in the exercise of this function by a christian. The implication regards the use of the traditional symbol of authority. The authority of the traditional elder derives from this symbol. In reference to the symbol of authority, Metuh writes:

> He owes his authority to the fact that he is the representative and mouthpiece of the ancestors. His staff of office, the 'ofo' is the symbol of the presence and of the authority of the ancestors since it has been handed down by the founder of the lineage through the succession of lineage heads . . . . Laws are promulgated by hitting it on the ground because the ancestors and the Earth-Deity are the guardians of traditional laws and customs and owners of the land.[88]

It is, therefore, clear why this symbol is essential for the traditional head, at least because of the historical value of its authority. But these symbols down the ages have been treated as objects of traditional religious worship. Religious attitudes have been addressed to them. It becomes a problem how a christian could freely make use of these symbols of authority in the ratification of decisions and policies, as well as in the traditional administration of justice. The 'ofo' has been traditionally used for taking of oaths as well, since no one would dare to tell lies on the authority of the ancestors. Once cases come up before the 'ofo' symbol, the truth will come out[89]. What must the christian eldest do in the administration of justice? As a christian, he is attached to the holy cross and the Bible as his standards of truth, with christian principles as his guide in taking decisions. These, however, may not be acceptable to many non-christians, who insist on a direct ancestral connection and authority. What symbols of truth and authority, having the lineage historical proof of authenticity, should the christian use to manifest the ancestral authority? The stamping of the 'ofo' on the ground over a point being discussed has an equivalent effect in the traditional community as the effect of the dictum: "Roma locuta est, causa

---

[88]E. I. METUH, Comparative Studies of African Traditional Religion, p. 150.

[89]This symbol is referred to as the 'guarantee of truth' for the Igbos. (Cf. F. A. ARINZE, Sacrifice in Ibo Religion, p. 16.)

finita" (When Rome speaks, that ends the case).

Also the symbol of 'ofo' represents the ordinances and customs of the land handed down by the forefathers. Guided by christian principles, the christian traditional head may see himself isolated when he takes some decisions contrary to the customs of the land, especially in the region of religious attitude to idols. As a christian he must uphold christian teachings, which, many a time, do not agree with traditional religious worship. It can really be problematic for him. Such problems would definitely always be surfacing for some time, until christianity permeates deeply into this cultural centre as to be able to influence the decisions taken. When the active presence of christians begins to be felt in the council of elders, the situation may change. It ought to be noted that, even though the oldest holds the last say over issues and ratifies decisions, he is, however, not a dictator, since democracy is the rule of the day in the council of elders.[90] In most cases, however, the decisions of the eldest is not disputed because, as the mouthpiece of the ancestors, to doubt him or disagree with him is tantamount to a confrontation with the ancestors, whose representative he is.

As we have seen, in as much as it offers an opportunity to the christian faith to penetrate and influence the political arm of the traditional system, the leadership of the christian has much political implications arising from the traditional symbol of authority. The implications would, however, melt away through a meaningful dialogue.

6.2.2.4   **General Synthesis**

Addressing oneself to the questions raised in the foregoing section, and their implications, with a mind to suggesting solutions, dialogue with the system has been considered very essential. It is even interesting to note that both parties see dialogue as essential. The Igbo non-christians, who have been living according to the old tradition, are aware of the crucial points and the dangers facing the traditional system on account of the spread of christianity in Igboland. It is clear to them that it is possible that the traditional system and their values may in the future die a natural death unless something is done. From the side of Christianity, it is equally clear that unless an inroad into the Igbo culture is made, all the efforts of these centuries would become a waste. Hence in so many parts of Igboland the non-christians are becoming more compromising with the christians, and are

---

[90]The powers of the eldest can be limited. "He is limited, first, by his councillors, the group of **ndishi** who are the heads of the patrilineages within the clan; without their support he cannot have his orders enforced, and as a rule he will not oppose them but will through persuasion, connivance, and often bribery, work hard to gain their consensus". - A. J. SHELTON, op. cit., p. 188.

prepared to come to dialogue for possible way out for both systems. One notes the changes already taking place in public gatherings that involve both christians and non-christians in this regard. For instance, where there are somethings to be consumed by everybody in the community, such items are no more offered to idols or used for libations, for, it is now certain to non-christians that the christians would refuse to touch the items if they are involved with idols. It is this changing attitude that emboldens one to confidently speak of the possibility of dialogue. The reaction of non-christians to innovations by way of inculturation is really encouraging. Chief Omeje, speaking of attempts at inculturation within the traditional Onyishi installation in Nsukka, where there is already a possibility of the Parish Priest taking part in the ceremony to pray for, bless, and install a christian as Onyishi, remarks, "The non-christians do not frown at this. In fact, they welcome this form of installation!".[91]

Granting the possibility of dialogue, certain measures could be taken to ensure a salutary participation of christians as well as the continuity of the traditional system. First and foremost, one recommends a change of attitude with regard to the sacred symbols of the community. Without mellowing down the strong relationship of the Igbos with their ancestors, which is a positive potential, the attitude of sacrificial worship should be diverted from the ancestors or even from the symbols to the Supreme God, who alone should be worshipped. When God alone is worshipped, it would not prevent a devoted tendency towards the ancestors, in whose honour one can pray to God. In this respect, changes of attitude have to be effected in the ambient of personal behaviour regarding the symbols. Shelton describes the superfluous attitude and much concern given to the symbols:

> . . . he carries them with him to his sleeping house at night, where they rest above the doorway to his house so that their spiritual powers control all who might enter the house; and in the morning when he awakens he carries them with him to his public reception house called **uloarua**, 'house of the arua', where they are given offerings at dawn and where they remain erect all day, their points . . . stuck into the earth of the altar or . . . their butts set on the earth of by the altar.[92]

One would see this treatment as unworthy and as an expression of confidence and trust which should be reposed and sought for only in God, to a created thing. When a change of attitude is assured, then and only then should one focus interest on the historical aspect of the traditional symbols. To arrive at this, the symbols must be subjected to purification and special blessing, exorcising all the superstitious practices and false worships to which they have been subjected for ages. Only on this

---

[91]Research Findings given by Chief P. Omeje of Nsukka.

[92]A. J. SHELTON, op. cit., p. 104.

condition are they recommended to be accepted by a christian for custody during his installation, which should be rid of all non-christian sacrifices and rituals. When that is done, these symbols become for him actual symbols of a direct historical and physical connection with his ancestors, which he ought to preserve and treasure as things very valuable, but not to be worshipped. The historical fact of the unbroken ancestral lineage and relationship of these symbols remain undisputable, and should be accorded much importance. By this way, one would not see any reason that would debar one from praying to God even in the presence of these memorial symbols of the past ancestors, who are thus honoured without veneration or worship. A christian traditional head could say his normal daily prayers in the presence of such symbols, since they are no longer objects of his prayers, hence they do not constitute any obstacles to his faith any more. Even if he is to pray over the kola-nut during his normal morning prayer, asking for God's blessings for himself, his family, lineage and the community, which is an aspect of our cultural heritage, good in itself, he simply prays, breaks it and shares to every person around without any further ritual implication. This is already done today in christian circles.

On feast days that demand the killing of animals as meat for feasting, for instance, in honour of the ancestors, celebrated once in the year, instead of the food offerings and series of sacrifices over the symbols, which the onyishi with the assistance of the elders of the lineage used to perform, the eldest could simply pray over the animals expressing sentiments of gratitude to God in honour of the ancestors, whom he can even enumerate in remembrance.[93] Afterwards, the animals would be unceremoniously killed and used for meals. With a change of attitude, this feast can still be celebrated even on a superlative tone, except for the various blood sacrifices and libations, which should be dropped. This would leave the feast to be a clean Thanksgiving feast by the whole of the lineage in honour of their dead ancestors.

It is interesting to note that, in some areas of Igboland, attempts have already been made for the inculturation of some annual ancestral feasts such as Akanni festival in Ezeagu area. It involved intensive dialogue between the traditional rulers and chiefs of the place and the christians, after which an agreement was reached, drafted and signed. A new inculturated ancestral feast was thus promulgated, and is now known and celebrated as Ekene Nna Thanksgiving festival (Thanksgiving to the forefathers festival), replacing the Akanni Festival.[94]

Even with a changed attitude, the eldest still performs his role as the chief priest of the lineage. The only difference is that instead of the blood sacrifices and idol worships, he now functions with a new attitude of prayer

---

[93]It should be no sin to call the names of one's dead fathers and ask God to bless their offspring on earth.

[94]Cf., The Agreement for the Ekene Nna Festival of Umana Parish, in Enugu Diocese of Igboland, signed on 6th Feb. 1982.

now rightly channelled to God. He diverts the attention given to the traditional symbols as objects of worship to God, while regarding the symbols with honour and respect in honour of the ancestors. This is in line with the expectations of the fourth Commandment of God, which recommends attitude of love and respect to our parents and seniors, limiting all attitudes of worship to God and God alone.

In keeping with the attitude of love and respect for the dead ancestors, the traditional symbols representing this relationship with the ancestors could be treated as symbols and relics in memory of the dead, which are gracefully and honourably preserved, even adorned with lighted lamps, as is witnessed in the European cemeteries. These remain symbols of the dead ancestors, which ought to be preserved as a historical evidence of the past generations. This could serve as the symbols of the origins and passage of what is the present-day Igbo culture. From the religious point of view, they could be seen even as the humble beginnings of the search for God by the Igbos, which gave birth to the present-day fructification of the christian faith in Igboland.

The purification of these traditional symbols removes nothing of their historical value and cultural significance. Only their spiritual aspect and attitude towards them are subjected to change. This is the goal of all inculturation: that the christian, while practising his religion feels comfortable also in his culture; without losing his faith he lives his culture, which supplies a foundation for his faith. Hence, the christian traditional head can handle the 'ofo' which has been purified and blessed. Purification and blessing removes nothing from the historical symbolism of the ancestral authority, which is the reference point in the administration of justice in the Igbo community.

Where there is no possibility of admitting of the traditional symbols by christian traditional head, there is yet another alternative. Since the office of the traditional head is a corporate responsibility, it is possible to provide or erect an accommodation quite distinct from the ancestral abode in the sacred precincts for the traditional head, while the symbols would remain in the ancestral abode, inhabited by no one as long as the christian is the head. There the symbols remain untouched, and not catered for until the death of the incumbent head. This may signify an indirect destruction of these symbols, because where christians become the head successively, one after the other for a long time, it becomes everybody's guess what happens with these symbols. In that case, however, the christian head must furnish himself with a specific symbol of authority, which must have an equivalent historical authenticity as the traditional symbols of authority, which derives authority from the ancestors. Such an acceptable substitute would be difficult for the christian to obtain. In this light, alternatives are meanwhile being considered. Some think of compiling a detailed register containing all the names of ancestors, whose memory still remains in the lineage, which the christian elder keeps in his custody as a proof of his authority. Another alternative would be to collect and preserve the photographs of the past ancestors up to the present head. Both of these would, however, lack the personal concrete aspect of each of these ancestors. The indisputable reality of the traditional symbols is that these successive ancestors had physical contact with the symbols and these have been handed down to the present-day ancestor representative. The last alternative is for the christian head to completely build a new symbol orientated in the form of the holy cross, the symbol for christians, and which could remain as the symbol for prospective christian heads, thus becoming a departure point from the use of the non-christian traditional symbols. This serves not only for his tenure of office, but also for the future christian heads. It is, however, doubtful what degree of authoritative influence such innovated symbols could wield in the exercise of his traditional role in the administration of justice among the traditional community. Definitely these would lack the power of coercion which the traditional symbols have. The christian does not force anybody to his view-point, instead, he appeals to the power of conscience. This method does not, however, impress so much the Igbo, who are a bit more pragmatic.

All said and done, dialogue remains the only key to the solutions of the implications of the traditional headship for the christian. Inculturation is a natural consequence of such serious-minded dialogue between the christian faith and the Igbo traditional system.

6.2.3 Can the Traditional Headship Installation be accompanied by the Christian Liturgy?

The event which concretely launches the oldest person in the traditional community to formally accept and take possession of the new office, is referred to as the Installation ceremony. This can be compared to the enthronement of a chieftaincy or the installation of a chief shepherd into his new office. It has always the character of a joyous and festive occasion. Among the Igbos, such an event pulls together the entire traditional community, in line with the we-concept and the solidarity mentality of the Igbos. When a christian accedes to this traditional lofty position, it becomes an event where the christian is set on a privileged pedestal, and launched into an influencing status in the traditional society. It becomes imperative that christians rally around him in christian solidarity, to boost his christian pride, give the occasion a christian imprint, as well as advertise christianity in the show-case of the traditional community. This is bound to register a thought-provoking impression in the traditional community. It is to be expected, then, that in such an event, solidarity, which characterises the Igbos ought to be looked for among the christians, who are bound together in Christ with the candidate to be installed. Every meeting of this brotherhood in Christ should always have the christian character.

Before surveying grounds for a possible inculturated installation ceremony, it is important to examine the structure of the normal traditional installation ceremony. We shall take the installation of a new head - 'Onyishi' - in the Nsukka area of Igboland as a concrete case.

When an incumbent onyishi dies, even before the announcement of his death, the traditional symbols of the ancestors are removed and transferred to a place unknown to the succeeding person. In this new site, some women would be detailed to a constant care and inspection of the symbols. Meanwhile, at the burial of the dead onyishi, the succeeding elder is made to declare and denounce publicly having played any part in the death of the dead onyishi and manifest his innocence of the death. Then he would be confined to his house for some time, pending the fixture for his installation. During this time, he solicits the assistance and support of his extended family, who now make all preparations for the big feast coming up.

On the eve of the fixed date, there is an entire-night wake keeping, during which, amid singing and dancing, all present - friends, relations, village daughters, and the entire community - would be sumptuously fed with food and drinks. On the fixed day, in the presence of all the other traditional elders and all present, the new head formally announces his acceptance of the Onyishi title and takes possession of the traditional symbols. Sacrificial rituals are then offered. The feasting aspects of eating, drinking, dancing and merry-making follows. This could last for days.

This survey reveals three fundamental structural aspects: the sacrificial aspects, the formal acceptance and possession of the office, and the festival aspects. Even though the traditional sacrificial aspects are so important for the Igbos, they should, however, not be admitted nor negotiated for in the installation of a christian. No room should be given for the sacrificial rituals either privately or publicly. The main interest should lie in the fruitful use of the good cultural structure. In order to avoid all dangers of syncretism, the elements that are in opposition with the true worship of God ought to be discarded. Therefore, in the installation of a christian as the traditional head, taking account of the recommendations of the foregoing section, an inculturated installation ceremony is possible. With a changed attitude towards the traditional symbols, which leaves them as purely cultural and historical values of the society, or the provision of an alternative christian orientated symbol of authority, an installation ceremony situated within a christian liturgy is not only possible, but most desirable.

In the midst of this positively charged communitarian context, a christian liturgy can be situated. This would utilise the communitarian solidarity, which, as was demonstrated already, is a powerful and sensitive wavelength in the Igbo psychology. The christian Liturgical celebration should take the place of the false worship. The Igbo would normally not accept the abrogation of his religious attitude to his deity without being offered an alternative. The situation of a liturgical ceremony in the installation would provide for the spiritual quests of the Igbo. One has in mind here the incorporation of the installation within the celebration of the Eucharist in the compound of the new christian traditional head, and in the context of this festive mood. The celebration of the Eucharist in this context is not out of place especially in mission lands. It should be noted that in some extraordinary circumstances, the local ecclesiastical authority do permit the celebration of the Eucharist, for such evangelisation purposes. The momentous installation of a christian as a traditional head is worth more than an extraordinary circumstance that would deserve and demand an exceptional and preferential celebration of the Eucharist. Besides the spiritual benefits and moral fortification it could serve for the candidate, it dignifies and uplifts the ceremony, and even promotes the existing unity and solidarity of the Igbos.[95] This would definitely pave a way for the flourishing of the faith. In areas where innovations of this kind are introduced to a traditional context, the effect it has on the non-christians is enormous. They normally see such innovations as an upliftment and recognition of their cultural tradition.

Where it is not possible to celebrate the Eucharist, the simple fact of the physical presence of the christian community adds to the communitarian solidarity. That can also be an eloquent sermon. What could be more impressive and spiritually nourishing as even a celebration of the liturgy of the Word in the midst of this installation in the compound of the eldest, during which the parish priest specially prays for him, blesses him and his house and surroundings? One envisages the possibility of using this context to publicly and formally purify, bless and hand over the old symbols of authority to the new head by the parish priest. If the second alternative suggested above is the case, then, the context could be utilised to bless the newly made christian orientated symbol or image of the cross, and even install this new symbol in an erected dignifying altar in the house of the new head. This could furnish him with a spiritually healthy surrounding for the performance of his religious role and spiritual care of his community, for whom he should always pray, to God, and in memory and honour of the dead ancestors.

The festival aspect of the ceremony, consisting of eating, drinking, dancing and merriment should remain to serve as the concluding part of the installation. One has only to make sure that none of the food items to be used for the festival would be ritualised or offered in idol worship. If living animals are provided for the feast, they should be unceremoniously killed and used for general consumption. In order to ensure this, as well as to borrow a leaf from the solidarity mentality of the Igbos, one recommends that the christian community takes over the sponsorship of the feasting aspects. This should be an expression and a manifestation in concrete terms of the sense of solidarity, which christianity must copy as a very positive potential of the Igbos. This would fall in line with the Igbo way of behaviour.

In effect, then, such a celebration becomes an installation of an Igbo christian traditional head within a liturgical celebration in the traditional communitarian context. It could also be seen as a liturgical celebration in the context of an Igbo traditional installation of a christian as head of the community. This would arouse the sense of pride in the Igbo christians, restore to them a sense of cultural identity, and make them feel at home in

---

[95]This agrees with the teaching of the Church that the people of God by the sacrifice of the Eucharist, show themselves as "a people who grow together in unity by being united with his Body and Blood . . .". (Cf., VATICAN II, Sacrosanctum Concilium, no. 5.)

their culture as well as in their christian religion. Besides, it would help to open up christianity to Igbo traditional system. This is the goal of the much desired Inculturation in Igboland.

6.3 **Conclusion**

In this chapter, we have attempted to take a leap in the dark. This is not always easy to do on account of the insecurity involved.

This venture has been provoked by the importance which the Igbos attach to the beginnings and end of the most precious gift of Life. In setting out the framework of what we refer to as models, which one sees only as provocations for an eventual consolidated reaction in the direction of Inculturation in Igboland, efforts were made to avoid any syncretism. Syncretism is quite different from Inculturation. While Inculturation has as an objective to make the christian faith penetrate the root of culture, so that a christian can feel at home in his culture and from this as a basis practice fully his faith, syncretism is an attempt solely to accommodate two different systems. Inculturation attempts to boost the faith with the use of the positive potentials of the culture, while syncretism endangers and destroys the faith. With this in mind, one has attempted to situate the christian faith within the cultural pressure points of the Igbos. The Igbo birth rites are the entrance gates to the Igbo culture for an individual. If the faith can be situated in order to influence this cultural gate, the flourishing of a culture-centred faith would be assured.

Also the traditional Headship is a very strategic potential for the Igbos and relates to the ancestors, a very sensitive pressure point in the traditional religion. To bring the christian faith directly to influence these cultural pressure points has been the strong motive for the recommendations made. As intended, these lines of suggestions are meant to be only indications for a concerted and actual inculturation of Christianity within the various fertile aspects of Igbo Culture. The particular areas delved into in this work could even be recommended as experimental cases to test on. The fact of the Incarnation of Jesus Christ among men remains, however, the best model in any inculturation work. It is to Him that all should look up to, for guide, direction, encouragement and execution of any Inculturation. On this note, then, one ends with a call to the Church in Igboland, to use all the opportunities, trained and devoted experts, teeming and conscious laity, indigenous quality of the episcopal conference, and the provocations that should come from this work to launch deep into the inculturation of the Church in Igbo Culture. May the Lord through whose enlightening inspiration this project was undertaken, make Inculturation in Igboland possible. May He be praised both now and forever. Amen.

CHAPTER 7

7   GENERAL CONCLUSION

At the very beginning, the set objectives of this work were delineated. The work is supposed to be an enquiry into the reasons for the unfortunate but observable fact in the Christianity in Igboland. It was clearly manifested that there were some mistakes made at the beginning of evangelisation in Igboland. With the aim of sowing the seeds of Christianity the cultural roots of the Igbos were dislodged. The christians were alienated from their cultural roots. Hence, Igbos became christians without cultural roots. Alienated from each other, the Igbo christians could not feel at home in their culture, and on the other hand, the faith remained strange to them. On such an existence without roots, the result was the shallowness of the faith. The christian faith remained in the air or on the surface level and made only a peripheral influence on the people. At the face of concrete human problems and traditional demands on them as citizens of the land, because there was no established relationship with traditional system, they either abandon the faith completely, or see themselves serving two masters at the same time. This has the natural effect of not being faithful to any of the two.

The research set out to look into the very foundations of Igbo Culture to seek for the authentic missing foundations. The double and parallel loyalty of the Igbo Christians is the object of concern. It revealed a dichotomy between the faith professed and the life lived. One confesses faith in God but is compelled to act according to the traditional demands. This necessitated the search for a synthesis. Fundamental questions were raised, the indications of the solutions of which the thesis set out to make. There was need to look into the structure, mentality, philosophy and the psychology of the Igbos[1] as well as to make an exposition of the essential aspects of the Igbos. The aim was to scan the pressure points, which would furnish the basis for influencing the culture. It is the positive use of such pressure points as firm foundations, that can help in preserving the authentic cultural heritage, on which a strong christian faith ought to be constructed.

---

[1]". . . the gospel message must be inculturated in **psychological** territory as well as in **geographical** territory. In other words, it must also link up with the ways of thinking, judging, and acting that characterize human collectivities." - HERVÉ CARRIER, Gospel Message and Human Cultures, trans. JOHN DRURY, Duquesne University Press, Pittsburgh,Pennsylvania, 1989, p. 131.

The Igbo rites of passage emerged as the entrance gates to the roots of the pressure points. No other way was appropriate to redress, unify and integrate the faith of the Igbos and their solid cultural roots than the inculturation method. It is understandable, then, why this subject was given much attention in the work. It is only through inculturation, that one succeeds in reconciling the christian faith with the Igbo Culture, which have remained in isolation from each other right from the early days of evangelisation. Inculturation aims at recuperating the positive values of Igbo Culture, ameliorating, beautifying, and boosting them in order to make Christianity really feel at home. The objective is to restore in the Igbo christian the lost sense of cultural identity, as well as pave a way for a convinced christian life and a flourishing of the faith in Igboland.

In the proposed models, one has tried simply to make indications for the future concrete challenges of the Church in Igboland. The proposals are meant to arouse some provocations for the Church, which would lead to a systematic, unified and concerted action in the direction of Inculturation in various aspects of the Igbo Culture. The work has not been an easy one, since inculturation, being a new attitude and terminology, is only now being given a literary attention. It has, however, been an interesting study, and very eye-opening indeed. If this work registered any success, it is to be seen in the fact that it exposed the dangers, difficulties, risks, hopes and promises, as well as the possibilities for any inculturation work.

Briefly, in the above pages, special attention has been paid to the positive values of the Igbo Culture. The deep sense of the sacred and of religion, which propels active religious sentiments of the Igbos were judiciously and properly protected in re-channelling a right attitude to the worship of God.

One has also given serious thoughts to the facts and recommendation expressed by Sawyerr, who observed that,

> The African sees himself as part of a cultic community - a community which is incomplete without the supernatural world. The worship of the ancestors, the attitude to birth and death, sin, sickness, forgiveness and health all converge on the central role of the community. Here doctrine and liturgy intersect and the role of the Church as a worshipping community with a message and mission can be made real, both to Christians who are already within as well as those outside the faith.[2]

Aware of this, therefore, the communitarian factor and sense of solidarity were expressed, recognised, and encouraged in the proposals made. The festive mood and attitude of the Igbos, always punctuated by hilarious feelings, which is a very powerful expression of human sentiments that prop

---

[2]HARRY SAWYERR, "What is African Theology", in JOHN PARRATT, ed., A Reader in African Christian Theology, SPCK, Great Britain, 1987, pp. 23 - 24.

up religious convictions, are accommodated in restoring the sense of feeling at home in both Igbo culture and in the christian religion.[3]

However, in the proposals, some features are exposed which are repugnant to the christian faith. No compromise was made with regard to these. Instead, the indifferent aspects of the cultural values intermingled with superstition were proposed for purification by the faith, so that their positive aspects will shine out. Over and above all these, the traditional contexts are positively recommended to be utilised as backgrounds to which the christian faith could take flesh. This would have the overall effect of assuring a traditionally orientated christian faith. With the guarantee of this, the double-way practice of the Igbo christians disappears. It is this goal that we set out from the onset to achieve.

However, in order that Inculturation in Igboland succeeds, some points have to be taken note of. First and foremost, a change of attitude is called for. This is expected from the part of the christians, especially all those who are involved directly or indirectly with the evangelising work, as well as from those spearheading and piloting the traditional affairs. While one expects these to be ready to compromise, the evangelising personnel must also be prepared to look after the culturally and anthropologically based spiritual needs of the Igbos in order to succeed.

> The Nigerian christian faithful generally do not make jokes of sacred things nor disdain them. Holy water, blessings of all sorts in sickness, at work, at childbirth, at planting and harvest, at school and examinations, etc. are hotly sought after by the faithful.[4]

Christianity must be ready to feed the deep spiritual quest of the Igbos in order to control them, and be able to divert their attention from the superstitious and false worships. It must be clearly understood that the Igbo is not satisfied with an impersonal, abstract and indifferent treatment of his human problems. It is on account of this that the Igbos want to be personally treated when they approach any of the sacraments. For instance, they would like to be directly touched when they are being blessed, really

---

[3]"Music in Nigeria is usually connected with dance. Nigerian music calls forth not only the voice but the whole person to expression and movement" - (PETER SCHINELLER, op. cit, p. 86).

[4]"And yet, today, no rituals have been compiled to take good advantage and maximise the pastoral benefits of the situation. It is not surprising that many Catholics often abandon their church to seek relief in church 'healing' homes and other prayer meetings which address their needs directly and existentially." - BASIL K. NWAZOJIE, "The Nigerian Hierarchy and Liturgical Inculturation in the Nigerian Church", in CATHOLIC SECRETARIAT OF NIGERIA, Inculturation in Nigeria, Proceedings of Catholic Bishops' Study Session, Nov. 1988, p. 75.

treated as 'this particular person', directly touched by the sprinkled holy water. They want the symbolism of the Sacraments and the sacramentals to be vividly and physically manifested and transmitted. The celebrations ought to be clearly expressed in symbols real to them. The recuperation of this spiritual sense is important in making them to be personally committed and convinced. In this light, the development of Igbo Liturgy becomes a big challenge for inculturation purposes.[5] Such a Liturgy should reflect and incorporate Igbo psychology and their symbolic values in the christian worship. This work has concerned itself in a special way with the rites of birth and the traditional headship. There are yet so many other areas that pose similar challenges for Inculturation, such as the use of the linguistic elements of the Igbos in formulating the doctrines of the faith, and the translation of the sacred literature. The use of proverbs and Igbo metaphors could manifestly bring the meanings of the doctrines very home to the people in their thought patterns. The etiological values of the stories and folklore could be put to use in the formulation of the Catechism books and christian moral teachings.

Aware of the problems encountered in the proposed models, one recommends as an important requisite for inculturation, a basic and thorough knowledge of the culture in question by all who are involved in the work of evangelisation. Since it properly belongs to the indigenous clergy to initiate and carry out the inculturation of the faith in their own culture, one strongly advocates that special training which give adequate attention to studies in missionary anthropology and Culture in general, should be given to all those preparing for the apostolate in any capacity, but more especially for the candidates for the priesthood. One acknowledges here the recommendations of the Nigerian Bishops' Conference, which among other things, have opted for more "exposure to Inculturation . . . in the formation of Seminarians and Religious".[6]

Inculturation demands a critical knowledge of Culture. As Luzbetak confirms,

> The moralist with only common-sense and a knowledge of Theology and Philosophy to rely on, but with little or no knowledge of culture and the particular cultural context, is indeed a dangerous 'expert' in the Missions.[7]

---

[5]"Despite the greatest progress that has been made in the development and propagation of our cultural languages, the liturgy still lags behind in their utilisation. What has been done so far is the translation of trans-literation of liturgical books from Latin into the traditional languages, paying as much fidelity as possible to the nuances and cultural background of the original Latin". - BASIL K. NWAZOJIE, op. cit., p. 74.

[6]CATHOLIC SECRETARIAT OF NIGERIA, Inculturation in Nigeria, p. 101.

[7]LOUIS J. LUZBETAK, op. cit., p. 9.

This would enable the evangeliser to be able to evaluate well the culture he is encountering, for a judicious use of the positive elements of the culture. There is also the need to develop an inculturated Catechism manual, which would express and integrate the faith in the thought patterns and cultural framework of the people. This would have the effect of relating the faith directly with the concrete cultural situation of the people. Awareness of the intimacy of the faith and culture even at the early impressionable stages of child development would lead to a conscious living of a culture-oriented faith.

Cultural awareness should be created in the minds of christians, so that more interest be shown in the various aspects of their culture. In this light one commends the spirit of competition in the exhibition of certain cultural aspects by christians, which practice is noticeable already in some dioceses in Igboland. These exhibitions take the form of cultural dances, music, acrobatic display, drumming, traditional arts, dressing etc. That is a step in the right direction. Such cultural conscious-raising would have the overall effect of cultural revival, and eventually lead into inculturation in these aspects of the culture. It is in the exposition of the various aspects of the culture that the positive and negative values are manifested and criticised, and eventually purified and uplifted.

Since Igboland is made up of nearly twelve dioceses, of people sharing the same language and cultural pattern, it is expected that the project of Inculturation should be given a unified and a concerted treatment by the whole ecclesiastical region. Instead of every diocese tackling the problem alone, all the dioceses should see it as a common problem demanding a uniformity of approach. One is glad that the ecclesiastical authorities in Nigeria are aware of this need for a unilateral approach to the subject of Inculturation, hence it was remarked in their Study Session on Inculturation that "it is only through a concerted effort that the Church will make herself able to bring the hope of Christ into today's cultures and mentalities".[8]

In the light of this, it is highly recommended the establishment of Cultural Commission in all - diocesan, parish, town and village levels in each of the dioceses of Igboland. For the purposes of coordination, a regional cultural commission is advocated, whose function would be to streamline, criticise and synthesize the cultural activities in the various dioceses. It is this regional level that ought to carry out intensive research that would lead to inculturation. These Commissions should be adequately staffed by specialists in all the disciplines which are demanded for Inculturation of the faith. Specialists in the field of Theology, Cultural Anthropology, Liturgy, music, literature etc. are important tools for any successful inculturation work. A coordinated interaction and dialogue between these specialists and the personnel also from the traditional system would lead to a simplified inculturation in Igboland. The Commission needs enough funds to be able

---

[8]CATHOLIC SECRETARIAT OF NIGERIA, op. cit., p. 25.

to carry out the long research which inculturation demands, and which even Francis Cardinal Arinze advocates,

Long research has to be conducted into various customs, rites and ceremonies. Internationally accepted local experts in theology, sacred liturgy, catechetics, anthropology, music, poetry, literature and fine arts must apply the tools of their trade to the various facets of our culture. And they must themselves have drunk deep from the genuine Catholic spirit.[9]

This is not going to be an easy task. However, Joseph McCabe gives the assurance that,

By working together on this, and by accepting our mission of incarnating the message of Jesus Christ for the peoples of every nation and age, we are accepting our prophetic call and to reawaken, in the People of God, a deep faith experience grounded in their own cultural milieu and yet, unified with the faith experience of the whole Church.[10]

Aware of the worth and value of the Igbo positive potentials, one is optimistic of the end result of inculturation carried out in the direction of the good potentials. One is convinced and united with Mbiti in asserting that:

Christianity which is 'indigenous', 'traditional', and 'African' . . . holds the greatest and the only potentials of meeting the dilemmas and challenges of modern Africa, and of reaching the full integration and manhood of individuals and communities.[11]

It is confidently hoped that if the inculturation of Christianity moves in the direction of these indications, the alienation of Igbo Christians will disappear and the faith would more convincingly be lived, such that there would be no need for any neo-evangelisation in Igboland as is greatly needed in Europe today after decades of centuries of christian practice. One is confident also that, in spite of the difficulties on the way, inculturation within the Igbo cultural potentials is an exercise that would ensure a consolidation and fructification of the christian faith in Igboland if it is given adequate attention and a trial.

Finally, one reminds the Church in Igboland that **NOW** is the chance

---

[9]FRANCIS A. ARINZE, The Church and Nigerian Culture, Lenten Pastoral, 1973, p. 28.

[10]JOSEPH V. McCABE, "The Challenge of Liturgical Inculturation: Directions", in SPEARHEAD, no. 92, June 1986, p. 11.

[11]J. MBITI, African Religions and Philosophy, p. 277.

for Inculturation of Christianity in Igboland. With Shorter, one reiterates and insists that,

> The only way in which inculturation can possibly be realized is through experimentation. If experimentation is prohibited, inculturation is delayed. Church leaders may be afraid of mistakes being made, or of losing control, but these are risks that have to be taken. Without the possibility of making mistakes and of learning by mistakes, nothing can be achieved.[12]

May the Good Lord, who took flesh and dwelt among men in order to uplift the whole of humanity, guide and direct all efforts geared towards this arduous task of Inculturation especially in Igboland, so that He finds a comfortable home within the Igbo Culture in order to transform Igbos into authentic and convinced sons and daughters of God.

---

[12]A. SHORTER, Towards a Theology of Inculturation, p. 252.

BIBLIOGRAPHY

SOURCES

Sacred Scripture

The Jerusalem Bible, Darton, Longman & Todd, London, 1968 edition.

Conciliar Documents

Constitution on the Sacred Liturgy, *Sacrosanctum Concilium*, AAS 56 (1964) : 97 - 138.

Dogmatic Constitution on the Church, *Lumen Gentium*, AAS 57 (1965): 5-75.

Decree on the Relation of the Church to non-Christian Religions, *Nostra Aetate*, AAS 58 (1966): 740 - 744.

Decree on the Church's Missionary Activity, *Ad Gentes*, AAS 58 (1966): 947 - 990.

Pastoral Constitution on the Church in the Modern World, *Gaudium et Spes*, AAS 58 (1966): 1025 - 1120.

Papal Documents

BENEDICT XV, Apostolic Letter, *Maximum Illud*, 30 Nov. 1919, AAS 11 (1919): 440 - 455.

--------, Apostolic Letter, *Epist. Perlibenti equidem*, AAS 1950: 727.

PIUS XII, Encyclical, *Evangelii Praecones*, 2 June 1951, AAS 33 (1951): 497 - 528.

JOHN XXIII, Encyclical, *Princeps Pastorum*, 28 Nov. 1959, AAS 51 (1959): 833 - 864.

--------, *Message to Humanity*, Oct. 1962

PAUL VI, Message, *Africae Terrarum*, 29 Oct. 1967, AAS 69 (1967):1073 - 1102.

--------, Address to the Closing Session of the Symposium of the African

Bishops in Kampala, Uganda, 31 July 1969, AAS 71 (1969): 573 - 578.

--------, Address to the African and Madagascar Episcopal Conference, Rome, 1975, AAS 67 (1975): 569 - 572.

--------, Apostolic Exhortation, *Evangelii Nuntiandi*, 8 Dec. 1975, AAS 68 (1976): 5 - 76.

JOHN PAUL II, Encyclical, *Redemptor Hominis*, 4 March 1979, AAS 71 (1979): 257 - 324.

--------, Apostolic Exhortation, *Catechesi Trahendae*, 16 Oct. 1979, AAS 71 (1979): 1320.

--------, Apostolic Exhortation, *Familiaris Consortio*, 22 nov. 1981, AAS 74 (1982): 90 - 95.

--------, *Papal Message to Nigeria*, 12 - 17 Feb. 1982, AAS 74, (1982) : 608 -624.

--------, Address to the Nigerian Bishops in Lagos, 15 Feb. 1982, AAS 74 (1982): 611 - 618.

Other Documents

CATHOLIC BISHOPS OF THE ONITSHA ECCLESIASTICAL PROVINCE, *Put out Into Deep Water*, Pastoral Letter, 1985.

CATHOLIC SECRETARIAT OF NIGERIA, *Inculturation in Nigeria*, Proceedings of Catholic Bishops' Study Session, Nov. 1988.

--------, *New Era of Evangelisation*, Seminar Proceedings, 1 - 3 May 1984.

Collectanea Sacrae Congregationis dei Propaganda Fide, I, Rome, 1907.

ENEJA, BISHOP M. U., *My Involvement in Evangelisation*, Lenten Pastoral, Enugu Diocese, 1984.

--------, *On Fire for Christ*, Lenten Pastoral, 1985.

NWEDO, BISHOP ANTHONY G., *Centenary Celebration in Eastern Nigeria 1885 - 1985*, Homily delivered at Onitsha, 7 Dec. 1985.

Ordo Initiationis Christianae Adultorum, General Introduction, IV, no. 88, Vatican City, 1972.

THE EXTRAORDINARY SYNOD OF BISHOPS, *Message to the People of God*, St Paul's Editions, Boston, 1985.

Dictionaries and Encyclopedias

Concise Encyclopedia of Psychology, Abridged edition, 1987.

Encyclopedia of Educational Research, 5th edition.

Encyclopedia of Religion and Ethics, ed. JAMES HASTINGS, vol. VIII, T & T Clark - Morrison & Gibb Ltd.

International Encyclopedia of the Social Sciences, vols. 3 & 4, 1972 edition.

Oxford Advanced Learner's Dictionary of Current English, ed. by A. S. HORNBY, Oxford University Press, Oxford, 1974.

The New Catholic Encyclopedia, 1981 edition.

The Encyclopedia of Religion, 1987 edition.

WORKS

Theological Anthropology Books

AA.VV., *Temi di Antropologia Teologica*, Teresianum, Roma, 1981.

AA.VV., *Portare Cristo all'uomo*, vol. 1, Studia Urbaniana, 22, Urban University, Rome, 1985.

ABEYASINGHA, NIHAL, *A Theological Evaluation of Non-Christian Rites*, Theological Publications in India, Bangalore.

ADASU, MOSES ORSHIO, *Understanding African Traditional Religion*, Dorset Publishing Company, England.

AGUWA, J. U. C., *The Anthropological Challenges of Christianity in the changing African Culture: The Nigerian Case*, (Ph.D. dissertation, Universit`a Teresianum, Rome, 1987).

ANDERSON, G. H. & T. F. STRANSKY, eds., *Mission Trends*, (Nos 1 - 5), Paulist Fathers, Inc.,1981.

ANISIOBI, H. N. M., "Igbo Religiousness: Its Virtues and Limitations in the Light of Christianity", Teresianum, 1978.

ANOZIE, I. P., "The Religious Import of Igbo Names", (Ph.D dissertation), Urban University, Rome, 1968.

APPIAH_KUBI, KOFI & SERGIO TORRES, African Theology en route, Orbis Books, Maryknoll, 1983.

ARBUCKLE, GERALD A., Earthening the Gospel, Geoffrey Chapmann, London, 1990.

ARINZE, CARDINAL FRANCIS, Church in Dialogue, Ignatius Press, San Francisco, 1990.

ARINZE, F. A., Sacrifice in Igbo Religion, University Press, Ibadan, 1970.

--------, The Church and Nigerian Culture, Lenten Pastoral, 1973, Archdiocese of Onitsha, Tabansi Press, Onitsha.

AZEVEDO, MARCELLO DE CARVALHO, Inculturation and the Challenges of Modernity, Gregorian University, Rome, 1982.

AZORJI EUGENE E., Some Recurrent Problems of Christian Inculturation in Nigeria with Special Reference to the Igbo People, Urban University, Rome, 1988.

BUCH, P.H., Anthropology and Religion, New Haven, Conn., 1940.

BÜHLMANN, W., All Have the Same God, Orbis Books, Maryknoll.

--------, The Coming of the Third Church, Orbis Books, Maryknoll, New York, 1978.

--------, The Missions on Trial, Orbis Books, Maryknoll, New York, 1979.

Bulletin of African Religion and Culture, published by National Association for African Traditional Religion, vol. 1, no.1, April 1987.

CARRIER, HERV'E, Gospel Message and Human Cultures, Duquesne University Press, Pennsylvania, 1989.

CHRISTENSEN, THOMAS G., An African Tree of Life, Orbis Books, Maryknoll, New York, 1990.

CHUKWULOZIE, VICTOR, Muslim - Christian Dialogue in Nigeria, Daystar Press, Ibadan, 1986.

CHUPUNGCO, ANSCAR J., Cultural Adaptation of the Liturgy, Paulist Press, New York / Ramsey, 1982.

--------, Liturgies of the Future, Paulist Press, New York, 1989.

COSTA, RUY O., ed., *One Faith, Many Cultures*, orbis Books, Maryknoll, New York, 1988.

CROLLIUS, ARIJ A. R., ed., *Inculturation, Working Papers on Living Faith and Cultures*, vols. I - XI. Roma, 1982 - 1989

de CHARDIN, TEILHARD, *The Divine Milieu*, Fontana Books, 1957.

DICKSON, KWESI A., & PAUL ELLINGWORTH, *Biblical Revelation and African Beliefs*, Orbis Books, Maryknoll.

DÖRMANN, J., *Die Eine Wahrheit und die vielen Religion*, Josef Kral Verlag, Abensberg, 1988.

DUCRUET, JEAN, et. al., *Faith and Culture: The Role of the Catholic University*, Gregorian University Press, Rome, 1989.

EDEH, EMMANUEL M. P., *Towards an Igbo Metaphysics*, Loyola University Press, 1985.

EJIZU, CHRISTOPHER I.,*'Ofo': Igbo Ritual Symbol*, Fourth Dimension Publishers, Enugu, 1986.

EKECHI, F. R., *Missionary Enterprise and Rivalry in Igboland 1857 - 1914*, Frank Cass & Co Inc., London, 1972.

ÉLA, JEAN - MARC, *La mia Fede di Africano*, Edizione Dehoniane, Bologna, 1987.

--------, *My Faith as an African*, Orbis Books, Maryknoll, New York, 1989.

--------, *African Cry*, Orbis Books, Maryknoll, New York, 1986.

ERSHINE, NOEL LEO, *Decolonising Theology*, Orbis Books, New York, 1981.

EZEANYA, S. N.*A Handbook of Igbo Christian Names*, C. M. S. Press, Port Harcourt, 1967.

FITZPATRICK, J. P., *One Church Many Cultures*, Sheed & Ward.

FOWLER, JAMES W., *Stages of Faith*, Harper & Row, Publishers, San Francisco, 1981.

GITTINS, ANTHONY J., *Gifts and Strangers: Meeting the Challenge of Inculturation*, Paulist Press, New York, 1989.

GREMILLION, J., ed., *The Church and Culture since Vatican II*, University of Notre Dame Press, Indiana, 1985.

GROOME, THOMAS, *Christian Religious Education*, Harper & Row Ltd.,

1980.

HACKER, PAUL, *Theological Foundations of Evangelization*, Steyler Verlag, St Augustin, 1983.

HÄRING, BERNARD, *Evangelization Today*, St Paul Publications, England, 1990.

HICKEY, R., ed., *Modern Missionary Documents and Africa*, Dominican Publications, Dublin, 1982.

HUNT, ARNOLD D., *Christ and the World's Religions*, The Joint Board of Christian Education, Melbourne, 1984.

IDEM, E. O., *Inculturation of Leadership in the Nigerian Situation*, Lateran University, Rome, 1988.

IDOWU, E. B., *African Traditional Religion: A Definition*, SCM, London, 1973.

--------, *Towards an Indigenous Church*, Oxford University Press, London, 1965.

IGBOAJA, E. U., ed., *Enugu Synod I*, Lay Apostolate Publications, Enugu, 1985.

IGBOAJA, UGONNA & OBIORA IKE, eds., *Inculturation: Where do We Stand?*, Snaap Press, Enugu, 1990.

IKENGA-METU, E., *Comparative Studies of African Traditional Religion*, Imico Publishers, Onitsha - Nigeria, 1987.

ILOGU, EDMUND, *Christianity and Igbo Culture*, University Publishing Co., Onitsha.

IMASOGIE, OSADOLOR, *Guidelines for Christian Theology in Africa*, University Press, Ltd., Ibadan, 1986.

IRVINE & J. T. SANDERS, eds., *Cultural Adaptation within Modern Africa*, Teachers' College Press, New York.

IWE, NWACHUKWUIKE S. S., *Christianity and Culture in Africa*, University Publishing Company, Nigeria, 1976.

--------, *Christianity, Culture and Colonialism in Africa*, R. S. N. C. Port Harcourt, 1985

JORDAN, J. P., *Bishop Shanahan of Southern Nigeria*, Conmore & Reynolds, Ltd., Dublin, 1948.

KALU, OGBU U., ed., *West African Religions*, Department of Religion, University of Nigeria, Nsukka.

KRAFT, C., *Christianity in Culture*, Orbis Books, New York, 1979.

LONERGAN, B., *Method in Theology*, London: Darton, Longman & Todd, 1972.

LUZBETAK, L. J., *The Church and Cultures*, Divine Word Publication, Illinois, 1970.

MADU, I. C., "Christianising the Igbo Traditional Love and Morality Rites", (Unpublished Thesis for the Licentiate in Angelicum, Rome, 1983).

MAKOZI, A. O., & A. OJO, eds., *The History of the Catholic Churchin Nigeria*, Macmillan, Nigeria, 1982.

MARIA DE LA CRUZ AYMES et al., *Effective Inculturation and Ethnic Identity*, Pontifical Gregorian University, Rome, 1987.

MBITI, J., *African Religions and Philosophy*, Heinemann, London, 1969

.--------, *Concepts of God in Africa*, Praeger, New York, 1970.

--------, *Introduction to African Religion*, Heinemann, London, 1975.

METUH, E. I., *God and Man in African Religion*, Geoffrey Chapman, London, 1981.

--------, *African Religion in Western Conceptual Schemes : The Problem of Interpretation*, Claverianum Press, Ibadan, 1985.

METZ, JOHANN-BAPTIST, EDWARD SCHILLEBEECKX & PHILIP HILLYER, eds., *World Catechism or Inculturation?*, T & T Clark Ltd, Edinburgh, 1989

MILINGO, E., *The World in Between*, C. Hurst & Co., London, 1984.

MOZIA, MICHAEL I., *Solidarity in the Church and Solidarity among the Igbos of Nigeria*, Claverianum Press, 1987.

MULLAN, J., *The Catholic Church in Modern Africa*, Geoffrey Chapman, London, 1965.

MUZOREWA, GWINYAI H., *The Origins and Development of African Theology*, Orbis Books, Maryknoll, New York, 1985.

NEIL, STEPHEN, *Christian Faith & Other Faiths*, Intervarsity Press, Illinois, 1984.

NGINDU, A. MUSHETE, *La Teologia Africana in cammino*, EDB, 1988.

NIEBUHR, H. R., *Christ and Culture*, Harper & Row Publishers, Inc., New

York, 1975.

NNABUCHI, NWANKWO, *In Defence of Igbo Belief*, Life Path Printing Press, Enugu, 1987.

NWABEKEE, A. I.A.N., *Liturgical-catechetical Formation of Children in the Light of Patristic Practice and Second Vatican Council Reform*, (Ph.D dissertation in Sacred Liturgy, Rome, 1986.)

NWOGA, DONATUS IBE, *The Supreme God as Stranger in Igbo Religious Thought*, Hawk Press, Ekwerazu, 1984.

NZOMIWU, P. C., *The Moral Concept of Justice among the Igbos*, Doctoral Thesis in Moral Theology, Alfonsianum, Rome, 1977.

OBI, C., ed., *A Hundred Years of the Catholic Church in Eastern Nigeria 1885 - 1985*, Africana - Feb Publishers, Onitsha, 1985.

OBIUKWU, S. C., "'Ala' (Earth Spirit) in Igbo Culture and Traditional Religious Beliefs", (Ph.D dissertation, Urban University, Rome, 1978.

ODUYOYE, MERCY AMBA, *Hearing and Knowing*, Orbis Books, Maryknoll, 1986.

OKOLO, CHUKWUDUM B., ed., *The Igbo Church and Quest for God*, Pacific College Press Ltd., 1985.

ONWUBIKO, OLIVER A., *The Church and Culture in an African Community*, Assumpta Press, Owerri, 1989.

ONYEHALU, M. C., *Government, Christianity, and Maskers: Encounters in Eastern Nigeria*, (Ph.D dissertation, Lateran University, Rome, 1987.

ONYENEKE, A. O., *The Dead Among the Living : Masquerades in Igbo Society*, Chuka Printing Co., Ltd., Enugu, 1987.

OPOKU, KOFI ASARE, *West African Traditional Religion*, Fep International Private Ltd., 1978.

OSUJI, C. C., *The Concept of Salvation in Igbo Traditional Religion*, Doctoral dissertation, Urban University, Rome, 1977.

PANNENBERG, W., *Anthropology in Theological Perspective*, Westminster Press, Philadelphia, 1985.

PARRATT, JOHN, ed., *A Reader in African Christian Theology*, SPCK, Great Britain, 1987.

PARRINDER, E. G., *West African Religion*, Epworth Press, London, (1949) 1969.

249

--------, *Africa's Three Religions*, Sheldon Press, London, 1969.

--------, *African Traditional Religion*, Sheldon Press, London, 1964.

RAHNER, KARL, *Uditori della Parola*, Edizioni Borla.

--------, *Grundkurs des Glaubens*, Verlag Herder, Germany, 1976.

RICHARD, L., D. T. HARRINGTON, & J. W. O'MALLEY, *Vatican II : the Unfinished Agenda*, Paulist Press, New York.

ROGUET, A. M., *Christ Acts Through Sacraments*, Liturgical Press, Collegeville, Minnesota, 1960.

SALDANHA, JULIAN, *Patterns of Evangelisation in Mission History*, St. Paul Publications, Bombay, 1988.

SCHINELLER, PETER, *A handbook on Inculturation*, Paulist Press, New York, 1990.

SHORTER, AYLWARD, *African Culture and the Christian Church*, Geoffrey Chapman, London, 1973.

--------, *Toward A Theology of Inculturation*, Orbis Books, Maryknoll, New York, 1988.

--------, *African Christian Theology*, Geoffrey Chapman, London.

SHORTER, A., AND OTHERS, *Towards African Christian Maturity*, St. Paul Publications, Africa, 1987.

SMALLEY, W. A., ed., *Readings in Missionary Anthropology*, 1978 edit., William Carey Library Publ., California, U.S.A.

THE VENERABLE BEDE, *A History of the English Church and People*, transl. by I. SHERLEY-PRICE, 1955, (Penguin ed.), Harmondsworth, Middx.

TILLICH, PAUL, *Systematic Theology*, vol. I, 1953.

UZUKWU, E. E., *Church and Inculturation*, Pacific College Press Ltd., Obosi, 1985.

--------, ed., *Religion and African Culture*, Spiritan Publications, Enugu, 1988.

VILADESAU, RICHARD, *Answering for Faith*, Paulist Press, New York, 1987.

VON RAD, GERHARD, *Old Testament Theology*, vol. 2, SCM Press Ltd., (1965), pp. 336 - 356.

WALIGGO, J. M., A. R. CROLLIUS, T. NKERAMIHIGO, J. MUTISO-MBINDA,

Inculturation : Its Meaning and Urgency, St. Paul Publications, Africa, 1986

WALSH, LIAM G., *The Sacraments of Initiation*, Geoffrey Chapman, London, 1988.

WALSH, M., & B. DAVIES, eds., *Proclaiming Justice and Peace*, Collins Liturgical Publications, London, 1984.

WESTERMANN, DIEDRICH, *Africa and Christianity*, Oxford University Press, 1937.

WIJNGAARDS, JOHN, *African Events*, August 1985.

Socio-Anthropological Books

ACHEBE, C., *Things Fall Apart*, Heinemann Educational Books Ltd., London, 1958.

ACUFF, F. GENE, DONALD E. ALLEN, LLOYD A. TAYLOR, *From Man to Society*, The Dryden Press, Hinsdalle, Illinois, 1973.

ADCOCK, C. J., *Fundamentals of Psychology*, Penguin Books Ltd., Great Britain, 1964.

ALEKE, C. E., "Social Psychological Integration of Adolescent Personality into Adulthood in Igboland", (Ph.D dissertation, Universitìoniana), Rome, 1978.

ALLAND, ALEXANDER, Jr., *To be Human*, John Wiley & Sons Inc., New York, 1980.

ANENE, J. C., *Southern Nigeria in Transition 1885 -1906*, Cambridge University Press, 1966.

ANIGBO, O. A. C., *Commensality and Human Relationship Among the Igbo*, University of Nigeria Press, 1987.

BARBU, ZEVEDEI, *Society, Culture and Personality*, Basil Blackwell, 1971.

BASDEN, G. T., *Among the Ibos of Nigeria*, Frank Cass & Co. Ltd., London, 1966.

--------, *Niger Ibos*, Frank Cass & Co., London, 1966.

BATES, DANIEL G., & SUSAN H. LEES, *Contemporary Anthropology*, Alfred A. Knopf, New York.

BATESON, G., "Cultural Determinants of Personality" in J. M. Hunt, ed., *Personality and the Behavioural Disorders*, new York, 1944.

BEALS, RALPH L., HARRY HOIJER & ALAN R. BEALS, *An Introduction to Anthropology*, Macmillan Publishing Co. Inc., New York, 1977.

BEATTIE, JOHN, Other Cultures, Routledge & Kegan Paul, London, 1964.

BELMONT, NICOLE, *Arnold van Gennep*, The University of Chicago Press, Chicago & London, 1979.

BENDERLY, BERYL LIEFF, M. F. GALLAGHER, JOHN M. YOUNG, *Discovering Culture: An Introduction to Anthropology*, D. van Nostrand Company, New York, 1977.

BOUYER, LOUIS, *Il Rito e L'uomo*, Morcelliana, 1964.

CHINAWA, PAUL OKECHUKWU, *Teachers' Role in Character Education of the Youth*, Ph.D dissertation, Universitìonianum, Rome, 1984.

COMBLIN, JOS9 *Retrieving the Human*, Orbis Books, Maryknoll, New York, 1985.

CROOKE, WILLIAM, *The Natives of Nordern India: Native Races of the British Empire*, A Constable, London, 1907.

CSIKSZENTMIHALYI, MIHALY, & REED LARSON, *Being Adolescent*, Basic Books, Inc., Publishers, New York, 1984.

DAVIS, RICHARD H., ed., *Aging: Prospects and Issues*, University of Southern California Press, los Angeles, 1976.

DIKE, AZUKA A., *The Resilience of Igbo Culture*, Fourth Dimension Publishers, 1985.

DOLGIN JANETH L., et al., eds., *Symbolic Anthropology*, Columbia University Press, New York, 1977.

DUBBS, PATRICK J., & DANIEL D. WHITNEY, *Cultural Contexts*, Allyn and Bacon, Inc., Boston.

DURKHEIM, EMILE, *The Rules of Sociological Method*, Trans by SARAH A. SOLOWAY & JOHN H. MeER, ed. GEORG E. E. CATLIN, (8th ed.), New York: Free Press, 1938.

EGWUONWU, ANI DIKE, *Marriage Problems in Africa*, Continental Services Ltd., 1986.
EJIOFOR, PITA N. O., *Cultural Revival in Igboland*, University Publishing Company, Onitsha, 1984.

ELIADE, MIRCIEA, *The Sacred & the Profane*, Harcourt Brace & World Inc.,

1959

--------, *Rites and Symbols of Initiation*, Harper Torchbooks, New York, (1958) 1965.

--------, *Man and the Sacred*, Harper & Row, Publishers, New York, 1974.

ELKIN, FREDERICK / GERALD HANDEL, *The Child and Society: The Process of Socialization*, Random House, New York, 1972.

EMBER, CAROL R., - MELVIN EMBER, *Cultural Anthropology*, Prentice - Hall, Inc., Englewood Cliffs, New Jersey, 4th ed., 1985.

ERIKSON, ERIK H., *Identity and the Life Cycle*, W. W. Norton & Company, New York, 1979.

--------, *Identity : Youth and Crisis*, W. W. Norton & Co., Inc., Great Britain, 1983.

--------, *Childhood and Society*, 2nd edit., W. W. Norton & Company, New York, 1963.

--------, *The Life Cycle Completed*, W. W. Norton & Company, New York, 1982.

ERIKSON, E. H., JOAN M. ERIKSON, HELEN Q. KIVNICK, *Vital Involvement in Old Age*, W. W. Norton & Company, New York, 1986.

FORDE, D., & G. JONES, *The Ibo and Ibibio Speaking Peoples of Eastern Nigeria*, London, 1950.

FRIEDL, JOHN, *Cultural Anthropology*, Harper's College Press, New York, 1976.

GEERTZ, C., *The Interpretation of Cultures*, Basic Books Inc., New York, 1973.

GILLIN, J., *The Ways of Men: An Introduction to Anthropology*, New York, Appleton-Century-Crofts, Inc., 1948.

GLUCKMAN, M., *Custom and Conflict in Africa*, Oxford, 1955.

GOODMAN, MARY ELLEN, *The Individual and Culture*, Dorsey Press, Homewood, Illinois, 1967.

GORMAN, MARGARET, ed., *Psychology and Religion*, Paulist Press, New York.

GREEN, M. M.,*Igbo Village Affairs*, Frank Cass & Co Ltd., London, 1964.

GRUNLAN, STEPHEN A. & MARVIN K. MAYERS, *Cultural Anthropology*,

Akademie Books, Michigan, 1988.

HAMMOND, PETER B., *Cultural & Social Anthropology*, Macmillan Publishing Co., Inc., New York, 1975.

--------, *An Introduction to Cultural and Social Anthropology*, Macmillan Publishing Co. Inc., New York, 1978.

HARING, D. G., ed., *Personal Character and Cultural Milieu*, Syracuse, New York, 1948.

HAVILAND, WILLIAM A., *Cultural Anthropology*, Holt Rinehart and Winston, Inc., USA, 1978 (2nd edition).

HERSKOVITS, M. J., *Cultural Anthropology*, Alfred A. Knopf, New York, 1955.

--------, Human Factor in Changing Africa.

--------, *Man and His Works*, New York, 1952.

HOEBEL, E. A., *Anthropology: The Study of Man*, McGraw, New York, 1972.

HOEBEL, E. A. & EVERETT L. FROST, *Cultural and Social Anthropology*, Mc Graw-Hill Book Company, New York, 1976.

HONIGMANN, J. J., *Culture and Personality*, New York, 1954.

ISICHEI, E.,*A History of Igbo People*, Macmillan, London, 1976.

--------, *Igbo Worlds*, Macmillan, London, 1977.

KALU, OGBU U., ed., *Readings in African Humanities: African Cultural Development*, Fourth Dimension Publishing Co. Ltd., Enugu, 1978.

KARDINER, A.0, *The Individual and His Society*, New York, 1939.

KARDINER, A., & EDWARD PREBLE, *They Studied Man*, Mentor Book.

KARP, IVAN, & CHARLES S. BIRD, eds., *Explorations in African Systems of Thought*, Indiana University Press, Bloomington.

KEESING, FELIX M., *Cultural Anthropology: The Science of Custom*, Holt, Rinehart & Winston, New York, 1966.

KING, NOEL Q., *African Cosmos*, Wadsworth Publishing Company, Belmont, California, 1986.

KITCHENS, J. A., LEOBARDO F. ESTRADA, *Individuals in Society*, Charles E. Merill Publishing Co., Columbus, Ohio, 1974

KLUCKHOHN, C., *Mirror for Man: The Relation of Anthropology to Modern Life*, New York & Torontto, McGraw Hill, 1944.

KOTTAK, CONRAD P., *Cultural Anthropology*, Random House Inc., New York, 1975.

LA FONTAINE, J. S., *Initiation*, Manchester University Press, Great Britain, 1986.

LAYE, CAMARA, *The African Child*, Fontana/ Collins, G.Britain, (1954) 1981.

LEITH-ROSS, S., *African Women*, Routledge and Kegan Paul, London, 1939.

LEONARD, A. M. G., *The Lower Niger and Its Tribes*, Frank Cass & Co. Ltd., London, 1964.

LEVI-STRAUSS, C., *The Savage Mind*, The University of Chicago Press.

LIDZ, THEODORE, *The Person. His and Her Development Throughout the Life Cycle*, Basic Books, Inc., Publishers, New York, 1983.

LINTON, RALPH, *The Cultural Background of Personality*, Routledge & Kegan Paul ltd., London, 1968.

LOWE, GORDON R., *The Growth of Personality: From infancy to Old Age*, Pelican Books, Great Britain, (1972) 1985.

LOWIE, ROBERT H., *The History of Ethnological Theory*, Rinehart, New York, 1937.

MACQUARRIE, JOHN, *In Search of Humanity*, SCM Press Ltd., London, 1982.

MEAD, M., *Coming of Age in Samoa*, New York, 1927.

--------, *Growing up in New Guinea*, Apollo Editions, New York, 1972.

--------, "The Implications of Culture Change for Personality Development", in *American Journal of Orthopsychiatry*, 17, 633 -646.

MEAD, M., & M. WOLFENSTEIN, *Childhood in Contemporary Culture*, Chicago, 1955.

MEEK, C. K., *Law and Authority in Nigerian Tribe*, Oxford University Press, London, 1937.

PHY, ROBERT F., *Cultural and Social Anthropology*, Prentice-Hall, Inc., Englewood Cliffs, New Jersey, 1986.

NDUKA, OTONTI, *Western Education and the Nigerian Cultural Background*, Oxford University Press, 1964.

NKWO, MARIUS, *Igbo Cultural Heritage*, University Publishing Co., Onitsha, 1984.

NOUWEN, HENRI J. M. & WALTER G. GAFFNEY, *Aging: The Fulfilment of Life*, Image Books, New York, 1976.

NWEKE, R., *An Optional Philosophy for a Nigeran Educational System*, Antonianum, Rome, 1979.

OBIECHINA, E., *Culture, Tradition, and Society in the West African Novels*, Cambridge University Press, Cambridge, 1975.

O'DEA, THOMAS F., *The Sociology of Religion*, Prentice-Hall, Inc., Englewood Cliffs, New Jersey, 1966.

OGBALU, F. C., *Omenala Igbo*, (Igbo Customs), University Publishing Co., Nigeria, 1960.

OGBALU, F. C., *Igbo Institutions and Customs*, University Publishing Co., Onitsha - Nigeria.

--------, ed., *The Igbo as seen by Others*, University Publishing Co., 1988.

OGBALU, F. C., & E. N. EMENANJO, *Igbo Language and Culture*, vol.2, University Press Ltd., Ibadan, 1982.

OKAFOR, FESTUS C, *Africa at the Cross-Roads, Philosophical Approach to Education*, Vantage Press Inc., New York, 1974.

OLISAH, O., *Igbo Native Law and Custom*, New Era Press, Onitsha.

OPPONG, CHRISTINE, *Middle Class African Marriage*, George Allen & Unwin (Publishers)Ltd., U. K., (1981).

PELTO, GRETEL H., & PERTTI J. PELTO, *The Cultural Dimension of the Human Adventure*, Macmillan Publishing Co. Inc., New York, 1979.

PIAGET, JEAN, *The Moral Judgement of the Child*, The Free Press, New York, 1965.

PIDDINGTON, RALPH, *An Introduction to Social Anthropology*, (2nd ed.), vol. 1, Edinburgh: Oliver & Boyd, (1950) 1952.

RADCLIFFE-BROWN, A. R., *Structure and Function in Primitive Society*, Routledge & Kegan Paul, London & Henley.

RADCLIFFE-BROWN, A. R., & DARYLL FORDE, eds., *African Systems of Kinship and Marriage*, Oxford University Press, London.

SCHNEIDERS, A. A., *Personality Development and Adjustment in*

Adolescence, Milwaukee, Bruce Publishing Co., 1960.

SHELTON, A. J., *The Igbo-Igala Borderland*, State University of New York, Albany, 1971.

SPRINTHALL, NORMAN A., & W. ANDREW COLLINS, *Adolescent Psychology -A Developmental View*, Random House, New York, 1984.

STEINBERG, LAURENCE, *Adolescence*, Alfred A. Knopf, New York.

STEWART, F. H., *Fundamentals of Age-Group Systems*, Academic Press, New York.

SWARTZ, MARC J., & DAVID K. JORDAN, *Culture: The Anthropological Perspective*, University of Washington Press, Chicago.

TAIWO, OLADELE, *Culture and the Nigerian Novel*, Macmillan Education Ltd., 1976.

TALBOT, P. A., *The Peoples of Southern Nigeria*, Frank Cass & Co., London, 1969.

--------, *Some Nigerian Fertility Cults*, Frank Cass & Co. Ltd. 1967.

TAYLOR, R. B.,*Cultural Ways*, Allyn and Bacon, Inc., Boston, 3rd edition.

TYLOR, EDWARD B., *Primitive Culture*, New York, Haper Torchbooks, (1871)1958.

TULIO-ALTAN, C., *Antropologia*, Feltrinelli, 1985, Milano.

TURNER, V., *The Forest of Symbols*, Cornell Paperbacks, Cornell University Press, Ithaca and London.

--------, *The Ritual Process*, Aldine Publishing Company, Chicago, 1969.

UBAHAKWE, EBO, *Igbo Names*, Daystar Press, Ibadan, 1981.

UBESIE, TONY, *Odinala ndi Igbo*, Oxford University Press, Ibadan, 1978.

UCHENDU, V. C., *The Igbo of Southeast Nigeria*, Holt, Rinehart & Winston, New York, 1965.

VAN der POEL, CORNELIUS J., *The Search for Human Values* Paulist Press, New York, 1971.

VAN GENNEP, ARNOLD, *The Rites of Passage*, The University of Chicago Press, 1960.

WARNER, W. LLOYD, *The Living and the Dead*, New Haven, Yale University Press, 1959.

257

WARNOCK, MARY, *Existentialism*, Oxford University Press, (1970) 1986.

ARTICLES

AKPABOT, SAMUEL, "The Conflict Between Foreign and Traditional Culture in Nigeria", in Pr+nce Africaine, no. 81, 1972, pp. 177 - 182.

AKPUNONU, PETER, "The Religion of the Ibos Yesterday and Today", in *LUX*, vol. 11, no. 1, 1965.

ALLI, BILLIAMIN A., "Acculturation in a Post-Traditional Society", in **MISSIOLOGY**, vol. III, no. 1, 1975, pp. 71 - 75.

ANIH, STAN, "Social Impact of our Christianity", A Paper for Centenary Celebration, 1985.

ARBUCKLE, GERALD A., "Communicating through Ritual", in *Human Development*, vol. 9, no. 2, Summer 1988.

ARINZE, FRANCIS CARDINAL, "Incarnation of the Gospel in Cultures", in *Echo From Africa and Other Continents*, Jan. 1986.

--------, "L'incarnazione del Vangelo nelle culture", in *Studi Cattolica*, no. 290/91, 1985.

ARRUPE, PEDRO, "On Inculturation", A Paper to the whole Society, Rome, 14 May 1978, Cur. Gen. 78/5, pp. 1 - 2.

BIBAKI, NZUZI, "In Africa Nera Dio ¡he Madre", in *Gentes*, Marzo 1988, pp. 140 - 149.

BLOMJOUS, JOSEPH, "Development in Mission Thinking and Practice 1959-1980 : Inculturation and Interculturation",in *AFER*, vol.22, no.6, 1980, pp. 393-399

BURRIDGE, W., "Making the Faith at Home", THE OUTLOOK, vol. XVIII, no. 7, 1983, pp. 173 - 177.

CRONIN, BRIAN, "Religious and Christian Conversion in an African Context", in *CHIEA : AFRICAN CHRISTIAN STUDIES*, vol 3, no.2, June 1987, pp. 19-35.

CULLEN, MALACHY, "Adaptation of Infant Baptism", in *AFER*, vol.21, no.1, 1979, pp.44-54.

D'COSTA, G., "Christianity and Other Religions", in *DIALOGUE & ALLIANCE*, vol. 2, no. 2, 1988.

DICKSON, K. A., "Christian and African Traditional Ceremonies", in *PRACTICAL ANTHROPOLOGY*, vol. 18, no. 2, 1971, pp. 64 - 71.

DI GIACOMO, FILIPPO, "Lezioni di Antropologia Culturale", Teresianum, Roma, 1987.

DOCUMENTO DI LAVORO SULL'INCULTURAZIONE, "Sintesi di Riflessioni e Interrogativi", *P.I.M.E.*, 24, 1982, pp. 89 - 99.

DROOGERS, A., "The Africanization of Christianity, An Anthropologist's View", Missiology, vol. V, no. 4, 1977, pp. 443-456.

EJIZU, C. I., "Liminality in the Contemporary Nigerian Christian Religious Experience". in **MISSION STUDIES**, JOURNAL OF THE IAMS, vol. IV-2, 11987, pp. 4-14.

--------, "Continuity and Discontinuity in African Traditional Religion : The Case of the Igbo of Nigeria", **Cahiers des Religions Africaines**, vol. 18, no. 36, july 1984, pp.197-214.

EKOWA, PAUL C., "The Background of Igbo Catholicism: A Historical Survey", The Presentation Paper of the doctoral Thesis in Gregorian University, Rome, 28 April 1989.

EKWUNIFE, A., "African Culture : A Definition", in **CHIEA : AFRICAN CHRISTIAN STUDIES**, vol 3, no.3, Sept 1987, pp. 5-18.

ENEM, E. O., "What are we Anglicans Doing?", A Lecture at Diobu, Port Harcourt, Nigeria, 1950.

ERIVWO, SAM U., "Traditional Culture and Christianity", in *AFER*, vol. 21, no.4, 1979, pp. 216-222.

EZEANYA, S., "'The Sacred Place' in the Traditional Religion of the Igbo People of the Eastern Group of Provinces of Nigeria", in *West African Religion*, 6 (August) 1966.

GARCIA, S. R., "The Incarnation of the Church in Indigenous Cultures", Missiology, vol. 1, no.2, 1973, pp. 21 - 31.

GREEN, MARGARET M., "The Present Linguistic Situation in Ibo Country", in *Africa*, vol. IX, no. 1, 1936, pp. 508 - 523.

HARTLE, DONALD D., "Archeology in Eastern Nigeria", in *Nigeria Magazine*, 93, June 1967, pp. 136 - 137.

HERING, WOLFGANG, "Interreligi+r Dialog und Inkulturation", in *Bonifatius-Einigung*, Sept. 1989, pp. 204 - 214.

HERSKOVITS, M. J., "The Culture Areas of Africa", in *Africa*, vol.III, no.1,

Jan 1930, pp. 59-77.

HICKEY, R., "Decline of African Traditional Religion", *THE OUTLOOK*, vol. XX, no. 2, 1986, pp. 36 - 41.

HILLMAN, E., "Approcci Missionari alle Culture Africane Oggi", P.I.M.E., 24, Marzo 1982, pp. 63 - 74.

HILLMAN, EUGENE, "Missionary Approaches to African Cultures Today", in *AFER*, vol.22. no.6, 1980, pp.342-356.

HORTON, W. R. C., "God, Man, and Land in Northern Ibo Village-Group", in *Africa*, 26 (1956), p. 18.

IGBOAJA, E. U., "From Uka Fada to Uka Anyi", A Centenary Celebration Lecture, Enugu Diocese, 1985.

JONES, J. I., "Dual Organisation in Ibo Social Structure", in **AFRICA**, vol. XIX, 1949, pp. 150 - 156.

--------, "Ecology and Social Structure Among the North Eastern Ibo", in **AFRICA**, vol. XXXI, 1961, pp. 117 - 134.

KAKUBA-KAPIA, "Complementarity of infant & Adult Baptism", in *AFER*, vol. 30, no. 5, 1988, pp. 313 - 315.

KALU, WILHELMINA, "The Church and the Challenge of Childhood in Contemporary Nigeria", in *AFRICA THEOLOGICAL JOURNAL*, vol. 9, no. 3, pp.41 - 49.

KAPENZI, GEOFFREY Z., "Rites of Passage in Four African Tribes", in MISSIOLOGY, vol. III, no.1, 1975, pp. 65 - 70.

KIRISWA, BENJAMIN, "Interaction between African and Christian Moral Values", *AFER*, vol.29, no.6, 1987, pp. 361-371.

KLUCKHOHN, C., "Myths and Rituals : A General Theory", in *Havard Theological Review*, 35, pp.45 -79, 1942.

KNIPE, BILL, "Inculturation in Africa", in *Missi*, Dec.1985, no.47

KONGOCHA, CHIWANGU, "The Funeral Rites and Inculturation", in *SPEARHEAD*, no. 92, June 1986, pp.40-48.

KRAFT, CHARLES H., "Christian Conversion or Cultural Conversion?", in PRACTICAL ANTHROPOLOGY, vol. 10, no.4, 1963, pp. 179 - 187.

KREIGISCH, RUDY, "Christian Initiation and Inculturation", in *AFER*, vol. 30, no.1. Feb.1988.

KROEBER, ALFRED L., & CLYDE KLUCKHOHN, "Culture: A Critical Review of Concepts and Definitions", Harvard University Peabody Museum of American Archeological Papers, vol. 47 (1952), p. 18

LA CIVILT`A CATTOLICA, "Il Problema dell'inculturazione Oggi", P.I.M.E., 24, Marzo 1982, pp. 22 - 30.

--------, "Condizioni e Limiti dell'inculturazione", op. cit., pp. 31 - 41.

LAUDAZI, CARLO, "L'uomo nel Rapporto con Dio", Lectures in the Theological Faculty, Teresianum, Rome, 1986.

LEJEUNE, MICHEL, "Towards a Ritual of Marriage", in AFER, vol. 22, no. 3, 1980, pp. 151-158.

LUMBASI, GABRIEL, " Ordination and Initiation Rites", in AFER, vol. 18, no. 2, 1976.

MAKOTA, GEROLD & GROUP , Peramiho Seminary, "Liturgical Incarnation in African Culture", SERVICE, no. 5, 1983.

MAMA, SILAS C. "Making of Onyeishi in Ubollo", Research Findings, University of Nigeria, Nsukka, March 1989.

MANUS, CHRIS U., "The Concept of Death and the After-life in the Old Testament and Igbo Traditional Religion :Some Reflections for Contemporary Missiology", in Mission Studies, Journal of the IAMS, vol. III-2, 1986.

MAKOTA, GEROLD & GROUP , Peramiho Seminary, "Liturgical Incarnation in African Culture", SERVICE, no. 5, 1983.

MBEFO, LUKE, "Theology and Inculturation - Problems and Prospects, - The Nigerian Experience", in The Nigerian Journal of Theology, vol. 1, no. 1, CATHAN.

McCABE, JOSEPH V., "The Challenge of Liturgical Inculturation: Directions", in Spearhead, no. 92, June 1986, pp. 6 - 11.

MEEK, C. K., "Marriage by Exchange in Nigeria - A Disappearing Institution", in Africa, vol. IX, no. 1. Jan 1936, pp.65-74.

--------, "An Ethnological Report on the Peoples of Nsukka Division, Onitsha Province", Manuscript, Lagos, 1931.

MOORE, ROBERT O., "Towards an African Catholic Culture", in AFER, vol. 19, no. 4., 1977.

MORICONI, BRUNO, "Gesu di nazareth, Paradigma dell'uomo", Lecture Notes in Teresianum, Rome, 1987.

NEBECHUKWU, A., "Beginning Inculturation Theology of Life (in Igbo

Culture)", in *Lucerna*, vol. 6, no. 1, p. 22.

NTHAMBURI, Z., "Making the Gospel Relevant Within the African Context and Culture", THE OUTLOOK, vol. XVIII, no. 8, 1983, pp. 219 - 225.

NWABARA, SAMUEL N., "Christian Encounter with Indigenous Religion at Onitsha (1857-1885)", in Cahier d'Etudes Africaines, cahier 41 - 44, vol. XI, 1971, pp. 589 - 601.

NZOMIWU, J.P.C., "The African Church and Indigenisation: An Igbo Experience", in *AFER*, vol. 28, no. 5, pp.323-334.

OBIJOLE, BAYO, "Infant Baptism : A Critical Review", in *AFER*, vol. 30, no. 5, 1988, pp. 299 - 312.

OKOLO, CHUKWUDUM B., "Traditional African and Christian Values", in *AFER*, vol 29, no. 2, 1987., pp. 81-93.

OKOYE, JAMES C., "A New Era of Evangelization", Paper delivered at the National Seminar, Ibadan, 1 - 3 May, 1984.

OKWOR, J., M. OSAI, C. OHAERI, "Christian Adaptation and Cultural Heritage", Research Findings for Enugu Diocese.

OKWU, A.S.O., "The Weak Foundations of Missionary Evangelisation in Precolonial Africa : The Case of the Igbo of Southeastern Nigeria 1857-1900", **Missiology**, vol. VIII, no. 1, Jan. 1980, pp. 31-50.

OLISA, M. S. O., "Political Culture and Stability in Igbo Society", in *The Conch*, III, Nsukka, Nigeria, 1871, p. 19.

ONAH, GODFREY, "Baptised but not Converted", An Address delivered at the Centenary Lectures in Enugu Diocese, 1985.

ONAIYEKAN, JOHN, "Why a New Era of Evangelisation?", Lecture at Seminar 1 - 3 May 1984.

ONUNWA, U., "Gospel, Culture and Study of Traditional African Religions : An Evaluation of Strategy of Mission", in IMR, vol. 10, no. 3, July 1988, pp. 223 - 254.

ONYENEKE, AUGUSTINE, "The Omu Liturgical Use: Igbo Inculturation Initiatives", in *AFER*, vol.30, no.1,1988.

POBEE, J. S., "I am First an African and second a Christian ?", in IMR, vol. 10, no.3, pp.268 - 277

--------, "The Word Became Flesh : The Meeting of Christianity and African Cultures", THE OUTLOOK, vol.XX, no. 2, 1986, pp. 42 - 46.

RAPONI, S., "L'immagine-somiglianza nei Padri", in E.

ANCILLI, ed., *Temi di antropologia teologica*, Teresianum, Roma, 1981, pp. 241 - 341.

RAYAN, SAMUEL, "Inculturation and the Local Church", in *Mission Studies*, Journal of the IAMS, vol.III-2, 1986

REYBURN, WILLIAM D., "Christianity and Ritual Communication", in PRACTICAL ANTHROPOLOGY, vol. 10, no. 4, 1963, pp. 145-159.

RIESMAN, P., "The Person and the Life Cycle in African Social Life and Thought", AFRICAN STUDIES REVIEW, vol. 29, no. 2, June 1986, pp. 71 - 138.

SALAMONE, FRANK A., "Continuity of Igbo Values After Conversion : A Study in Purity and Prestige", in MISSIOLOGY, vol. III, no. 1, Jan. 1975.

SAWYER, HARRY, "What is African Christian Theology?", in *African Theological Journal*, 4, (1971), p. 19.

SEKWA, BISHOP CASTOR, "Guidelines and Strategies for Liturgical Inculturation", in *SPEARHEAD*, no.92, June 1986, pp.49-57.

SHELTON, A. J., "Recent Interpretation of Deus Otiosus: Withdrawn God in West African Psychology", in *Man*, Jan. 1964, p. 53.

SIMMONS, DONALD C., "Sexual Life, Marriage, and Childhood among the Efik", in AFRICA, vol. XXX, 1960, pp. 153 - 165.

Special Report on Nigeria in *Time*, 2nd March 1987.

SPol, J., "Marriage Custom among the Ibos." in ANTHROPOS, vol. XXXVII-XL, 1/3, 1942 - 45, pp. 113 - 121.

SUNDERMEIER, THEO, "Death Rites Supporting Life : The Process of Mourning in Africa", *AFRICA THEOLOGICAL JOURNAL*, vol.9, no.3, pp. 50 - 64.

TIMIRA, ALPHONSE, "Religious Themes in 'The African Child' of Camara Laye", in CHIEA : AFRICAN CHRISTIAN STUDIES, Occasional Paper no.2, June 1985, pp. 8-14.

TIPPETT, ALAN R., "Initiation Rites and Functional Substitutes", in PRACTICAL ANTHROPOLOGY, vol. 10, no. 2, 1963, pp. 66 - 69.

TOMKO, JOSEPH CARDINAL, "Inculturation and African Marriage", in *Afer*, 28, no 3/4 (June/August 1986), p. 155.

TRACY, D., "Ethnic Pluralism and Systematic Theology: Reflections", in A. M. GREELY & G. BAUM, eds., "Ethnicity", in *Concilium*, no. 101, New

263

York, 1977, pp. 91 - 99.

UBAH, C. N., "Religious Change among the Igbo during the Colonial Period", in *Journal of Religion in Africa*, vol. XVIII- Fasc. 1, Feb.1988, pp. 71 - 91.

UCHENDU, VICTOR C., "Missionary Problems in Nigerian Society", in **PRACTICAL ANTHROPOLOGY**, vol. 11, no. 3, 1964, pp. 105 - 117.

UKAEGBU, ALFRED O., "The Role of Traditional Marriage Habits in Population Growth : Then Case of Eastern Nigeria", in **AFRICA**, vol. 46, 1976, pp. 390 - 398.

UKPONG, JUSTIN S., "Contextualizing Theological Education in West Africa : Focus on subjects", in **CHIEA : AFRICAN CHRISTIAN STUDIES**, vol 3, no. 3, 1987, pp.   59-75.

--------, "The Emergence of African Theological Theologies", in *Theological Studies*, 45 (1984), p. 510

UZUKWU, ELOCHUKWU E., "African Personality and the Christian Liturgy", in **CHIEA : AFRICAN CHRISTIAN STUDIES**, vol 3, no.2, June 1987, pp. 61-74.

VAZ, ARMINDO, "Per una Antropologia dell'Antico Testamento", Lectures, Teresianum, Rome, 1987 - 88.

WALIGGO, J. M., "Inculturation of Christianity in Africa", in CHIEA: AFRICAN CHRISTIAN STUDIES, Occasional Paper no.3 & 4, Nov/Dec 1985, pp. 51 - 68.

WELTON, MICHAEL R., "Themes in African Traditional Befief and Ritual", in **PRACTICAL ANTHROPOLOGY**, vol. 18, no. 1, 1971, pp. 1 - 18.

--------, Review of "The Igbo of Southest Nigeria", in **PRACTICAL ANTHROPOLOGY**, vol 18, no. 2, 1971, pp. 95 - 96.

EMAN, H., "African Folkmusic in Christian Churches in Africa", A Paper to "All-Africa Conference of Churches, Nairobi/Kenya" for Liturgy and Church Music in Africa, 1974.

WIESCHHOF, H., "The Social Significance of Names Among the Ibo of Nigeria", in *American Anthropologist*, vol. 43, 1941, p. 212.

WILSON, GODFREY, "An African Morality", in *Africa*, vol. IX, no.1, 1936, pp.75-98.

ZVAREVASHE, IGNATIUS M., "The Problem of Ancestors and Inculturation", in *Afer*, vol. 29, no. 4, August 1987, pp. 242ff.